*The Transitions in American Thought Series
seeks to explain the changes in values, expression,
and intellectual currents which characterized
significant turning points in American history.*

TRANSITIONS IN
AMERICAN THOUGHT SERIES

William Goetzmann, General Editor

Robert M. Crunden, author of this volume in the Transitions
in American Thought series, is Associate Professor of History
and American Civilization and advisor to the Graduate
Program in American Civilization at the University of Texas
at Austin. He is the author of *The Mind and Art of Albert Jay
Nock* and *A Hero in Spite of Himself: Brand Whitlock in Art,
Politics, and War.*

Transitions in American Thought Series

FROM
SELF
TO
SOCIETY
1919-1941

ROBERT M. CRUNDEN

A SPECTRUM BOOK

PRENTICE-HALL, INC., *Englewood Cliffs, New Jersey*

ISBN: P 0–13–331413–8   C 0–13–331421–9

Library of Congress Catalog Card Number 78–168740

10 9 8 7 6 5 4 3 2 1

PRENTICE-HALL INTERNATIONAL, INC., *London*
PRENTICE-HALL OF AUSTRALIA, PTY. LTD., *Sydney*
PRENTICE-HALL OF CANADA, LTD., *Toronto*
PRENTICE-HALL OF INDIA PRIVATE LIMITED, *New Delhi*
PRENTICE-HALL OF JAPAN, INC., *Tokyo*

For Wendy,
whose arrival during
chapter 2 probably
contributed to its tone,
and
for Pat,
who bore that burden
and several others

CONTENTS

vii

PREFACE

This study is one volume in a series of reinterpretations of American intellectual and cultural history. Its purpose is to analyze the culture as a whole in the period between 1919 and 1941 and to show through detailed examples how and why the mind of the country that went to war in 1941 differed from the mind of the country that emerged from World War I.

Although it is part of a series, my book is in some ways more personal and idiosyncratic than one might expect under the circumstances, and not at all a homogeneous "textbook" summary of other scholars' work. It is designed to supplement the material usually covered in textbooks by including areas often omitted and by adopting an interdisciplinary focus that attempts to see the culture of the period as a whole. We do not yet have many useful secondary sources for this recent period and what sources we do have usually deal primarily with literature and politics. The history of such other areas as the social sciences and the fine arts is still in the beginning stages. As a result, in my attempt at a synthesis I have had to form conclusions in several areas where the basic scholarship still remains to be done. This lack of precedents creates both a certain freedom and a certain constriction. But it is one purpose of this series to encourage attempts at cultural synthesis and to open up areas for further study.

The unifying focus of this book is the problem of the relationship between the individual and society. My thesis is that three distinctive views of this relationship succeed one another in the period. In the Progressive Era, intellectuals saw the individual as an integral part of society; his values were not opposed to the values of the majority. In the postwar period, intellectuals thought that the individual was alienated from society, and they valued individualism in all its manifestations. In the depression years, intellectuals insisted that society should engulf the individual, and for them communitarian values gained precedence over individual values. In brief, the transitions are from the self in society, to the self apart from society, to the self submerged in society. At any given time, many figures ignored or opposed the prevailing temper, and I have tried to take these exceptions into account as often as possible. In assessing the prevailing temper of the culture, I have used "culture" to refer primarily to the activity of the intellectuals, who leave written records, music, pictures, and buildings. The scope of the book precludes consideration of "popular" culture except where it reflects a prevailing attitude. I have understood "intellectual history" to mean the study of ideas that cross disciplinary boundaries. In this view, Freudian ideas were part of the history of medicine until they influenced critics, novelists, sociologists, and laymen and so became part of intellectual history.

On the same principle, I have ignored certain topics that might at first seem relevant. I do not treat the role of the little magazines in any detail nor the rise of American history nor American literary history. These topics would be important in another book on the period but they are less important to my purposes here than other, more neglected subjects. Likewise, I have ignored the influence of Ezra Pound, which had considerable importance for American culture before 1919 but afterwards became increasingly confined to the history of literature rather than to the history of ideas in American culture. For the same reasons I have omitted the influence of the fiction of James Joyce and the poetry of T. S. Eliot, but I do discuss Eliot's critical and social ideas. I have neglected politics for similar reasons: the twenties stimulated political discussion but it was largely negative and unproductive. The New Deal stimulated a variety of schemes for economic and social planning, which I do discuss, but even during that period "politics" in the strict sense of the word was less influential in intellectual history than it was, say, between 1900 and 1915. As a child of the forties and fifties, I have also been surprised by my neglect of science and technology. I had thought, when I began the book, that they would have considerable importance but I discovered that most scientific and technological ideas remained a part of the history of their own disciplines throughout the period covered and only during the 1940s became a part of "intellectual history" in my sense of the word.

Even within the limitations created by the scope of the work, its place in a series, and my own understanding of the nature of intellectual and cultural history, I considered a number of ways of writing a book of this kind. I have tried to use an approach that steers a middle way between a list of a large number of figures and influences treated only in the most cursory fashion and a study in depth of a very few representative figures or abstract ideas. This approach is designed for the intelligent, liberally educated college or graduate student who wants a brief introduction to the period and to the intellectual history of culture. Such an audience, in my judgment, needs to know something about the major figures in each area of knowledge. They do not need descriptions of all figures in any area, but they do need a "representative man" to keep in mind as a specific example and a bibliography to point the way for further work in each area.

In structuring the book, then, I have built my argument around portraits of men who are representative of a general position. I have not, and I wish to emphasize this, tried to paint well-rounded portraits of whole men in all their complexity. No one reading this book should assume that they "know" H. L. Mencken, for example, from my brief and rather critical description of his work as a literary critic. I am fully aware of Mencken's importance in other roles such as editor, philologist, memoirist, critic of the New Deal, popular anthropologist, and culture hero for the younger generation of the twenties. But Mencken's work as a literary critic is especially useful for my purpose because it is an important example of one of the legacies of progressive culture to the twenties. He was influential, he was intelligent, his ideas crossed disciplines, and no one to my knowledge had analyzed his criticism successfully in print. I have used these criteria in choosing other figures, and thus make no pretence of having been "fair" to those parts of their lives that I do not describe directly. I have also on occasion taken a certain delight in ignoring men with reputations already established, and describing men who have been ignored by other historians. My purpose was to describe the intellectual history of culture, and for this purpose any man who fitted the general category could sit for his portrait.

In a similar fashion I have regarded the men I chose as "replaceable" or "movable." Hemingway here stands for the exile who made a cult of youth, of certain social codes, of hunting and fishing and bull fighting as a way of insulating himself from the shock of war and hypocrisy. Had I wished, I could have concentrated instead on E. E. Cummings and *The Enormous Room,* or John Dos Passos and *Three Soldiers.* I could also have moved Hemingway into the next chapter, and discussed *For Whom The Bell Tolls* as a picture of social solidarity and revolutionary awareness in the novel. In this case, Hemingway made a transition just as his culture did, and my pragmatic method makes any part of his career "usable" where it fits. This approach is certainly open to serious criticism. But after experimenting with several other quite different schemes of organization, I decided on the one that best fitted the editorial demands of the series.

For making the book as useful and comprehensible as I hope it is, I have several debts to acknowledge. The American Civilization program at the University of Texas at Austin is remarkably rich in scholars in intellectual history or related fields, and I have called on several of them for help. Delmer Rogers gave me several useful suggestions about how to tackle Edgard Varèse. Palmer Wright let me read his enormous study of the American mind since 1940, which will, when published, open up this whole, untouched area; he also gave me the benefit of a searching critique of the manuscript. C. Hartley Grattan, who has with great reluctance seen his name included in my portrait gallery, did not let friendship stand in the way of a devastating analysis of one draft, complete with personal memories and suggestions that have certainly influenced my choice of figures and their handling, especially in literature and the social sciences. Vivienne Wright gave the manuscript an attentive critical reading, in an attempt to make my diffuse style say what I mean.

My greatest debts are to William H. Goetzmann and Patricia Crunden. Prof. Goetzmann had the confidence in me to ask that I do a volume, the patience to prune away some of my excesses of both rhetoric and interpretation, and the tolerance to accept a book that he finds more than slightly eccentric. Mrs. Crunden, as usual, took valuable time from her more important efforts to help with both style and content; but then, she already knows how much I owe her.

PROLOGUE:
HEADHUNTING
WITH
MABEL
DODGE

"You have a certain faculty," Lincoln Steffens said to Mabel Dodge, one autumn day before the war. They were chatting before her white marble chimney piece and its glowing fire. "It's a centralizing, magnetic, social faculty," he went on. "You attract, stimulate, and soothe people, and men like to sit with you and talk to themselves! You make them think more fluently, and they feel enhanced." Surely we should do something about that, he insisted. What? "Why not organize all this accidental, unplanned activity around you, this coming and going of visitors, and see these people at certain hours. Have Evenings!" It was a lovely idea. Mabel Dodge was a rich, neurotic, and confused woman, but she had for her friends and acquaintances a remarkable number of the younger American intelligentsia. The solution was perfect. It gave a bored woman something to do besides fret about her ego and her love life, and required her to do little but sit and be hospitable. The result was the most famous salon in American history. In the development of her plans, Mabel Dodge brought together under one roof not only the chief intellectual currents of the day, but also the men who later enunciated the ideas of the next three decades. "I wanted, in particular, to know the Heads of things," she wrote later. "Heads of Movements, Heads of Newspapers, Heads of all kinds of groups of people. I became a Species of Head Hunter. . . ."[1]

At times, Mabel Dodge hunted her "Heads" in the outside world, visiting them in the homes of her friends, meeting them at parties, visiting them in salons, or seeking them out at art exhibitions. In this fashion she encountered the first examples of the modernist painting that became so important during the 1920s. She was a friend of William Macbeth, for example. He was the dealer for many of the new artists, "the most courageous man in the New York art-dealing world," who went to considerable lengths to get showings for his favorite painters. One of his special favorites, and one of Mabel Dodge's, was Arthur Davies, who "painted very strange and poetic figures wandering in allegorical scenes." Mabel Dodge found "a great beauty in his pictures, half-domesticated and half beyond the pale." Alfred Stieglitz—another "Head" hunted at times—had begun the introduction of modern European art to America with his "291" exhibitions, and encouraged American painters like John Marin and Arthur Dove, whose work seemed to rate inclusion with the best of the newer European paintings. Given this precedent, Davies one day found himself nominated to help produce what became the most significant art exhibition ever put on in America—the famous Armory Show of 1913—and naturally Mabel Dodge was a fascinated observer in this as in everything else. One of Davies' friends in the Armory Show adventure, James Gregg, even persuaded Mabel Dodge to do her bit for modernity, and after considerable dawdling, she did in fact strike her small blow for the cause. She was friendly with Gertrude Stein, and at Gregg's insistence wrote an article for *Arts and Decoration* that helped set the tone for the experimentation that soon followed. Mabel Dodge called her times "an age of communication," and Gertrude Stein was representative of the age. "In a large studio in Paris, hung with paintings by Renoir, Matisse, and Picasso, Gertrude Stein is doing with words what Picasso is doing with paint. She is impelling language to induce new states of consciousness, and in doing so language becomes with her a creative art rather than a mirror of history." With two such indomitable ladies at the front of the avant-garde, the pieties of Victorian Americans, their realistic art forms, their faith in reason

---

[1] Mabel Dodge Luhan, *Movers and Shakers* ("Intimate Memories," III), (New York, 1936), pp. 80–84.

and progress, their matter-of-fact assumptions about normality, all were about to die. The heads of these Victorians, Mabel Dodge would cheerfully cut off.[2]

But she did her most famous headhunting at home, and three of the prize "Heads" she brought there represented the main trends in most of American intellectual life for the years to come. Lincoln Steffens was the first. One of his friends remembered him as a "little paradoxical man, lively and incalculable as quicksilver," who was "the most attractive and plausible man in the world. . . ." Once a single-taxer, a social-gospeler, a newspaperman, and a muckraker, he was slowly moving toward the position that made him a hero to the young men of the Left in the 1930s. Even then he was concerned with social reform and the economics of the class struggle, although he still thought in conventional Progressive categories. In his slow trip to the totalitarian Left in the years after the First World War, he demonstrated the power that social solidarity, particularly the communitarian kind described in Marxist literature, had over even the most open and supple minds of the time.[3]

Steffens, as a "Headhunter" himself, introduced a young Harvard socialist into the group. Walter Lippmann, as one of his college friends said, was "a Manhattan Zeus, steady, massive, impassive, hurling his thunderbolts judiciously among the herds of humankind." Lippmann was less at home in bohemia than Steffens and others at the salon, and he was less popular. People respected him, were perhaps a little in awe of him, but they did not like him the way they liked Steffens. His own representative idea was pragmatism of a rather austere variety. Originally, the idea came from William James, his friend and teacher at Harvard, but in Lippmann's hands the warm, religious pragmatism of James became the cold, scientific pragmatism associated with John Dewey. As Steffens became more and more authoritarian, his young friend Lippmann became a prophet first of the scientific method, and then of a pragmatism that wandered uncertainly between a mild endorsement of state power to solve social problems, and a mild condemnation of that power whenever it seemed that the state might go too far.[4] According to John Reed, Lippmann was "calm, inscrutable,"

---

2 Ibid., pp. 25–27; Jerome Myers, *Artist in Manhattan* (New York, 1940), pp. 35–36.

3 Mary Heaton Vorse, *A Footnote to Folly* (New York, 1935), p. 29; Lincoln Steffens, *The Autobiography of Lincoln Steffens* (New York, 1931), p. 654 and passim; Ella Winter and Granville Hicks, eds., *The Letters of Lincoln Steffens* (New York, 1939).

4 Granville Hicks, *John Reed* (New York, 1936), quoting E. E. Hunt, p. 48; Charles Forcey, *The Crossroads of Liberalism* (New York, 1961), ch. 3.

and "our all unchallenged Chief." Nevertheless, Reed complained, Lippmann dreamt "a pageant, gorgeous, infinite," only to leave out "all the color," with his humorless formulas for social betterment.

Reed could not have said that about a third famous figure at Mabel Dodge's salon. Max Eastman was without question the handsomest radical in New York, and although a pupil of Dewey and a convinced socialist, he had little in common with Steffens and Lippmann. For all his philosophy and radicalism, Eastman was most comfortable as a hedonist, an individualist whose politics seem in retrospect to be chiefly an attempt to help everyone enjoy poetry and women as much as he did. As such, he was a major prophet of Freud and the new psychology for many of his friends: he popularized the new attitudes toward sex, offered his own aesthetics, and eventually published more books with titles containing the word "enjoyment" than anyone else in memory. He was, as his friend Claude McKay remembered, "an ikon for the radical women," but his religion was only an attempt to practice what he preached.[5]

The salon ended even before the war, but it had served its purpose. Mabel Dodge's "Heads" faced the postwar years well aware that their chief concerns were the impact of pragmatism and the related developments in social science; the impact of psychology, and what it meant for the unhappy and dissatisfied individual; and the impact of communitarian social ideas, and what they meant for a capitalist society that was in trouble.

---

5 John Reed, *The Day in Bohemia* (Riverside, Conn., 1913), on Lippmann; Claude McKay, *A Long Way from Home* (New York, 1937), p. 102.

I

LEGACIES OF THE PROGRESSIVE ERA

Of all the ideas propounded in Mabel Dodge's salon, the pragmatism advocated by Walter Lippmann was easily the most important legacy of the Progressive Era to the America of 1920. Many of the other important legacies of the Progressive Era found few people capable of exploiting them. The political achievements which had seemed so important in the years before the war were largely forgotten, and except for the Federal Reserve Act, they had little permanent effect on the government. Muckraking had lost most of its popular appeal even before the war. The painters of the Ashcan group found themselves largely neglected in the successive vogues of Fauvism, Dada, Expressionism, and the numerous other fads imported from Paris. The music of Charles Ives remained unpublished and unheard in a confused and dusty pile in the same room where it had been written. Even the law, once stirred by the ideas of Holmes, Brandeis, and Pound at the national level, and Ben Lindsey at the local level, became a relatively complacent interpretation of the status quo. Architects like Frank Lloyd Wright and Louis Sullivan found themselves without major commissions or reputations. But in the social sciences and closely related fields, and especially in education, the ideas formulated in the Progressive Era remained important forces.

No one represented the legacy of pragmatism to social science better than John Dewey, who was at once both the last of the great pragmatists and the first of the great influences on life after the war. He had been a pioneer in psychology, and a devotee of the philosophy of Hegel. William James had introduced him to his *Principles of Psychology,* and Dewey's own children made sure that their father applied those principles in his own home. Dewey had helped found and run one of the most important experimental schools in American history at the University of Chicago, only to find himself eased out by William Rainey Harper. Soon Dewey was introducing students at Columbia University to his ideas about philosophy and education, and through Columbia Teachers College these ideas eventually became the accepted doctrine for the most highly trained of the nation's secondary school teachers. With his necktie frequently askew, a hole in his coat, and his socks sagging about his ankles, he wandered around the campus like an incarnation of the absentminded sage. His hair looked as though he had combed it with a towel, and his prose was devoid of a single phrase of ingratiating beauty or sign of wit, but his students were devoted, his influence great, and his mind probably the most directly influential on the life of the nation in 1920.[1]

That mind sometimes seemed to have little but contempt for most of its predecessors. Traditionally, Dewey maintained, philosophers "made a fixed and fundamental distinction between two realms of existence," and in so doing effectively paralyzed productive social thought. They placed the "final source and sanction of all important truths and rules of conduct" in a metaphysical realm removed from the world of experience, and protected from criticism by unquestioned religious dogma. "Reality" for them was fine and clean and noumenal, unsullied by the world of daily living. That world was empirical and phenomenal, a world of "the practical affairs and utilities of men," and thus of little concern to the philosopher. Dewey termed this philosophical orientation "historic intellectualism, the spectator view of knowledge," and found it "a purely compensatory doctrine which men of an intellectual turn have built up to console themselves for the actual and social impotency of the calling of thought to which they

---

1 Max Eastman, "John Dewey: My Teacher and Friend," in *Great Companions* (New York, 1959); Jane M. Dewey, "Biography of John Dewey," in P. A. Schlipp, ed., *The Philosophy of John Dewey* (Evanston and Chicago, 1939).

are devoted." They were practicing not a viable and intelligent discipline but "a morally irresponsible estheticism." Their chief delight was to detain thought "within pompous and sonorous generalities wherein controversy is as inevitable as it is incapable of solution." At their worst, their intellectual antics "reduced philosophy to a show of elaborate terminology, a hair-splitting logic, and a fictitious devotion to the mere external forms of comprehensive and minute demonstration." [2] They were intellectually sterile and socially impotent.

In place of this outmoded dualism, Dewey flatly declared that the "interaction of organism and environment, resulting in some adaptation which secures utilization of the latter, is the primary fact, the basic category." Knowledge is not "something separate and self-sufficing," but a vital part of "the process by which life is sustained and evolved." The intelligent man, then, should devote his attention not to an abstraction but to a process; his true concern is not so much with the idea itself as with the way his concept or idea behaves under a great variety of circumstances. He should view the world "only as *material* for change," and not as anything permanent. His goal should not be perfection, "but the ever-enduring process of perfecting, maturing, refining. . . ." By such standards, his values become relative and in flux. If he wishes to decide whether a man is good or bad, for example, he should not ask about his past character and deeds, but about where he is headed. "The good man is the man who no matter how morally unworthy he *has* been is moving to become better." Dewey hoped the result of this new approach would be "a new temper of imagination and aspiration." [3]

In the course of this transformation of philosophical priorities, Dewey brought certain words into common philosophical discourse. "Experience," for example, meant to him "that which calls us away from adherence to the past, that which reveals novel facts and truths." Thus, if one had faith in experience, he was devoted not "to custom but endeavor for progress." He likewise altered the common meaning of words when he began talking of what was perhaps his favorite word in the language, "science." "Science," or "reason,"—he used the terms interchangeably—was the opposite of the ideas taught by the old philosophers. "Suggested and tested in experience, it is also employed through inventions in a thousand ways to expand and enrich experience." In this context, science, or reason, becomes a kind of benign substitution for the Deity that Dewey rarely invoked, blessing the

2 John Dewey, *Reconstruction in Philosophy* (Boston, 1948, c.1920), pp. 22-23, 117, 199. (Hereafter a publication date given in this fashion means "copyright, 1920," but that the pagination and text is from the 1948 edition.)

3 Ibid., pp. 87, 114, 177, 176, 73.

endeavors of all men of good will. Shaped by its hands, the human mind becomes something of a savior for society: "For reason is experimental intelligence, conceived after the pattern of science, and used in the creation of social arts; it has something to do. It liberates man from the bondage of the past, due to ignorance and accident hardened into custom." Dewey's prose seemed innocent of rhetoric, but he knew how to use words to persuade his reader that he was only insisting on the most reasonable of ideas. Once one accepted his terminology, one could scarcely attack Dewey on his own ground, for disagreement with his argument implied a defense of dead and useless ideas, ritualistic behavior, and the obscurantist mind that refused to appreciate the progress brought about by science.[4]

On the whole Dewey was right. The old philosophy had often been sterile, and one could hardly argue with a pragmatism that innocently declared that it only asked for results, and would gladly change its mind if an idea somehow did not work out. Dewey also redefined the key term "knowing" to be compatible with his own preferences for the experimental sciences. "Knowing" meant "a certain kind of intelligently conducted doing"; no longer contemplative, it was suddenly practical. Philosophy, therefore, had to change: "It must assume a practical nature; it must become operative and experimental." Reflecting these attitudes, Dewey's language became implicitly clinical in its metaphors—he called his task "diagnosis" of the ills of society—and explicitly reformist: "the task of future philosophy is to clarify men's ideas as to the social and moral strifes of their own day," and "to become so far as is humanly possible an organ for dealing with these conflicts."[5] The Dewey who wandered absently around the Columbia campus as though unaware of the time or the weather was remaking society inside his head.

Dewey was most successful in the schools, and at Chicago and Columbia he did more to change American society than any other man of his time. One of the key insights of the Progressive Era was that character was formed not by some sort of innate quality, but by environment. For all practical purposes, men were born without character; as they grew up, their character developed under the influences of their families, their friends, and their fellow workers. The result, in the work of thinkers like Charles H. Cooley, or Dewey's friend Jane Addams, was a reorientation of social thought away from the individual and toward society, and Dewey was an important figure in this change. To him, the schools were an obvious means of so controlling the environment of the child that he grew up to become a responsible

---

4 Ibid., pp. 93, 95, 96.

5 Ibid., pp. 121, 142, 26.

member of a democratic society. The job of the school, he insisted, was to become so much a part of the community that it really *was* the environment for its students, and was thus able to furnish a suitable set of models upon which the young could form their characters and their behavior.

Dewey detested the older schools. They were, he thought, the relics of a feudal and aristocratic past that had no proper place in democratic America. As a philosopher he insisted that nothing separated the world of ideas from the world of action. As an educator he insisted that nothing should separate the world of the "humanities" from the world of the "sciences" or the world of vocational training. Education, he said, was "a fostering, a nurturing, a cultivating process," and as such it must pay attention to growth; in a democracy all men were equally worthy and thus equally deserving of the opportunity to grow. A true democracy was "more than a form of government"; it was "primarily a mode of associated living, of conjoint communicated experience." The role of a truly progressive education, then, was to provide an environment that would not perpetuate but correct "unfair privilege and unfair deprivation." The old emphasis on the classics, on a mandarin kind of useless knowledge, he thought "futile, with something rotten about it," for it set one man apart from another, tore apart the social fabric, and insinuated that real knowledge and the world of mundane facts were somehow separate. If democracy had "a moral and ideal meaning," he wrote, it was "that a social return be demanded from all and that opportunity for development of distinctive capacities be afforded to all. The separation of the two aims in education is fatal to democracy. . . ." [6]

In reeducating teachers, Dewey also changed the language of education. Critics might argue with some justice that he also made it unintelligible, but certain of his definitions were clear enough. "The starting point of any process of thinking is something going on, something which just as it stands is incomplete or unfulfilled." In other words, a man should ignore abstractions and spend his time on actual problems. In this context, "to have an *idea* of a thing is thus not just to get certain sensations from it. It is to be able to respond to the thing in view of its place in an inclusive scheme of action." A "mind," then, "is precisely the power to understand things in terms of the use made of them; a socialized mind is the power to understand them in terms of the use to which they are turned in joint or shared situations." "Mind," he maintained, "is not a name for something complete by itself; it is a name for a course of action in so far as that is intelligently

---

6 John Dewey, *Democracy and Education* (Glencoe, Ill., 1966, c.1916), passim, quotations on pp. 10, 87, 119–22.

directed." In other words, if he had a mind, a man did not sit in a corner and brood; he found a social problem and tried to do something about it. If he were a teacher, he tried to bring up children so that when they came of age they would be able to help him or his fellow problem-solvers. Logically, then, "thinking" was the process someone used to confront the problem, "the accurate and deliberate instituting of connections between what is done and its consequences." It included four steps: "The sense of a problem, the observation of conditions, the formation and rational elaboration of a suggested conclusion, and the active experimental testing." Thought became operational, an activity with a purpose; it thus became all but synonymous with reform. Dewey the progressive had taken his science into the classroom.[7]

II

Dewey's work in the classroom was based on one vital pre-supposition: the environment was the key influence on character. But education was hardly the only field where this idea was winning converts; in anthropology it was becoming something of a religion. The Progressive Era in American anthropology was something of a one-man show as German immigrant Franz Boas laboriously set the standards for the new field from his desk at Columbia University. Like the initial phase of almost any new area of knowledge, this early period in anthropology was unexciting to outsiders. In contrast to a Gilded Age theorist like Lewis Henry Morgan, Boas grubbed patiently for the basic facts and techniques that were vital for genuinely scientific generalizing. His students slowly gathered the data of the lives of other cultures—the Kwakiutl, the Zuñi, the Manus—reconstructing their languages, writing down their myths and customs. The whole procedure was something of a salvage job—the cultures were slowly dying before the encroaching white man, and the next generation would be too late. Boas was in many ways a brilliant teacher and scholar, and his pioneering work in this area, especially *The Mind of Primitive Man* (1911) and *Anthropology and Modern Life* (1928), were widely read in more intellectual circles; but it remained for his students to capture the imagination of the whole literate reading public for anthropological ideas. The work of Boas's students, at its best, was read throughout the world, sold hundreds of thousands of copies, and had an incalculable influence on the course of world history.[8]

---

7 Ibid., pp. 146, 30, 33, 132, 151.

8 Melville J. Herskovits, *Franz Boas* (New York, 1953); see also Margaret Mead and Ruth L. Bunzel, eds., *The Golden Age of American Anthropology* (New York, 1960).

Of the members of this next generation, none became better known or more often taught in the schools than Ruth Benedict. She had come late to her professional training, and even then in a mood of a dilettante, not of a crusader. She had been a shy girl, withdrawn almost to the point of morbidity at times, and terribly afraid of a life without a husband and children. After teaching school for a few terms, she married; but even then she felt the malaise of uselessness that tortured so many of the women of the Progressive Era. But unlike Jane Addams or Frances Perkins, she did not turn to reform for her outlet. Childless and discontented in her marriage, she enrolled in the Columbia graduate school and took her doctorate under Boas. Although she entered Boas's program with little apparent motivation, she soon found graduate work in anthropology very satisfying. Shy, partly deaf, unhappy in her personal life, Ruth Benedict was clearly something of a misfit in an America soon devoted to Mah-Jongg and the stock market. She chose one of the few professions then available to her that not only accepted her on her merits but enabled her to work for the cultural understanding that would enable her to make a useful contribution to society.[9]

Boas had little trouble understanding her needs. During the war, when the egregious Nicholas Murray Butler was rooting out dissenters on the Columbia faculty, Boas had stood firm. A German himself, he knew full well that a whole culture, especially the one he grew up in, could not be composed of the mass rapists and looters portrayed by American propaganda. He spoke out publicly against the lies. America, he said firmly, had no right to assert its own moral righteousness and purity, and to judge others by irrelevant standards and bigoted ideals. Ruth Benedict needed little persuasion. Her own temperament, she was convinced, was incompatible with all the approved social roles available to her in America. She tried to find fulfillment in writing poetry; she attempted a biographical study of well-known women rebels, but made little headway. But in anthropology she found a way of vindicating individual differences without resorting to the obsolete individualism of Social Darwinism. In publishing her work, she was contributing to the education of a democratic people; nothing could be closer to Progressive ideals.

All of Boas's students were taught, almost as their first lessons, the theories that everything in a culture was related to everything else, and that each culture was equal in worth and dignity to every other culture. The first theory meant that anthropologists were firmly opposed to any psychoanalytic approach that insisted on the biological source of cul-

---

9 For biographical details, see Margaret Mead, *An Anthropologist at Work: Writings of Ruth Benedict* (Boston, 1959).

tural or personality traits. Like the Progressives, they insisted that man was a social animal, and that his character was the creation of his society and environment. The second theory, known as cultural relativism, was a standing rebuke to anyone who would impose his own standards on the culture of another people. Boas and his students never permitted anyone to assume that primitive-appearing people were really in a state of arrested development, as if they needed only time and education to become middle-class Anglo-Saxons. They were not the primitive predecessors of modern civilization, but modern members of a different civilization, with complex heritages, religions, and customs fully as functional in their individual circumstances as the comparable customs of Americans. The lessons for Americans were obvious: other cultures deserved as much respect as one's own culture—what Western people regarded as eternal principles were simply customs sanctified by time and usage, and had no necessary validity for other peoples. Those who seem aberrant or unconventional or even dangerous in one culture might well be the honored leaders in another.

For Ruth Benedict these doctrines had a peculiar force, since she regarded herself as an outcast. For her, these cultures so different from her own were really personalities writ large, groups of people who had formed viable social groups that valued certain types of people that other societies might find completely unassimilable. To her, tolerance of these cultures symbolized tolerance of people like herself. Normality, she insisted, was culturally defined, and while Americans might abhor the homosexual, the mystic, the cataleptic, or the paranoid, she could point to at least one group of people who considered such individuals the highest form of human development, or who at least found acceptable places for those who were scorned in her own country. That which a society called morally good was simply what that society was accustomed to. Boas had believed that the world must be made safe for differences; as Ruth Benedict phrased it, ". . . the inculcation of tolerance and appreciation in any society toward its less usual types is fundamentally important in successful mental hygiene." [10]

Throughout the 1920s she worked at Columbia and in the field, teaching classes and living with the actual peoples who supplied her with insights. The chief fruit of her work did not appear until 1934, but when it did, *Patterns of Culture* quickly became one of the most popular texts in its field. A culture, she wrote, was a consistent pattern of thought and action, and earlier anthropologists like James G. Frazer were fundamentally misguided. Where Frazer had remained in his arm-

---

[10] Ibid., passim, esp. p. 420 for Boas on Germany, and p. 278 for quote.

chair and collected the data of others, she had been to the tribes herself. While he had pasted together a kind of Frankenstein's monster, "with a right eye from Fiji, a left from Europe, one leg from Tierra del Fuego, and one from Tahiti," into a composite man labeled "primitive," she insisted that each culture was a separate entity, and deserved comprehension on its own terms. But chiefly what she wrote was her own *apologia pro vita sua.* She took three cultures, which she labeled as essentially Apollonian, Dionysian, and paranoid, and showed how each tendency formed the basis for a functioning culture. In one tribe, passivity and social congeniality were the chief traits, while despair, self-torture, and guilt were almost totally unknown. Another tribe exalted the use of drugs and alcohol, building up to religious frenzies and visionary experiences. A third made avarice and jealousy into national pastimes, and surpassed even Americans in the urge to show off and shame the neighbors. Some peoples encouraged sexual promiscuity or thought nothing of divorce; others found a useful place for the talents of homosexuals. The man who would be in jail as a drug addict in America might well be the religious leader of his people, were he born into the proper tribe. But what concerned Ruth Benedict fully as much as the acceptance of these "nonconformists" was the rejection of the individual "whose congenial drives are not provided for in the institutions of his culture." The discontented drug addict in the tribe that valued passive congeniality was an outcast; the generous man was equally out of place in the tribe that valued possessions. Like Ruth Benedict, they had been born in the wrong culture. Her final plea was for an understanding of all forms of possible human behavior, and a tolerance for that which seemed inappropriate. "Just as we are handicapped in dealing with ethical problems so long as we hold to an absolute definition of morality, so we are handicapped in dealing with human society so long as we identify our local normalities with the inevitable necessities of existence." Taught to generations of students, this doctrine of cultural relativism did almost as much to shape the thinking of intelligent Americans as the ideas of John Dewey.[11]

III

Under the influence of progressive ideas, not only the social sciences but virtually every area of American cultural thought became active in the criticism of life. Modern students expect to find sociolo-

---

11 Ruth Benedict, *Patterns of Culture* (Boston, 1961, c.1934), quotations on pp. 49, 262, 271.

gists and anthropologists talking about society, but they do not customarily think of literary critics, painters, or architects performing this task. Yet in the Progressive Era, the whole force of the waning Protestantism that was the chief religious heritage of most Americans seemed to be transformed into social criticism, heavily flavored with moralism, in almost every field of endeavor. Literary criticism became the criticism of life and society; painting became the criticism of life and society; architecture became the criticism of life and society. One of the chief legacies of the Progressive Era thus became the assumption that aesthetics was a branch of social science fully committed to the improvement of America.

In literary criticism, all the critical schools were patently criticizing society and its customs whenever they appeared to be discussing literature. The best critics of the period, men like Paul Elmer More and William C. Brownell, were conservatives who upheld their own versions of Victorian morality either explicitly in their asides, or implicitly in their praise or condemnation of the writers whose books they were discussing. Books were good that upheld moral standards, that seemed based on religious insight, and that were written in a chaste style. Books were bad that mentioned the vulgar in human life, that contained characters who acted immorally and were not punished for it, or that reminded the critic and the reader that man had anything in common with other biological creatures. All too often, books were acceptable only if they contained nothing offensive to the mind of a teen-aged girl, and the judge of offensiveness was her father, not the girl herself.

Such critics did not remain unchallenged at any time during the period. Their most distinguished and widely read opponent, however, the New York cosmopolitan critic of all the arts James Gibbons Huneker, was fully as much a covert social critic as any of the conservatives. He merely took the opposite side and tended to praise in his impressionistic way all art that opened up unknown possibilities for his audience—the new theater of Ibsen, the new art of Whistler, the new music of Wagner—and obviously hoped that his audience would follow him to a new life of awareness and sensuous freedom from the old dogmas. Late in the period he also discovered his most valuable ally and disciple, H. L. Mencken, and the two of them set about to reform American letters, art, and life. The result was a violent and amusing battle, often fought over extremely trivial literature. In the end, Mencken, with his great editorial prestige and power, won the day for Huneker and himself, but if his victory was a liberating experience for many readers and writers, it also had severe limitations for the development of American critical thought. Mencken, like Huneker, was a critic with crippling flaws, and if he helped make the literary renais-

sance of the twenties possible he also did not have the vaguest idea
what to do with it or say about it.[12]

Nothing better illustrates the limitations of Huneker and Mencken
than Mencken's ode to his critical hero. Huneker, he wrote, is "the
only critic among us whose vision sweeps the whole field of beauty, and
whose reports of what he sees there show any genuine gusto." Of all
the critics, he is the only one "who knows how to arouse his audience
to anything approaching enthusiasm." He is at his best in portraying
the character of the artist about whom he is writing: his Ibsen, for
example, is not the "pretty mystifier of the women's clubs," but "a
literary artist of large skill and exalted passion, and withal a quite
human and understandable man." Huneker is essentially a civilizer, a
man who searches out the cultural centers of the world and tells Americans what is going on in all the arts, not just in literature. His world
is "the whole universe of beauty," and if America has achieved any
sort of contact with the aesthetic life of the world, "there is surely no
man who can claim a larger share of credit for preparing the way.
. . ." Here are the first difficulties: Mencken judges Huneker for his
ability to enjoy life and to help others enjoy life. He shows people
how to be civilized and tells them what it is like to be an artist. But
he never says much about the text.

Mencken found himself becoming civilized when he listened to
Huneker's torrent of conversation and thought nothing could be
better. But he also found in Huneker many of his own values. Describing Huneker's *Old Fogy,* Mencken makes Huneker into his ideal critic:
"Here, throwing off his critic's black gown, he lays about him right
and left, knocking the reigning idols off their perches; resurrecting the
old, old dead and trying to pump the breath into them; lambasting on
one page and lauding on the next; lampooning his fellow critics and
burlesquing their rubber-stamp fustian. . . ." Entranced by the daz-
zling performance of the critic, Mencken forgets totally about the
literature involved. What he loves is the spectacle, the fireworks, the
"gargantuan gaiety," the "magnificent irreverence." At the same time,
and almost on the same page, Mencken finds that Huneker also shared
his tory prejudices in music. What Mencken values here is "a longing
for form, clarity, coherence, a self-respecting tune," and he yearns "un-
speakably for a composer who gives out his pair of honest themes, and
then develops them with both ears open, and then recapitulates them

---

12 For the background of this period see William Van O'Connor, *An Age of
Criticism* (Chicago, 1952); Arnold T. Schwab, *James Gibbons Huneker* (Stanford,
1963); Charles I. Glicksberg, *American Literary Criticism, 1900–1950* (New York,
1951); Floyd Stovall, ed., *The Development of American Literary Criticism* (Chapel
Hill, 1955; John P. Pritchard, *Criticism in America* (Norman, 1956).

unashamed, and then hangs a brisk coda to them and then shuts up."
Finally, as a kind of coda of his own, Mencken finds in Huneker the
assumption that he is dealing with an aristocracy of civilized men, and
a hatred for all that is cheap and philistine. The conclusion is inescapable that what attracted Mencken to Huneker were his own views
wrapped in a man he liked; such prejudice was not the act of a critic
but a friend, and like much of Mencken's other criticism, it was not
based on aesthetic grounds at all.[13]

Like most critical impressionists, Mencken lacked a satisfactory critical method; he was so busy purveying his own emotions with gusto that
he gave little thought to what his real job should be. When he did the
results were undistinguished. The motive of the critic who is worth
reading, he wrote about 1920, "is not the motive of the pedagogue, but
the motive of the artist. It is no more and no less than the simple desire
to function freely and beautifully. . . ." Here he was obviously analyzing himself again. Elsewhere he wrote that criticism was almost entirely
negative, "indistinguishable from skepticism," and thus the phrase
"constructive criticism" was a contradiction in terms. The critic should
abuse and shame people into doing better, and he should do it with
enthusiasm. But what was good? Mencken again looked into his soul,
and decided that "the primary aim of the novel, at all times and everywhere, is the representation of human beings at their follies and vil-
lainies. . . . It sets forth, not what might be true, or what ought to be
true, but what actually *is* true." [14] Apparently the critic was little more
than a frustrated realist. He wanted to portray life as he saw it, but
his talents did not run that way, so he criticized. Such an aesthetic was
extremely limiting, and had Mencken followed it closely he would
have been an even poorer critic than he was.

Mencken was at his best writing about his favorite contemporary
novelists. He was enthusiastic about Joseph Conrad, for instance, long
before the professors made him a minor industry. He liked the cool
aristocratic tone, the aura of masculine adventure with little sexual
romance or sentimentalism, the lack of any propaganda, and the sense
of the ultimate meaninglessness of the world. To Mencken, Conrad
was a realist, and his work was "not mere photography," but "interpretive painting at its highest." Likewise he valued the H. G. Wells of
Tono-Bungay, but lashed out in disgust when Wells became patriotic,
moralistic, and full of propaganda: these values were not "realistic,"
presumably because Mencken did not like them. Arnold Bennett, on
the other hand, received high marks for his detached irony, but low

---

13 H. L. Mencken, *A Book of Prefaces* (New York, 1917), pp. 151–96.

14 H. L. Mencken, *Prejudices* (New York, 1922), vol. 3, pp. 84, 97, 205.

ones for his lack of passion and gusto. The standard, obviously, was whether or not these writers had enough in common with Mencken to make them congenial to him and wrote well enough to qualify as literate artists. And at times, Mencken simply gave himself away, and excommunicated from the guild of artists all those he decided would be a bore over beer at Lüchow's: "No virtuous man . . . has ever painted a picture worth looking at, or written a symphony worth hearing, or a book worth reading. . . ." [15]

But at his best, Mencken could be perceptive indeed. Nothing illustrated his limited but genuine talent so well as his long essay on Theodore Dreiser. Dreiser was a very close friend of Mencken, but he was also a symbol of his time. To the genteel or moralistic critic, he stood for all the immoralities of animalism, crudity, and the sewer. But to the younger men, he was a hero, the novelist who wrote without fear about unconventional sexual activity, the slums, and the inner machinations of modern business. Mencken readily admitted that some of Dreiser's critics were right: the style was bad, the scenes often melodramatic, the books far too long, the tone humorless. Of *A Traveler at Forty,* for example, he wrote that it had a "furious accumulation of trivialities. . . . It is without structure, without selection, without reticence. One arises from it as from a great babbling, half drunken." He was equally devastating about the trial scenes shoveled into *The Financier,* or the maudlin *longueurs* of The *"Genius."* But Dreiser seemed to bring out the best in Mencken, even the Mencken who imitated Huneker and tried to evoke a feeling rather than analyze a paragraph. Although he contributed little in the way of critical analysis, Mencken did create a vivid impression of both Dreiser and his books:

> Writing a novel is as solemn a business to him as trimming a beard is to a German barber. He blasts his way through his interminable stories by something not unlike main strength; his writing, one feels, often takes on the character of an actual siege operation, with tunnelings, drum fire, assaults in close order, and hand-to-hand fighting. Once, seeking an analogy, I called him the Hindenburg of the novel. If it holds, the The *"Genius"* is his Poland. The field of action bears the aspect, at the end, of a hostile province meticulously brought under the yoke, with every road and lane explored to its beginning, and every crossroads village laboriously taken, inventoried, and policed.

He also paid attention to textual matters—*Sister Carrie,* he insisted, had a "broken back" structure, the story of Hurstwood interrupting

---

15 Mencken, *Prefaces,* p. 47; *Prejudices* (New York, 1919), vol. 1, p. 198.

the basic requirements of Carrie's story. But what made the essay mem-
orable, aside from its pioneering effect on Dreiser's critical reputation,
were the critical insights that proved Mencken a close reader. Dreiser,
he saw, did not reach his often lugubrious ideas by normal rational
thought processes: "There is vastly more intuition in him than intellect; his talent is essentially feminine," and "his ideas always seem to
be deduced from his feelings." Likewise, Mencken understood Dreiser's
portraits of old men: "In their tragic helplessness they stand as symbols
of that unfathomable cosmic cruelty which he sees as the motive power
of life itself." [16]

Perhaps the only way to sum up the mixed critical legacy that
Huneker and Mencken left to the twenties is to say that they were men
of great importance in the critical life of their times, but when their
work was done, little of lasting merit was left. Both men repeated
themselves frequently, and both wandered incoherently at times from
the subject at hand to their own emotions to a party they remembered
from years ago. Too often, like the typical progressive critics they were,
they confused the social critic with the aesthetic critic, and too often
they felt free to use the book or music they were reviewing as a club
for chastizing the professors and the philistines. Mencken was right in
exposing the aridity of much of his opponents' work; he was wrong in
attributing it to his favorite straw men, puritanism, and prudery.
America did not have enough good literature or enough good critics
for a meaningful debate at the time he wrote, and while Mencken did
his part with great flair and an unparalleled verbal fluency, he also
demonstrated his own ignorance several times too often. Lest anyone
doubt it, let him only look at his criticism of poetry: he snorted at the
work of Robert Frost, Edwin Arlington Robinson, Edgar Lee Masters,
and Vachel Lindsay, yet could write in all seriousness: ". . . Lizette
Woodworth Reese . . . has written more sound poetry, more genuinely eloquent and beautiful poetry, than all the new poets put together. . . ." [17]

IV

Just as an examination of Huneker and Mencken demonstrates how literary criticism could be an aesthetic masquerade for a
social criticism of national mores, so an examination of the most able
painter of the Progressive Era, John Sloan, shows how painting could

---

16 Mencken, *Prefaces*, pp. 67–148.

17 Mencken, *Prejudices*, vol. 1, p. 96. For a broader analysis of the whole subject
of American criticism, much of which I have had to neglect, see Richard Ruland,
The Rediscovery of American Literature (Cambridge, 1967).

also be a form of social criticism. American painting as a whole had always taken sides in the arguments about how to lead one's life. In colonial times, Benjamin West and John Singleton Copley painted chiefly in classical forms that emphasized moderation, form, rationality, and measure. Romantics like Thomas Cole and Asher Durand painted landscapes that told Americans how small man appeared when placed in his natural context, emphasizing the religious significance of the American natural environment and, especially in the case of Cole, expressly comparing America to other civilizations and creating sermons in paint on the subject of national destiny. After the Civil War, a naturalistic painter like Thomas Eakins stressed the importance of science and skepticism and ridiculed the American prejudices against the nude, against the showing of blood, or other forms of unpleasantness in art. At the opposite pole of aesthetic attitude, Mary Cassatt declared a kind of genteel war against any kind of unpleasantness in painting at all, and her work was a perfumed and feminine rejection of the whole course of modern industry and democratic political development. It was in this context that John Sloan became the painter of American socialism in its most attractive guise. He illustrated realistic stories about the poor and thus emphasized their importance in a democratic country. He drew topical cartoons that supported strikers or attacked selfish businessmen and exploiters. Perhaps most important, he led the school of American realist painters in their attempt to capture the city for modern art, and leave for dead the old, conventional, academic art that still stressed the painting of antiques, of idealized views, and the sculptural qualities of historical scenes.

Eakins had opened the way for painters like Sloan at the old Philadelphia Academy, and even after he was forced to resign, his influence lingered on in teachers like Robert Henri and Thomas Anshutz. Sloan knew and worked with both these men while he was an apprentice artist and newspaper illustrator in Philadelphia, and when he came to New York in 1904 he brought to the new center of American painting Eakins's old emphasis on common American subjects for painting, his dislike of prettification, and his willingness to represent the unattractive sides of life if they seemed appropriate. Eakins had never been particularly political. Henri had been something of a Jeffersonian or Emersonian individualist, only rarely mixing his art directly with what seemed to be his politics. With Sloan, however, life in New York included politics, and so did his art. His wife Dolly was an active socialist organizer and a tireless supporter of strikers and the impoverished. Sloan himself worked for minimal or nonexistent fees for the socialist publications *The Call* and *The Masses,* and his work included criticisms of war, of businesses that did not give in to strikers, and of politicians who were unfriendly to socialist principles. In this way his art was an instrument of social criticism like Mencken's literary criticism, Dewey's philosophy, or Ruth Benedict's anthropology.[18]

Yet it would be a serious mistake to see Sloan or any of the other artists of the Progressive Era strictly as propagandists. They were men of art, and they saw things in artistic rather than political or social terms. This artistic mind that so often produced socially relevant art is the crucial difference that separated Sloan both from the painters of the twenties, who tended to emphasize shape, form, and color to the exclusion of all "relevant" extra-artistic commentary, and from the painters of the thirties, who all too often ignored the formal aspects of art to stress the message they wished to convey. The progressive artist said, in effect, here is a scene I have artistically perceived which has relevance to your life; the twenties artist said, here is a work of the imagination that ignores social and worldly concerns and is better because it does; while the thirties artist said, art is a social weapon that is especially effective in reaching people who can't or who won't read. An oversimplification, to be sure, but these differences are there. Sloan's progressive combination of art and message appears clearly in many passages of his voluminous diary, but two views of poverty and misery illuminate most clearly, although perhaps unwittingly, how he saw pictures instead of social issues:

> . . . Walked through the interesting streets on the East Side. Saw a boy spit on a passing hearse, a shabby old hearse. Doorways of tenement houses, grimy and greasy door frames looking as though huge hogs covered with filth had worn the paint away and replaced it with matted dirt in going in and out. Healthy faced children, solid-legged, rich full color to their hair. Happiness rather than misery in the whole life. Fifth Avenue faces are unhappy in comparison.

> Started to paint from memory of the Wind and Dust Storm that we saw and felt Sunday. Across the backyards in a room on the second floor I saw a baby die in its mother's arms. The men of the house powerless, helpless, stupid. She held it in her arms after it had started to pale and stiffen. Hope tried to fight off Fact, and then Fact killed hope in her. They took it from her. The men smoked their pipes—sympathetic with her anguish and trying to reason her back to calmness. A bottle of whiskey, and a drink for her. I could hear nothing—but the acting was perfect.

---

18 Surveys of these years in painting include Oliver Larkin, *Art and Life in America* (New York, 1949, and later editions); Barbara Rose, *American Art Since 1900* (New York, 1967); and Sam Hunter, *Modern American Painting and Sculpture* (New York, 1959). The best of several biographies of Eakins is by Lloyd Goodrich. The only study of Henri is the recent and first-rate W. I. Homer, *Robert Henri and His Circle* (Ithaca, 1969).

Sloan obviously thinks these normal, lower-class people are important, and that real life is important. But he does not complain at every opportunity of the injustices of capitalism, nor does he propagandize about what he sees or paints. He is always an artist first and a reformer second, and the reform element is almost always an implicit rather than an explicit part of his paintings. By their very nature, his cartoons and commissioned drawings are of course something else.[19]

Sloan had been a key member of the Society of Independent Artists, and he had been represented in the Armory Show. As the years passed the new influences from Europe had their effect on his art and he moved at least a part of the way toward the spirit that predominated in the twenties. He became offended when the editors of *The Masses* persisted in printing his work with propagandistic subtitles, and finally quit over the issue. He never gave up socialism, but his new devotion to a purer art was obviously affected by the work of the Europeans that had been so prominent at the Armory Show: "I consciously began to be aware of the technique: the use of graphic devices to represent plastic forms. While I have made no abstract pictures, I have absorbed a great deal from the work of the ultramoderns." More and more, he came to emphasize that art should deal with things, not with their social effects, and things could only be painted for their own inherent interest. He never could abandon his progressive realism and passed it along to his many students during the twenties and thirties, but like any great artist he could change, and along with his customary street scenes, viewers could now see in his massive, muscular and metallic nudes a kind of compromise between realism and "thingness" that could pass for autonomous art. As he said, "Work which is purely non-representational loses some of the texture of life. Students cannot have too much training in cubism but there has to be an interest in life before the work takes on a healthy creative vigor." [20]

V

In architecture, as in literary criticism and painting, the most distinguished work of the Progressive Era had been often covertly, but sometimes quite blatantly, a criticism of American mores. The history of American architecture from its earliest days was, again and again, the story of ingenious adaptations by amateurs to solve whatever immediate problems they encountered in the New World. The severe

19 Van Wyck Brooks, *John Sloan: A Painter's Life* (New York, 1955); Bruce St. John, ed., *John Sloan's New York Scene* (New York, 1965), esp. pp. 13, 40, for quotations.

20 Lloyd Goodrich, *John Sloan* (New York, 1952), esp. pp. 48–49.

climatic extremes of hot and cold, the shortage of labor, and the in-
genuity of the people all combined to produce the genuinely American
architectural forms: the huge dominating chimneys, small rooms and
small windows, to keep the people warm in northern areas; the high
ceilings and the broad porches, often two or three stories high, to allow
for the maximum circulation of air, to keep the people cool in southern
areas. Such original developments, which Americans soon took for
granted, tended to be overshadowed during the dark years of nineteenth-century eclecticism, when phony Gothic, Egyptian, Byzantine,
and similar styles had a vogue that distorted American architecture for
generations. During the Progressive Era, however, the spirit of adaptation to real needs and the native environment returned, both as a
building style, and as a style of life.[21]

In Frank Lloyd Wright, the Progressive Era had its spokesman for
individualism, to contrast with the socialism of Sloan and the impressionism of Huneker and Mencken. Like most of the other progressives
Wright had a pioneer, largely midwestern heritage, and a firm ground-
ing in the values of the Protestant ethic and the Protestant religion.
He had even known the poverty and drudgery of life on a farm.
Largely untutored in any formal sense, Wright had attached himself
to several of the best architects of the period and discovered that, at
least in the matter of building private houses, he was the peer of the
best of them. The heritage of New England transcendentalism, with
its mystical devotion to nature and its obsession with organic notions
of growth, proved to be the key to his intellectual development. His
mother had educated him to be an architect and a lover of nature;
when he left home she told him: "Keep close to the earth, my boy: in
that lies strength." Wright never forgot this training, and his application of it in his work changed the face of America. By the start of the
First World War he was among the best-known American architects,
and the American who had the single greatest influence on the architecture of Europe and Asia.[22]

American building in the 1890s had been devoted to what Wright
later called "General Grant Gothic." He hated it: it "lied about everything. It had no sense of Unity at all nor any such sense of space as
should belong to a free man among a free people in a free country."
The houses were little boxes, bearing no relation to their surroundings

21 James M. Fitch, *American Building I: The Forces That Shaped It* (Boston,
1966, c.1948), provides the best background.

22 Peter Blake, *The Master Builders* (New York, 1960), part 3; Norris Kelly Smith,
Frank Lloyd Wright (Englewood Cliffs, 1966); F. L. Wright, *An Autobiography*
(New York, 1943), p. 71; Richard P. Adams, "Architecture and the Romantic Tra-
dition: Coleridge to Wright," *American Quarterly* 9 (Spring, 1957): 46–62.

and indescribably ugly. They were built without imagination and decorated without art. To Wright, they made the atmosphere threatening, and he endowed them with an animism that overwhelmed his imagery:

> Chimneys were lean and taller still—sooty fingers threatening the sky. And beside them, sticking up almost as high, were the dormers. Dormers were elaborate devices—cunning little buildings complete in themselves—stuck onto the main roof—slopes to let the help poke their heads out of the attic for air. Invariably the damp, sticky clay of the prairie was dug out for a basement under the whole house and the rubble stone-walls of this dank basement always stuck above the ground a foot or so—and blinked through half-windows.

In revolt against these structures that lived fretfully but could not grow, Wright threw out the attic with its dormer and the basement and most of the chimneys. He squashed down the roof so that it sloped gently or was flat, and lowered the ceilings so they fitted more precisely the size of a man. Servants were either thrown out of the house completely, or else relegated to more "suitable" quarters, usually tucked away behind the kitchen on the first floor. Indoors, he attacked the walls that separated people and divided families from themselves, experimented with new ways of heating and lighting, and even designed his own furniture so that no element in the house (except possibly a tenant who thought he knew his own mind) could conflict with this shelter that grew out of the soil. The result—horizontal, dark, "natural"—was the prairie house.[23]

The great symbol of Wright's accomplishment was Taliesin I (1911–14), an emblem as full of meaning for Progressive America as the Bull Moose or the City on a Hill. Taliesin was Wright's own home in Wisconsin, named after a Welsh druid poet who had sung the glories of fine art. Taking refuge from a marriage and family that he thought were constricting his freedom, Wright created his own Greenwich Village, where his free spirit could presumably roam unfettered by the demands of civilization, its laws and marriage contracts. The house he designed was explicitly *of* the hill, rather than *on* it, the logical fruition of his development of the prairie house. But as a symbol of its era Taliesin was more. Its very name hinted at the medieval heroics and romantic adventures of the days of chivalry, when great leaders led devoted vassals to victory. Woodrow Wilson dreamed of a world order, and led his people into battle to achieve it; Wright dreamed of a democracy of individualism close to the soil, and of the democratic

---

23 Wright, *Autobiography*, pp. 108, 139–42.

leader who would go into battle for the sake of beauty and the life of art. It breathed the spirit of Fourier and Brook Farm, and the dreams of human emancipation and development so precious to progressives like Tom Johnson and Brand Whitlock. The place would be self-sufficient, rural and voluntary; architects would flock like crusaders to their feudal baron, and learn the means for wiping out the infidel. Wright could thus solve his personal problems and live with his new companion; and he and his followers could emancipate themselves and their country at the same time, free from the demands and constrictions of the new world of industrial chaos and rising bureaucracy.[24]

Wright's brief idyll came to an end when a mentally deranged servant set a spectacular fire that destroyed Taliesin I, and murdered Wright's mistress, her children, and several others. His career was torn apart, his home and symbol destroyed, and his life a public scandal. The coming of the First World War meant fewer and fewer commissions anyway, but the newspapers never forgot him or his peculiar habits of dress and speech. In the 1920s, his status became just as symbolic as Taliesin I had been, but with a painful difference. Americans, misled by the British example, had long held tenaciously to moral and ethical views of art. The immoral man could not paint anything but an immoral picture, and good pictures were of necessity the products of good men. The architect who had run off to live in public adultery with the wife of a client was thus, *ipso facto,* an incompetent. His buildings were not only ridiculous, they were unsafe pollutants of the American landscape. The election of Warren G. Harding and the rise of businessmen to power in the twenties in a sense symbolized the resurrection of these barbarous aesthetic principles. They coincided, all too tragically, with Wright's adventures with another mistress, her increasing insanity, and a series of tragicomic lawsuits, harassments, arrests and other public indecencies and prevented Wright from producing a single commissioned work of merit in the United States in this period. His international reputation had enabled him to receive the commission to build the Imperial Hotel in Tokyo during and just after the war, but when that was completed he seemed to be through. He was immoral so his work must be bad. He refused to conform, and a nation of conformists ignored him, except for the scandals. One can scarcely make a more severe indictment of the United States in the twenties than to say that its greatest practicing artist was known across the land only as an adulterer. Other architects of the Chicago School, men like George G. Elmslie, William G. Purcell, and Walter Burley Griffin, tried with some success to spread Wright's concepts, and West Coast architects like Richard Neutra and Rudolph Schindler even

---

24 Ibid., pp. 167 ff.

adapted Wright's precedents to European innovations, but aside from these few exceptions, things looked bleak. Not until the 1930s were almost half gone did Wright begin to regain the stature that was his in 1910—by then he was safely and legally married, and presumably too old to do much damage.[25]

VI

The progressive legacy, then, was a distinctly mixed one: in social thought almost totally benign, preaching a democratic personality theory and the tolerance of cultural relativism; and in literature and the fine arts, stressing reform and immediate relevance, and portraying the common man in his myriad activities. True to progressive habits of thought, in all these areas men were devoted to criticism of the mores of society, and they always assumed that some socially relevant conclusions would definitely follow from their work. Unlike figures in the decade to come, who tended to proclaim loudly the irrelevance of art, politics, and social thought to any kind of reform, the progressives always took sides and thus were always at least obliquely involved in politics.

Unfortunately, politics *per se* was exactly the area where the progressive impulses were most exhausted in 1920 and after. Some legacy of reform remained: the farmers in particular agitated for government protection and price supports, and they and their allies also campaigned for such projects as publicly owned power plants and the construction of public works like the Tennessee Valley Authority. But the essence of progressive politics was the messianic, optimistic, revivalistic tone of the local campaigns for mayor and national campaigns for Roosevelt and for Wilson. The fairly meager results of these political struggles at all levels were slowly becoming more and more clear, and that was bad enough, but yet the real disaster was quite obviously the effect of the First World War. Strictly speaking, no event had been more "progressive" in its fervent idealism, its rhetoric, and its complete faith that good intentions would be sufficient to secure good results—ultimately the reign of peace on earth. After the debacle of Versailles and the election of Harding, progressives found themselves in a kind of shock. They had tried to make the world safe for democracy, but had only changed the names of the colonial powers in large parts of the world. They had wanted to remake diplomacy, and they found the old methods as entrenched as before. They had wanted to remake America, and had succeeded in achieving a society fit only

---

25 *Ibid.*, esp. pp. 275 ff; for the successors of Wright, see Mark L. Peisch, *The Chicago School of Architecture* (New York, 1964).

for businessmen. The result was an attitude totally at odds with the old progressivism, a skepticism that frequently made all political effort seem irrelevant.[26]

The experience of the Jeffersonian liberal Frederic C. Howe was typical. A Wilson man since his days with Wilson at Johns Hopkins, years before either man planned to enter politics, he had been swept into the progressive movement in Tom Johnson's Cleveland; and in that most progressive of towns he had become a strong believer in direct democracy, the single tax, and home rule. He became an expert on taxation and on cooperatives, in both America and Europe. He served in the Ohio legislature, in an often futile attempt to enable local cities to run their own affairs without rural interference. Wilson's election had been one of his answered prayers, and when the President asked him to be commissioner of immigration for the Port of New York, he joined the first really liberal administration in his mature lifetime. He sincerely wanted to extend the progressive ideals to the new Americans that streamed into Ellis Island, to find their hidden talents, and encourage whatever latent abilities he might discover, whether mechanical or intellectual. What he found almost destroyed him mentally and physically. The president had a closed mind that was basically uninterested in Howe's problems. Racketeers had for years been fleecing uncomprehending immigrants of their savings, through food concessions, phony points of embarkation, devious travel plans, and a host of harassments. But the petty clerks who ran the department, and who were protected by civil service, did not care and fought all change. Some were corrupt, others incompetent. Congressmen proved to be under the influence of lobbyists, and quite willing to attack Howe as a communist whenever he asked for reform.

As Howe's term went on, he found himself less a commissioner of immigration than a jailer. The country went through its convulsions of moral righteousness, and Howe found himself responsible for whichever groups had most recently fallen into public disfavor. First a load of "German spies" arrived, then a load of "white slavers," and a load of "Reds." That most of the men and women involved were totally innocent of the charges levelled against them was soon patently obvious, but every time Howe tried to treat them in a civilized fashion, granting them the barest minimum of judicial protection, he was denounced by all the patriots and profiteers within earshot. He wanted to protect communists, therefore he was a communist; he wanted to

---

26 The best general introduction to this subject is Arthur Link, "What Happened to the Progressive Movement in the 1920s?" *American Historical Review* 54 (July 1959): 833–51; see also Murray R. Benedict, *Farm Policies of the United States, 1790–1950* (New York, 1953).

protect Germans, therefore he was a spy. He protested to Washington, and even spoke to the president himself. Except for an occasional liberal in an appointive position, like Louis Post, Howe received no assistance at all. The government that he had loved and the president he had adored used spies and totalitarian methods to root out many of the men who had once worked side by side with them.

> The crushing of this movement and the men responsible for it made me hate in a way that was new to me. I hated the Department of Justice, the ignorant secret-service men who had been intrusted with man-hunting powers; I hated the new state that had arisen, hated its brutalities, its ignorance, its unpatriotic patriotism, that made profit from our sacrifices and used its power to suppress criticism of its acts. I hated the suggestion of disloyalty of myself and my friends; suggestions that were directed against liberals, never against profiteers. I wanted to protest against the destruction of *my* government, *my* democracy, *my* America.

Howe also went abroad and saw the death of liberalism at Versailles. He knew many of the diplomats personally and was aware at first hand of the shortcomings of Wilson's foreign policies and of his rigid and naive character. The conservative triumph at home and abroad, all endorsed by the man who had been his hero, produced a disillusion in Howe and the other Progressives so profound that it colored their attitudes toward politics and war for more than a generation. If that was the way liberal politics worked, they would have no more to do with politics of any variety. The state, once so benign, was no longer worthy of trust. "It seemed to want to hurt people; it showed no concern for innocence; it aggrandized itself and protected its power by unscrupulous means. It was not my America, it was something else." Second, the disasters in the war and the making of the peace meant that the lives of other peoples were no concern of Americans. We should leave them alone: "Righteousness meant getting off the backs of people; it meant extending to backward nations the same liberties we enjoyed at home." To do this we must not interfere; we should instead mend our own fences—"we must begin at home." The third casualty was the liberal faith in rational discussion. Howe had believed in facts, in dispassionate analysis, in persuasion. "We liberals had the truth. If we talked it enough and wrote it enough, it would undoubtedly prevail." But it obviously did not. People, apparently, were not as rational as the Progressives had thought. Even when they knew their own best interests, they frequently did not follow them.[27]

The end of faith in political action, the end of faith in interna-

---

27 Frederic C. Howe, *The Confessions of a Reformer* (New York, 1925), quotations on pp. 279, 282, 320, 322.

tionalism, the end of faith in rationality: the stage was set for new ideas, ideas that condoned an irrational, autistic narcissism that ignored social problems. In the transition from the Progressive Era to the 1920s, the most obvious change was just this: not only did politics seem hopeless to intelligent people after the war, but it was also quite absent from their personality theory and their art. The individual self replaced the moral reformer as the cynosure of the country.

II

WHEN
WE
WERE
VERY
YOUNG

The social science that so captivated intellectuals before the war had not been completely oriented toward the community. The ideas of the new psychology were just as present in Mabel Dodge's salon as the ideas of social thought, and may well have been more prominent. Mabel Dodge herself, obsessed as she was with her own mind and body, was particularly susceptible to the new ideological vogues coming over from Europe. Max Eastman wrote occasional articles in popular magazines, telling middle-class Americans what, for example, Freud might say about their slips of the tongue. Walter Lippmann probably encountered Freud's theories at Harvard, where William James was open to all the new ideas and willing to defend many of Freud's insights. The few trained psychologists who were working in the universities, however, were only rarely friendly to the new ideas, and for every William James or G. Stanley Hall willing to give Freud his due, a dozen men seemed ready to denounce his ideas as subversive of morality and religion. Yet so attractive were several of these new ideas that many intellectuals knew and used them even before America entered the war. The new psychology was thus one of those odd cases where the unprofessional intelligentsia adopted new doctrines before most of the learned men in the field had certified them. For Max Eastman, the repressions of society were an obvious evil, and his own hedonistic mentality absorbed the new psychology without difficulty. For Lippmann, Freudian psychology offered key insights into mass behavior, especially in politics, and his early books display at least some knowledge of the irrational basis of human behavior. But in the 1920s these educated, consciously Freudian people were in a distinct minority; the people of the country took up what they understood of the new ideas and made them stylish, a fad; only after they became popular did they filter up, as it were, into the training of professional medical men.[1]

Mabel Dodge was typical of these faddists insofar as a person so implacably exotic could be typical of anything. One of her earliest pet specialists was Dr. Smith Ely Jelliffe, who believed, she wrote, "that nearly all bodily illness is a failure of the spirit expressing itself at the physical level. . . ." He was, in other words, a descendent of the nineteenth-century spiritualists, with perhaps a dash of Mary Baker Eddy: disease was all in your mind, so to cure it, talk yourself out of it. Jelliffe, to this day, retains a certain professional reputation, but from the picture of his work that emerges from Mabel Dodge's memoirs, it is hard to understand why. Any new science is prone to aberrations as men follow false trails and then abandon them, but her version of Jelliffe's ideas makes him seem an unlikely candidate for immortality. He was, says Mabel Dodge, fascinated by the symbolism of the human body: the respiratory organs, for example, stood for human aspiration, and a man's breath was no less than the breath of God. Failure in aspiration meant that the lungs, the bronchial tubes, or the larynx would break down. "The creation, birth, and development of the soul could be reckoned in these parts, and they corresponded with the lower organs of sex where creation on another plan was effected." Jelliffe's slogan was, "As below, so above." If a person came down with

---

[1] Mabel Dodge Luhan, *Movers and Shakers,* passim; Frederick J. Hoffman, *Freudianism and the Literary Mind* (Baton Rouge, 1957, c.1945), ch. 1–3; F. H. Matthews, "The Americanization of Sigmund Freud: Adaptations of Psychoanalysis before 1917," *Journal of American Studies* (April 1967); David Shakow and David Rapaport, *The Influence of Freud on American Psychology* (Cleveland, 1968, c.1964), pp. 20 ff., 55 ff., 88 ff. Two useful dissertations are John C. Burnham, "Psychoanalysis in American Civilization Before 1918" (Stanford, 1958; Ann Arbor #58–2501); and Nathan G. Hale, "The Origins and Foundation of the Psychoanalytic Movement in America, 1909–1914" (Berkeley, 1966; Ann Arbor #65–13501).

cancer, he was really consumed by hatred: "It was a parasite eating away the vitality of man." The bowels, on the other hand, "were the vehicle of the money power, excrement was gold, hoarded or distributed in circulation. . . ." When presumably reputable and trained practitioners were handing out this sort of nonsense, however garbled the patient's version of it might be, psychology could scarcely help receiving not only vulgarization, but also ill-informed judgments both pro and con.

Max Eastman, also a friend of Jelliffe's, was considerably more responsible than Mabel Dodge in what he did with Freud's ideas, although even he was probably not orthodox enough for the serious medical practitioners of psychoanalysis. Eastman began reading Freud in 1914 and never stopped. His extensive autobiographical volumes consistently use Freudian terminology wherever it seems even faintly relevant. In addition, like many men of the Left, he was still attempting to "mix" Marx and Freud into a viable radical social program, regardless of their theoretical incompatibility. Thus, in *Marx, Lenin, and the Science of Revolution* (1926), he devoted a whole chapter to Marx and Freud which Freud himself found "really important, probably also right" (*"wirklich bedeutsam, wahrscheinlich auch richtig"*). But Eastman was the student of Dewey far more than he ever was of Marx or Freud. He was so totally pragmatic in his mental processes, so "scientific" in his orientation, that he sometimes did not seem to know his own true intellectual ancestors. He was really a Freudian only when it "worked," just as he was a Marxist only when Marxism "worked." In fact, Eastman and the Freud he so admired had such wildly varying temperaments that, looked at together, they provide more of an example of how America perverted Freud's theories than how it developed them.

Eastman, unlike most American intellectuals, actually managed to meet Freud, and he used the occasion to show how a genuine intellectual could analyze Freud in a detached fashion. In doing so he provided a useful alternative picture to place beside Mabel Dodge's bizarre impressionism. Eastman, as usual, was his scientific self in analyzing Freud, and he found Freud very unscientific. He criticized Freud for referring to the "unconscious" as an "it"—an entity, rather than the void left when consciousness was not present. For Eastman, this unscientific use of terminology provided an excellent means of getting at the "real" Freud, and he was apparently right. Psychoanalytic pietists would doubtless deny it, but Eastman in fact had a definite insight into Freud, and his remarks bear repeating. Freud, to Eastman, was not a scientist "but an artist—a demonological poet—who insisted on peopling an underworld with masked demons who move about in the unlocal dark, controlling our thoughts and the action of our bodies. . . ." Freud's demons were mysterious, but they were "endowed both with ideas and intentions, and behave at times almost exactly like little ghouls or demons." To Eastman, who had the soul of a poet and lover whatever the uses he made of "science," this Freudian troll kingdom was irresistible. He thus put his finger on the real impact that Freud would have in America and other countries: he would be far more a stimulator of the artistic intellect than a contributor to hard science. "To me he was less like Newton, or Darwin, or any of the great men of science, than like Paracelsus—a man who made significant contributions to science, but was by nature given to infatuation with magical ideas and causes." [2]

But for every serious writer on Freud, like Eastman or the well-known and responsible A. A. Brill, there were a dozen popularizers. None of them outdid André Tridon, a tireless producer of books that cheerfully mixed together whatever the author found attractive in Freud, Jung, Adler, or anyone else he had read. "Our unconscious," he wrote, "is like a pool into which dead leaves, dust, rain drops, and a thousand other things are falling day after day, some of them floating on the surface for a while, some sinking to the bottom, and, all of them, after a while, merging themselves with the water or the ooze." Or, changing the metaphor and the mood, "Our unconscious is a tremendous storage-plant full of potential energy which can be expended for beneficial or harmful ends. Like every apparatus for storing up power, it can be man's most precious ally. . . ." With commendable thoroughness and unfortunate lack of discrimination, Tridon wandered through all the standard concerns of psychoanalysis, including repression, dream interpretation, symbols, everyday actions, wit, hysteria, and perversion, in an effort to understand the theory further and to give people a kind of guide for the game of life. The new learning could be enjoyable as well as helpful.

Rice and old shoes at a wedding, Tridon reported cheerfully, were obvious symbols of the semen and the female genitals. Cinderella stories blended sex and ego satisfaction: "They all emphasize the conflict between the young girl and her mother or stepmother, and all end with the humiliation of the mother and the other daughters and Cinderella's marriage to a beautiful prince." Still other stories "seem to be compensation stories for women compelled to marry some repulsive man who reminds them of an animal." Jokes, he said, were a key to character: obscene ones revealed exhibitionism, aggressive jokes sadism, and cynical jokes a craving for selfish hedonism. At times,

---

2 Dodge, *Movers*, quotations on pp. 20, 440; Max Eastman, *Love and Revolution* (New York, 1964), pp. 461, 485–87; *Great Companions* (London, 1959), esp. pp. 124–25, 132–34.

Tridon offered a comment that showed a certain insight into the progress of history: "A few hundred years ago the insane man was treated as a criminal. In a hundred years every criminal will be treated as a diseased man." But at other times, he gave off the air of a sciolist pontificating with inadequate evidence: "The passive male homosexual is in every case the son of a widow or divorced mother"; puritanism he called "a dignified neurosis"; the gossip "is either an oversexed person or an unconscious thief or an unconscious murderer." No one, he insisted, *"has to become insane unless he unconsciously wishes to do so."* As his contribution to social therapy, Tridon also suggested that exhibitionists could be used with social benefit if they were encouraged to go into dancing or the theater, that masochists would do well in nursing, and sadists "would wield harmlessly a butcher's knife or a surgeon's scalpel." If, as seems likely, Tridon was the most widely read of the popularizers of psychoanalysis, the average conception of the new ideas was scarcely likely to be a comfort to a newly practicing psychoanalyst.[3]

II

The new narcissism practiced by the intelligentsia meant a whole new series of interests. *"We have all been educated—and just look at us!"* Floyd Dell snorted in 1919. *Were You Ever a Child?*, his first book after the war, was often coy and sentimental, but it indicated the changes in store for progressive ideas about children, education and the life of art. Dell never mentioned Dewey by name in this book, but his influence was pervasive. The purpose of education was to facilitate mastery of the present environment, not memorization of dead facts, and school buildings were to be a part of community life, and not abandoned after school hours. The concept of continuous growth, and the desire to equate education with life were clearly central. The key question, Dell said, was "How can education encourage and develop, not in a few individuals, but in the masses of the people, the creative faculties which are the source of beauty?—for it must conceive its task in these broad terms if it is to be a democratic education." Dell solved the problem neatly: the artist and the child were essentially the same thing, differing only in chronological age. "The child is an artist; and that artist is always a child," and the

---

3 The quotations and paraphrases are taken from André Tridon, *Psychoanalysis: Its History, Theory and Practice* (New York, 1923, c.1919); *Psychoanalysis and Behavior* (New York, 1920); *Easy Lessons in Psychoanalysis* (New York, 1921); *Psychoanalysis and Man's Unconscious Motives* (New York, 1924). Tridon wrote at least three other books at this time on similar topics.

greatest outbursts of artistic effort have always come from artists who retained the "naive, unspoiled vision of the child." The child/artist was "one who *plays* with his materials." The meaning for the school-room was obvious—it should become a theater, so that "the spirit of creative play" could permeate all schoolwork, and the school itself become "a gorgeous, joyous, dramatic festival of learning-to-live." Dell himself had been a child and an artist. He had also been an avid reader of psychoanalytic literature and had gone through psycho-analysis. Where progressives had believed in the rational order of man and his world, Dell believed that ". . . man is not primarily a thinking animal—he is a creature of emotion and action." As such, the child, who was emotional and irrational, and the artist, who captured these currents in art, should become the ideals for men in general: ". . . we must treat children as our equals. Education must embody a demo-cratic relationship between adults and children." In other words, since Dell and his friends in Greenwich Village were the ideal types of social development in the 1920s why could not children grow up to be like them? The narcissism of psychoanalysis could scarcely go farther: his ideas, Dell concluded, involve "no less a heresy than the calm assumption that the artist type is the highest human type, and that the chief service which education can perform for the future is the deliberate cultivation of the faculty of 'creative dreaming.' " [4]

It was only a small step from bohemian idealization of the child to the schools' attempt to make the child into a bohemian, and geography conspired to make it even smaller. While Dell and his friends theorized about their love affairs at the south end of Broadway, at the north end one of their number, Harold Rugg, was spreading the gospel from his post at Columbia Teachers College. With a dualism worthy of Vernon Parrington or Charles Beard, Rugg was at work dividing schools and scholars into those who browbeat children and those who nourished them, those who believed in discipline and those who believed in growth, those that were teacher-centered and those that were child-centered. Rugg idealized the child-as-artist fully as much as Dell, and his work did far more to bring such a phenomenon into existence. The aim of the old schools, he argued, was to force the child into the mold society had prepared for him—the child had to adapt to society, and "growing" meant only increasing the ability to conform. The new school was quite different. It saw in every child a well of untapped

---

4 For the biographical and psychoanalytic background, see Floyd Dell, *Home-coming* (New York, 1933), pp. 291 and passim; for the quotes here, see *Were You Ever a Child?* (New York, 1919), pp. 9, 98–99, 100, 102, 129, 139, 156, 198. For more Village background, see also Joseph Freeman, *An American Testament* (New York, 1936), esp. pp. 158, 274–75.

creativity and individuality, and did what it could to bring out this unique, creative capacity. Where the old schools insisted on rote memorization in standard subjects such as Latin and mathematics, the new schools gave the child what he most enjoyed doing: the dance, handicrafts, music, graphic arts, or trips to businesses or institutions in the nearby community to stimulate interest in the larger environment. The ultimate goal was a society of child-artists, just as Dell had dreamed: "The artist in Everyman's child is being discovered, not only in the unusual, the gifted, the genius; the lid of restraint is being lifted from the child of the common man in order that he may come to his own best self-fulfillment. The new schools are providing 'drawing-out' environments in sharp contrast to the 'pouring-in' environments of the old." The goal was to have the child say not "I know" but "I have experienced."

Rugg insisted throughout *The Child-Centered School* that he was only elaborating on the ideas set forth in the Progressive Era by John Dewey. Increasingly, as the decade wore on, the parallels with Dewey wore thinner and thinner, and even Dewey's patience with some of his so-called disciples disappeared. Dewey had stressed the growth of the child of Everyman in his earlier books, and Rugg was correct in seeing his ideas implicit in much that Dewey wrote. But Dewey's work must be considered in its historical context, and only as experimental plans to be tested before becoming permanent. Rugg, like his students, was innocent of historical perspective. He insisted that he was following Dewey when he argued that "personality evolves from within. It cannot be imposed from without," and that "it's the feel inside, the urge to create, the occasional glimpses of some personal ideal . . . — these the new education seeks to evoke and to build upon." But he was only half right, and thus often wrong. Dewey neatly counterbalanced his emphasis on the child's unique capacities with his notions that the child grew up by modeling himself on the adults and teachers around him and became a useful and cooperative member of the community. If anything, he stressed social conformity rather than individual idiosyncracy. Above all, Dewey's child was a socialized child. Both Dewey and Rugg stressed that schools should be involved in community affairs, and both men downgraded traditional disciplines in favor of physical and artistic work. But Dewey was fighting the pioneer's battle against entrenched methods, while Rugg was merely annotating and consolidating work already mapped out. Rugg was doubly culpable for not seeing more clearly the aimless, mindless, and indiscriminate activity that many of his pet institutions were encouraging. Instead, he railed against the "Reactionary Right" of academic, college-minded people, and made juvenility into a national institution. Certainly Dewey himself knew the difference. After studying certain aspects of the child-centered schools, he wrote: "Such a method is really stupid. For it attempts the impossible, which is always stupid; and it misconceives the conditions of independent thinking." As the years passed his skepticism increased, even as he found himself held responsible for the very views he himself was attacking.[5]

The influence, of course, cut both ways. The bohemians influenced Rugg and his schools, and the schools influenced the bohemians. As Joseph Freeman wrote, about a decade later, "For us, at this time, the child was a symbol of incredible importance. In the Village the artist was supposed to be free of conventional obligations because he was a child, and the child was the bohemian's substitute for the simple and happy savage of the eighteenth-century romantics, the "natural man" endowed with boundless goodness and creativeness which were corrupted by conventional society." For Freeman the school was the one which his mistress Laura helped run in Stelton, New Jersey. The school itself was run by a radical group, including many of the poorer laborers in the city. Freeman spoke of his trips there as "pilgrimages"—obviously the combination of intellectual radicalism, the participation of the workers, and the presence of the artist-children were all tied together in a symbolic veneration that amounted to a religion for men like Freeman. The school was a Rugg prototype: "The child learned through play. He was expected to master hammer and nail, crayon and paper, acting and dancing through the open avenues of 'self-expression.'" The teachers used no creed to indoctrinate the child and volunteered no ideas unless the child requested them—the child did not even see a book until he asked to learn to read. His natural instincts presumably guided him safely through the educational process, and physical contact with his world gave him an interest in his work presumably denied to the merely bookish. That such an education of necessity involved its own kind of indoctrination, no one seemed to realize; that it isolated the child from the real world even as it tried to introduce it to him, escaped all of Freeman's friends. The child "was treated tenderly, respectfully, seriously; but it was forgotten that someday he would become an adult in a world utterly different from Stelton. No provision was made for a transition to that world." Like Greenwich Village, Stelton was an adolescent "dreamworld," which actually bound the hands of its children for the coming struggle with reality. In fact, the whole enterprise was as reactionary as the Luddite movement or the medievalism of William Morris. The hand-

---

5 Harold Rugg and Ann Schumaker, *The Child-Centered School* (Yonkers-on-Hudson, 1928), passim, esp. pp. 62–63, 5–6; on Dewey see esp. Lawrence A. Cremin, *The Transformation of School* (New York, 1961), pp. 234 ff.

made clothes, the self-conscious sandals, the studious avoidance of the whole modern industrial world were really reversions to Fourierism, or even Jeffersonian agrarianism. "For many of them art was not an attempt to express contemporary civilization, but to escape from it into dreams of a nonindustrial world assumed to be full of peace, beauty, and love." [6] That was just not what Dewey had intended.

III

Not to mention what Freud had intended. The reception of his ideas in America was a subject that always irritated Freud. He did not trust the country as a whole, he loathed Woodrow Wilson and his war policies, and he found intellectual life shallow and self-indulgent in all but a few special areas of academia. For Freud was precisely the opposite, in his own character, of the popular image associated with his name in America: he was austere, moralistic, rationalistic and extremely conservative in many of his views, yet in America his name symbolized freedom, enthusiasm, license, aimless growth, and the life of art. Compressing the doctrine of a seminal thinker into a few paragraphs is risky business at best, but few will deny that America perverted Freud, and nothing shows this better than a brief summary of his basic views. Freud viewed the activities of the human body as the results of the biological demands that motivated people. In his analyses of his patients' dreams and neuroses, he discovered what seemed to be an inherent conflict between the demands of human instinct, and the demands of society as a whole. The individual said, "I want," and society, from its broader experience, said, "You can't." The conflict began at birth and was most important for character development in childhood. If the parents were unsuccessful in easing the child past the crises involved in civilizing him, his adulthood would be haunted by the ghosts of his unhappy past. Problems that were essentially unresolved were repressed into the unconscious, where they remained, unverbalized but persistent. They could disturb a man's dreams, cause him anxiety, invade the privacy of his sexual life, motivate him into religion or art, and cause him to deviate from what common experience led people to call "normal" life. In a sense, Freud led people to become the literary critics of life: from him they learned to look at the actions of characters and determine the deeper meaning of their acts. In the hands of an André Tridon, this meant discussing the symbolism of rice at weddings or the desirability of sadists becoming surgeons. In more discriminating hands, it meant that people could

---

6 Joseph Freeman, *An American Testament* (New York, 1936), esp. pp. 280–82, 288.

seek medical help for emotional problems as well as for physical ones.[7]

Freud was at his most accessible in *The Psychopathology of Everyday Life*. The tone of this work was conversational and untechnical, and the wealth of personal examples from Freud's own life, from his patients, and from his friends provided an excellent mask for the radical ideas that lay behind the surface commonsense of the prose. For example, when Freud wrote that in his analysis of name-forgetting in himself, "I find almost regularly that the name withheld shows some relation to a theme which concerns my own person, and is apt to provoke in me strong and often painful emotions," he could be read on the popular level as saying that he tended to forget things that bothered him. He could also be read at a somewhat higher level as saying that painful emotions tended to become part of the unconscious, the unverbalized part of the human mind, and thus introduce this new and radical psychoanalytical concept. His illustrations were equally apt at both levels, as is shown by one given him by A. A. Brill, one of his most eminent American followers, which would be equally comprehensible to a Mabel Dodge:

A wealthy but not very generous host invited his friends for an evening dance. Everything went well until about 11:30 P.M., when there was an intermission, presumably for supper. To the great disappointment of most of the guests, there was no supper; instead, they were regaled with thin sandwiches and lemonade. As it was close to Election Day, the conversation centered on the different candidates; and as the discussion grew warmer, one of the guests, an ardent admirer of the Progressive party candidate, remarked to the host: "You may say what you please about Teddy, but there is one thing—he can always be relied upon, he always gives you a *square meal*," wishing to say *square deal*. The assembled guests burst into a roar of laughter, to the great embarrassment of the speaker and the host, who fully understood each other.

This sort of anecdotal trip into the unconscious was obviously a key attraction of the new psychology for intellectuals, and as many memoirs show, they applied it immediately to their friends, their slips of the tongue, and their use of their hands. But a far more important point that many of them also grasped was that in these little stories Freud was trying to describe the irrationalities of outward life in the most rational way possible. He insisted that there was a reason for even the most trivial things, and that all would be clear if only men

---

7 The best introduction to Freud is the Lionel Trilling–Stephen Marcus abridgment of Ernest Jones's three-volume biography; for Freudianism, the best guide is Phillip Rieff, *Freud: The Mind of the Moralist* (New York, 1961, c.1959).

could understand and analyze perceptively enough. These mistakes, he wrote, were not "psychic arbitrariness," but in fact followed "lawful and rational paths." When an individual forgot a name, he did so because of "intimate and painful things in the person analyzed." All of his cases, he insisted, had in common "the fact that the forgotten or distorted material becomes connected through some associative path with an unconscious stream of thought which gives rise to the influence that comes to light as forgetting." People forgot because they were displeased, and this displeasure took root in the unconscious but appeared and disappeared to the view of the onlooker in the form of the little problems of everyday life. In this outwardly offhand manner, the new reinterpretation of the old concept of the unconscious—now the most important concept in the history of modern thought—came to America and helped foster the cult of the child, the vogue of stream-of-consciousness literature, of nonobjective art, and many of the other ideas of the twenties. As Freud summed it up (his italics): *"Certain inadequacies of our psychic functions . . . and certain performances which are apparently unintentional prove to be well motivated when subjected to psychoanalytic investigation, and are determined through the consciousness of unknown motives."* 8

The step from everyday life to dreams gave Freud his next major insights into the unconscious. In *The Interpretation of Dreams* he described the dream as "a psychological structure, full of significance, and one which may be assigned to a specific place in the psychic activities of the waking state," and dream interpretation as "capable of yielding information concerning the structure of our psychic apparatus which we have hitherto vainly expected from philosophy." No matter how condensed or distorted the outward appearance of a dream might be, no matter how much it might look like the realization of an apprehension or simply a random memory, "if the method of dream-interpretation here indicated is followed, it will be found that dreams do really possess a meaning." For Freud, dreams were not the disorganized expressions of cerebral activity emphasized by other writers: *"When the work of interpretation has been completed the dream can be recognized as a wish-fulfillment."* In addition, he found that in all cases the dream was based on material supplied since the last period of sleep, regardless of what might be evoked with apparent randomness by these events working on the unconscious. As he worked out

---

8 Since the Modern Library edition of Freud's works contains examples of everything I discuss in this brief summation, all references are to A. A. Brill, translator and editor, *The Basic Writings of Sigmund Freud* (New York, 1938); for these paragraphs, see especially pp. 50, 82, 35, 49, 150. For further material on Freud's literary style, see Stanley Edgar Hyman, *The Tangled Bank* (New York, 1962), part 4.

the scheme, Freud found that the source of these keys to the unconscious could be:

(a) A recent and psychologically significant event which is directly represented in the dream.

(b) Several recent and significant events, which are combined by the dream into a single whole.

(c) One or more recent and significant events, which are represented in the dream content by allusion to a contemporary but indifferent event.

(d) A subjectively significant experience (recollection, train of thought), which is *constantly* represented in the dream by allusion to a recent but indifferent impression.

Or, phrased somewhat more succinctly elsewhere: *"The dream is the (disguised) fulfillment of a (suppressed, repressed) wish."*

Even more important to the intellectuals, however, was the system of dream symbolism that Freud used to poke into the nineteenth-century consciousness. Kings and queens, for example, were usually the dreamer's parents, while the dreamer was a prince or princess. And then came the repeated jabs:

All elongated objects, sticks, tree-trunks, umbrellas (on account of the opening, which might be likened to an erection), all sharp and elongated weapons, knives, daggers, and pikes, represent the male member. . . . Small boxes, chests, cupboards, and ovens correspond to the female organ; also cavities, ships, and all kinds of vessels.—A room in a dream generally represents a woman; the description of its various entrances and exits is scarcely calculated to make us doubt this interpretation. . . . Steep inclines, ladders, and stairs, and going up or down them, are symbolic representations of the sexual act. . . . Of articles of dress, a woman's hat may very often be interpreted with certainty as the male genitals. In the dreams of men one often finds the necktie as a symbol for the penis. . . . All complicated machines and appliances are very probably the genitals. . . . Children, too, often signify the genitals, since men and women are in the habit of fondly referring to their genital organs as "little man," "little woman," "little thing."

During the cult of the child, intellectuals had to have their little intellectual playthings, and it was perhaps inevitable that the decorously hatted females of the previous generation took the brunt of the attack. Elsewhere, just to balance the scales slightly, Freud did insist that not all dreams called for a sexual explanation, and he was highly critical of writers like Stekel and Adler who thought they did. Intellectuals scarcely noticed, but they did perceive decently well the key insight of the book: that "the unconscious must be accepted as the general basis of the psychic life" and as "the true psychic reality." [9]

But for some of his other doctrines, Freud received little or no approval or even attention in America. The nation as a whole, despite the world war and the Versailles treaty, was essentially an optimistic group of people who thought a man could change his life and improve himself if he wished. Average Americans did not believe that early childhood was that important in determining adult character; nor did they take very seriously—except as broad humor—all Freud's talk about infantile sexuality, Oedipus complexes, seduction fantasies, and father fixations. They did not think people were so sexual in their characters, although they generally ignored or did not know that Freud used the word in a far broader sense than merely the genital. Nor did they feel much concern over the death wish, the division of the psyche between the id, the ego, and the superego, or the zonal progress of the young from mouth to anus to genitals. Conventional Christianity, Victorian morality, the Protestant ethic and the business mentality all conspired to make people ignore what they did not want to see. Instead, they found in Freud, and with more legitimacy in Carl Jung and Alfred Adler, ideas more in line with typical American assumptions.

What these Americans wanted was a club they could use to beat their parents and all the hated ideas of the previous decades: sexual repression, patriotism, fundamentalist religion, war-making idealism, and reticent artistic expression. Among such people, Freud had little trouble in finding followers for his psychoanalytic method: what could be more liberating than talking over your sex life, your parents, and your problems with an understanding medical man who said he knew all about them, and that really, you had few problems that thousands of other Americans did not share? Likewise, the importance of the unconscious was soon taken for granted, and as Floyd Dell and Sherwood Anderson and their friends remembered it, everybody was soon deep in parlor games involving jokes, dreams, mannerisms, and other idiosyncrasies. The doctrine that nothing was basically nonsense soon created more nonsense than ever. Even a few of Freud's more complex ideas gradually became accepted: the lovable, artistic child, so symbolically important, was so obviously frustrated and furious at his toilet training that its importance was soon a household shibboleth: certainly it could make parents neurotic, if not children. Infant masturbation was clearly a problem in the middle-class, repressive homes in which the artists had grown up; and the ambivalence of love and

---

9 Brill, ed., *Freud*, pp. 183, 224, 209, 207, 249, 235, 271–73, 392, 542.

hate was also the perfect tool for analyzing the tangled love affairs of the period. Other, less optimistic or strictly environmental aspects of Freudian theory received less acceptance, as far as these things can be measured. The Oedipus complex and the death wish, to name two of the most obvious, received more treatment in art than acceptance in genuine self-analysis. An artist or bohemian was perfectly willing to write stories about the love of a son for his mother; whether or not he accepted the idea as relevant to his own development was a more complex question. Even more difficult was the problem of whether such behavior was really universal, as Freud insisted, or merely the result of special circumstances peculiar to the late nineteenth-century in Vienna, and the Victorian period in Anglo-Saxon countries.

IV

In a sense, Freud's influence was stronger than this account has suggested. Even his chief opponents in the intellectual world found themselves adopting some of his ideas and emphases to improve their means of attacking him. Throughout the period between the world wars, anthropologists led the intellectual world in criticizing Freud's personality theories, while absorbing his emphasis on the young and growing child, its conflicts with its social milieu, and its difficulties in adapting its selfish personality to the demands of social coexistence. Curiously, a chief result of this anthropological work was to reinforce popular misconceptions of Freudian theory and to add to the attractiveness of the spontaneous, unspoiled child as a kind of culture hero, even as that culture hero received strong criticisms in the very books that became popular.

The chief figure in this intellectual feuding in America was Margaret Mead, the most widely read and honored of Ruth Benedict's many students. But whereas Benedict, like most of her generation, was concerned with problems of adult vocation and the nonconforming personality, Mead concentrated on the process of growing up, examining how the young members of another culture experienced the various biological stages of existence, and whether they had the same problems as American children. Like Freud, she was very much concerned with the formation of personality within the family and social circle, with sexual adjustment and marriage customs. Yet if she shared Freud's focus of interest, her interpretations were radically different. For Mead, as for most anthropologists, the all-important force in the determination of character was not infant frustration, the Oedipus complex, or a childhood trauma—not, in short, biological and inevitable—but the result of cultural expectation. A child's personality was formed by what

adults commanded it to do and was thus infinitely malleable, reform-
able, and full of possibilities.

At first glance, then, Mead should have been within the ranks of
child-worshippers like Harold Rugg and Floyd Dell, but in fact she
was not. In her examination of the Manus of New Guinea, for example, she found a group of children who quite literally had nothing to
do all day long. They could amuse themselves in any way they wished,
and no repressive adult came along to forbid their behavior. The physical environment was ideal, with both ocean and woods nearby, and not
especially dangerous, and there were plentiful quantities of materials
available for use in play activities. They had canoes, palm leaves, bark,
seeds, flowers, coconut shells, herbs, reeds, and some of them had even
seen a white man's store in operation. But these children never organized boat crews, never set up stores, never made up games of hunt-
ers and hunted, never imitated the dance activities of their elders,
never made music by themselves. They could join in when elders led
such activities but they did nothing original on their own. Mead
nowhere mentions the proponents of the child-centered school, but
they clearly were at the back of her mind when she came to her conclusions: "Those who believe that all children are naturally creative,
inherently imaginative, that they need only be given freedom to evolve
rich and charming ways of life for themselves, will find in the be-
haviour of Manus children no confirmation of their faith." Without
the suggestions of adults provided in other cultures, these children
"have a dull, uninteresting child life, romping good humouredly until
they are tired, then lying inert and breathless until rested sufficiently
to romp again." For her, the conclusions were obvious: in any culture,
adults had to decide for themselves what the norms for their children
should be and must make themselves into models proper for the child
to form his personality upon. In opposition to both Rugg and Freud,
she regarded human nature as "the rawest, most undifferentiated of
raw material, which must be molded into shape by its society, which
will have no form worthy of recognition unless it is shaped and formed
by cultural tradition." [10]

Mead's greatest contribution to the cult of the child in the 1920s
was the way she put these ideas to work in her best-known book, *Coming of Age in Samoa*. A study of the sexual maturation of the young
girl, the book not only had a phenomenal success in the popular press,
but, with a brief, approving introduction by Franz Boas, presumably
had scholarly acceptance. Here, Mead set out to examine the tradi-

---

10 Margaret Mead, *Growing Up in New Guinea* (New York, 1962, c.1930), pp.
120–21, 7–8, 212.

tional belief of the Western world that adolescence was a period of storm and stress due to biological processes associated with puberty, and that therefore little could be done about it. Teenagers were presumably full of idealism and rebellion, their sexual capacities matured before their ability to control them, and all parents and teachers could do was hang on until the young could be married off or gainfully employed and out of the house. Mead, as an anthropologist, was supremely skeptical of this view and may well have gone to Samoa more than half convinced that adolescent stress was the result not simply of coming of age but of coming of age in America. Regardless of such possible prejudgment, the questions she asked in Samoa were scientifically important: "Are the disturbances which vex our adolescents due to the nature of adolescence itself or to the civilization? Under different conditions does adolescence present a different picture?"

The culture she examined had an extremely diffused sense of family authority and social customs that enabled the child who felt abused or put-upon to escape the disagreeable situation and take refuge with understanding relatives. Very young girls were expected to serve as baby tenders for a term, but except for this preadolescent chore, they were largely ignored by the culture until they were fifteen or even older. The society was largely peaceful and had few taboos, so a great variety of behavior was permissible without social censure. Thus, puberty and initiation into sex and marriage, Mead discovered, were taken far more matter-of-factly in Samoa than in America, and the result was an almost total lack of what Americans saw as the neurotic problems associated with sex and maturation. Most girls received their sexual initiations from older men, most boys from older women, romantic love was an unknown concept, divorce was common, adultery frequent, and social disapproval of extramarital affairs minimal. In addition, open and communal living conditions meant that children became sexually knowledgeable very early, often from having witnessed adults on the other side of the living quarters. Such a low-pressure, permissive environment, Mead insisted, produced "a scheme of personal relations in which there are no neurotic pictures, no frigidity, no impotence, except as the temporary result of severe illness, and the capacity for intercourse only once in a night is counted as senility."

In America, the pressures of an acquisitive, capitalistic society, always conscious of upward mobility and fearful of failure, produced too many choices for the growing child, too many taboos that he must not violate. The parental group was restricted, social deviance not often permitted, and escape extremely difficult. Thus, Mead rather neatly cut the ground from under the advocates of the creative child, even as she produced a utopian alternative that appealed to many of them. They too wanted a sexually permissive society tolerant of de-

viance and with less pressure to succeed and conform. Where they
went wrong, Mead implied, was in their eighteenth-century assumptions that children were naturally good and creative and only needed
to have adults get out of their way. She insisted that what they needed
was to have intelligent parents adopt a life-enriching mode of existence, tolerant of deviant children and able to encourage them into
proper and rewarding activity. She managed to bring John Dewey up
to date in his progressive educational theories, even as she found she
had to oppose those like Harold Rugg who claimed that they were
acting in Dewey's name. Her book re-created Dewey's socialized child,
with a new sexual dimension and a new marriage of biology and social
theory. Adolescence in Samoa, she concluded, "represented no period
of crisis or stress, but was instead an orderly developing of a set of
slowly maturing interests and activities." The minds of the young
girls "were perplexed by no conflicts, troubled by no philosophical
queries, beset by no remote ambitions." The "uniform and satisfying
ambitions" in Samoa were "to live as a girl with many lovers as long
as possible and then to marry in one's own village, near one's own
relatives and to have many children. . . ." Dewey's social school had
read Freud, taken out his biological determinism, and produced in
Margaret Mead's Samoa a utopian adolescent vision that expressed very
well indeed the yearnings of intellectuals in the 1920s.[11]

V

But Mead and other anthropologists had to wait several
more years before their ideas, in the form of neo-Freudianism, replaced the biological determinism that was the more immediate result
of Freud's ideas. Indeed, relatively "pure" Freudian doctrine had a
great appeal even to intellectuals presumably aware of the currents of
opposition. Oddly enough, this appeal extended even into the very
arts where "creativity" was presumably most valued, and where Freud
had been most critical. Artists might well have avoided Freud simply
out of an instinct for self-preservation. Had not Freud insisted that
artistic creation was simply a form of sublimation, of value only as a
form of personal therapy? But in fact artists were fascinated by Freud,
particularly the Freud who talked of dream symbols and the unconscious. He had not really introduced these ideas into art: in the novel
they go back at least to Flaubert and Dostoyevsky, and in Freud's own
time both D. H. Lawrence and James Joyce apparently reached similar
conclusions before encountering Freud. What the new psychology did

---

11 Margaret Mead, *Coming of Age in Samoa* (New York, 1949, c.1928), pp. 11–12,
16, 82, 33, 50, 54, 58, 92, 67, 69, 83–84, 92, 95, 119, 138–39.

was to give a coherent vocabulary and systematization to ideas that literary men had long known by intuition. In so doing, it made these ideas available to lesser artists, as well as to the reading public. In America, no artist of the first rank was an obvious Freudian, but a great many—like Sherwood Anderson at his best—were psychologically acute in a way that resembled Freud, and a few found in Freud ideas that revolutionized their own creative work. In this latter group, Conrad Aiken was the most prominent.

". . . I told her my dreams about the sea. I'm always dreaming about the sea. We all know what that means, don't we? I'm going to be born again one of these days. Oh, yes, we rise again. Back to the womb, and forth once more we swim. . . ." mutters the central character of Aiken's novel *Great Circle* (1933) as he attempts to talk out his neurosis. In so doing he pointed out the central metaphorical contribution of Freud to art: the reemphasis on sea symbolism or voyage imagery that had had importance in literature at least since *The Odyssey*. Conrad Aiken took Freud's ideas about the artist as neurotic very seriously: the author was a man driven by his own past to a cathartic experience, in the hope of therapy; the reader, by identification with the characters and situations in the work of art, could help himself by sharing the catharsis. For Aiken, life became a voyage, a choppy, often aimless and fruitless sailing in search of the security of early childhood and a character reintegrated and made whole after the shattering experiences of life. In his autobiographical narrative *Ushant*, surely one of the handful of great memoirs in English, and in *Blue Voyage* (1927) he based whole books on the idea of life as a voyage. The movement of the ship came to be the process of memory, of free association therapy, of the forces of the unconscious past, as Aiken and his autobiographical counterparts in his fiction tried to navigate, with little success, the problem-filled sea of the present.[12]

Aiken had a strong personal reason for becoming a Freudian: if ever anyone had a childhood trauma, it was he. One morning, when he was still a boy, he heard his parents quarrelling, then "came the half-stifled scream, and then the sound of his father's voice counting three, and the two loud pistol shots; and he had tiptoed into the dark room, where the two bodies lay motionless, and apart, and, finding them dead, he found himself possessed of them forever." His life, he wrote later, became an attempt to create an art that would be "an equivalent to it all, in terms of his own life, or work; and an equivalent that those two angelic people would have thought acceptable." In trying to do this, Aiken evolved certain methods that gave some indication of the effect of Freud on the American novel. He con-

---

12 Conrad Aiken, *Collected Novels* (New York, 1964), esp. pp. 245, 116–18.

structed his longer works of fiction as therapeutic models; beginning with his central characters in the present, he slowly went deeper into their subconsciouses, probing into the sources of their life habits, the symbols used by their minds, their neuroses, and compulsions. Central chapters tended to be long streams of consciousness, evoking in an apparently random way all the bits and pieces of trivia that concern men and that mold their lives. In less sophisticated hands, the device became hackneyed as the "flashback," an often cliché-ridden dip into the past, used in a popular book or movie to provide a facile explanation of some current perversion. In Aiken's books and stories, plots tended to disappear as the "story" disappeared, and the stuff of art increasingly became the interior of the central character. No one ever saw buildings or trees or beautiful girls; instead, they saw one usually twisted sensibility registering these phenomena. Reading a novel became an often difficult attempt to keep up with a mind as it kept up with life. Society disappeared; all that remained were the random family, lovers, or outsiders who accidentally impinged on the central sufferer.

Freudian doctrine and the therapeutic work of art might seem to be the antitheses of romanticism and the bohemianism of Greenwich Village, yet all these ideas shared a common obsession with the child. Youth had been all-important to Freud and remained so to Aiken. Aiken's own youth had been traumatic, and his art, in its narcissistic fashion, once more returned to early life in the search for clues to the present. No longer trailing clouds of glory, no longer the delicate sensibility in the child-centered school, the child in Aiken's work was the sufferer, the abused and defenseless boy of *Great Circle* who discovered his mother in infidelity; or the imaginative schizophrenic of "Silent Snow, Secret Snow," who slowly severed his mental connection with an incomprehending world and retired into his own autistic world. Likewise, love suffered. Demarest, the central character in *Blue Voyage*, tortured himself between his idealized Cynthia and the earthy Faubion, and could never be happy with either. In *Ushant*, Aiken himself went from woman to woman in a compulsive and joyless search for fulfillment. He was unsparingly honest about his own infidelities in approved psychotherapeutic fashion; but clearly, the new realism of the Freudian novelist meant portraying the unsmiling aspects of American life, aspects which were the more typically human. The boy haunted by the image of his mother or the authority of his father was doomed to dissatisfaction: the child was father to the man, and both were miserable.[13]

---

13 Conrad Aiken, *Ushant* (New York, 1962, c.1952), pp. 302–3, 141.

VI

Intellectuals thus found themselves caught between opposing visions of the child and the artist. They could indulge themselves psychologically, take up the child-centered schools, Greenwich Village bohemianism, or a Samoan ideal of sexual freedom, and rest in the assumption of their own superiority; or they could take the more intellectually rigorous path outlined by Freud, regard art as the expression of a neurotic need, and themselves as potential misfits. In characteristically American and artistic fashion, what actually happened was more an untidy series of compromise positions than a neatly organized series of ideas. Creative personalities in all fields—art, music, literature, criticism, law—find their own forms, regardless of what the intellectual historian might say, and the creative leaders of the twenties were no exception. The earliest reaction was plainly an extension of the Greenwich Village instinct. Only a limited number of people, no matter how much they hated a Babbitt-run society, could operate child-centered schools or philosophize in the half-baked fashion of a Floyd Dell about love in Greenwich Village. The world war, however, had introduced a number of creative people to the idea of exile, and thanks to the opportunities for ambulance service a number of Americans had managed to experience the war esthetically without getting themselves blown up. After their return they gravitated to New York, and many always retained at least minimal contact with the publishing center of the country. But, as the years passed, more and more tourists invaded the area, businessmen raised the rents and restaurant prices, and the exodus began for many.

Some writers and artists moved to suburban and rural New Jersey, Connecticut, and Long Island, but to others only one place was really attractive—Europe. For many, Europe meant Paris, which they had seen while in military service and loved for its cheap prices and tolerance of the eccentric lives they hoped to lead. For others, it was the Riviera, or Munich, or Rome, or Brussels, or even Berlin. And it became increasingly clear as the decade went on that artists in America had to be internal emigrés, at odds with the world around them. Those who found this situation intolerable could leave, and often did so. America, Glenway Wescott declared, was oriented toward money, success, social acceptability, and conformity. Its writers, on the other hand, "have a mania for writing; they cannot be discouraged; they go on doing it." Despite the discouragement they meet, they continue, for "they are in love with something, in heaven or on earth, or in themselves; and their tribute to the thing they love is its equivalent, as exact as may be, in written words." Thus, American writers "are spiritual expatriates. Their position in this commonwealth is that of a band of revolutionaries or a cult of immoralists." If they stay home, "they exist by suffrance, by their willingness to endure poverty, or by 'protective coloration.' " [14]

One of the most attractive of these emigrés was the young Ernest Hemingway, with his typical hero, the young man of great sensitivity who has received some traumatic wound, and whose resulting styles of life and literature gave the twenties an alternative to the other more juvenile youth images. Like many of his fellow exiles, Hemingway grew up in the Middle West, in his case Oak Park, Illinois. His father was a doctor, and his mother a would-be opera singer whose eyes were too poor to endure stage lights, and who was thus condemned to home and children. On the one hand, the father introduced Ernest almost from birth to the rough masculine life of country living, especially during the summer trips to a lakeside home in northern Michigan. On the other hand, the mother—largely incompetent in the normal tasks of clothes-buying and housekeeping—insisted on a more aesthetic training, and the home always had its share of art and music. Ernest's obsessive concern with writing demonstrated how well some of his mother's training prepared him for his later career, but outwardly he was far more his father's son, always boastful, eager to show off his boxing prowess, and proud of his physique and his hunting and fishing skills.[15]

Hemingway graduated from high school in 1917, and decided that work as a reporter on the *Kansas City Star* would be preferable to college. While there, he immersed himself in the lowlife of the city, but he was happy only briefly and soon became extremely eager to get into the war. Despite his youth and a bad left eye, he finally managed to join a Red Cross ambulance unit destined for service in Italy. "I was an awful dope when I went to the last war," he said many years later. "I can remember just thinking that we were the home team and the Austrians were the visiting team." One of his friends at the time, however, remembered as well that Hemingway was "extremely conscious of the war as a 'crusade for democracy,' and burning with the desire to have a share in it." At his own insistence, he operated as close to the front lines as he could, and after weeks of boredom and fear that the war would pass him by, he was severely wounded on

---

[14] Glenway Wescott, "The Quarter's Books," *Transatlantic Review* 2 (1925): 446–48.

[15] For Hemingway's wounds and the whole psychiatric problem presented by his career, see especially Philip Young, *Ernest Hemingway* (New York, 1966, c.1952), esp. pp. 162–71. For biography, I have relied on Carlos Baker, *Ernest Hemingway* (New York, 1969), part 1.

July 8, 1918, by a random Austrian missile, followed by machine gun bullets in his right leg. While convalescing in Italy, he fell in love with a nurse, Agnes Hannah von Kurowsky, a situation he later developed into *A Farewell to Arms* (1929). He returned home, and as part of his therapy he renewed his acquaintance with northern Michigan and was provided with some of his best short story material. But life in both America and Canada proved as unrewarding to him as it had to Wescott and the other sensitive young men of the day, and so he went off to Paris with a bride and little else but faith that he could be a creative writer.[16]

While other intellectuals and artists were apparently motivated by social or psychological theories, Hemingway, odd as it now may seem, was motivated in large measure by religion, its loss, and the need for a replacement. The Hemingway home, like many homes in the Protestant Middle West, had been extremely religious, and its religion had been of the oppressive, moralistic variety that worried about liquor, girls, Sunday baseball, and the horrors of the card table. "The wonder to me," one of Hemingway's teachers later reflected, "is how a boy brought up in Christian and Puritan nurture should know and write so well of the devil and the underworld." The town was devoutly middle class, completely dry, and Hemingway's parents obviously approved and encouraged this repressiveness. No one will be surprised to learn that Hemingway quickly rejected his parents' religion, and that this rejection was at least partly why he fled to Paris, but Hemingway's critical readers have less readily recognized how "religious" so many aspects of his work became. Both *The Sun Also Rises* (1926) and *A Farewell to Arms* have repeated references to religious medals, rituals, and codes of proper behavior even in the most secular contexts; and it is quite clear that Hemingway and his characters felt a craving for something to replace the religion that had died within them. His parents, of course, were incapable of understanding their son and his problems, not to mention his literary solutions. When his father read *In Our Time* (1924), he found the book lacking in spiritual uplift and hoped that Ernest would "see and describe more of humanity of a different character in future volumes." Now that he had described the brutal in life, he should "look for the joyous, uplifting, and optimistic and spiritual in character. It is present if found. Remember God holds us each responsible to do our best." When *The Sun Also Rises* came out, his mother doubted that it was much of an honor to have produced "one of the filthiest books of the year," invoked the name of

---

16 Baker, *Hemingway*, quotation on p. 38; the second quotation is from Charles Fenton, *The Apprenticeship of Ernest Hemingway* (New York, 1961, c.1954), p. 57.

God, and exhorted Ernest to "try to find Him and your real work."
Ernest was not amused and stayed in Paris.[17]

Hemingway had been chafing under his parents' rule even before
the war, but like many young Americans he found that the violent
patterns of life he saw made any return to the old values simply impossible. "I got hurt in the war," Jake Barnes said laconically—for
Hemingway the most understated remarks are the ones that convey the
most pain. Hemingway really was seriously hurt in the war, and again
and again his characters suffered similar wounds, and lived close to
hysteria in trying to cope with the memory. The result came through
most clearly in the Hobbesian nihilism of a crucial passage in *A Farewell to Arms,* which in its evocative savagery recalled the battle of the
lobster and the squid in Dreiser's *The Financier.* As Frederic Henry
summed up the meaning of the war:

> Once in camp I put a log on top of the fire and it was full of ants. As
> it commenced to burn, the ants swarmed out and went first toward the
> centre where the fire was; then turned back and ran toward the end. When
> there were enough on the end they fell off into the fire. Some got out, their
> bodies burnt and flattened, and went off not knowing where they were
> going. But most of them went toward the fire and then back toward the
> end and swarmed on the cool end and finally fell off into the fire. I remem-
> ber thinking at the time that it was the end of the world and a splendid
> chance to be a messiah and lift the log off the fire and throw it out where
> the ants could get off onto the ground. But I did not do anything but
> throw a tin cup of water on the log, so that I would have the cup empty
> to put whiskey in before I added water to it. I think the cup of water on
> the burning log only steamed the ants.[18]

A nihilist by faith, a writer by vocation: the combination meant
that Hemingway sublimated all his religious energies into his art, and
took the act of writing with all the seriousness of a priest performing
a sacrament. As Hemingway said to Morley Callaghan, "A writer is
like a priest. He has to have the same feeling about his work," and
for Hemingway that meant the search for the perfect word, the perfect
sentence, that would be worthy of this religious function. When things
went badly in those early days in Paris, he repeated to himself: "Do

---

17 Baker, *Hemingway,* esp. pp. 71–72, 160, 179; Fenton, *Apprenticeship,* pp. 14–
15. On Hemingway's rather temporary and token Catholicism, see Baker, p. 185; and
Morley Callaghan, *That Summer in Paris* (New York, 1964, c.1963), pp. 89–90; as
well as Philip Young, *Hemingway,* p. 161. For just a few of the many references to
religion, see *The Sun Also Rises* (New York, 1926), pp. 22, 26, 97, 124, 245; and
A Farewell to Arms (New York, 1929), pp. 43–44, 116.

18 *The Sun Also Rises,* p. 17; *A Farewell to Arms,* pp. 327–28.

not worry. You have always written before and you will write now. All you have to do is write one true sentence. Write the truest sentence that you know." In part, the resulting "Hemingway style" came from his old journalism training on the *Kansas City Star,* with its preference for short sentences and paragraphs, its insistence on the active voice and crisp Anglo-Saxon expressions, and its hatred of any kind of extravagant adjectives. In part, the style came from Ezra Pound and Gertrude Stein, with their insistence that works of art be as concentrated as possible, with key passages often left out completely but still presumably "felt" in the final, truncated version of the work. But in greatest part the style came from the war and the inability of the old words to convey the new ideas to young men. When Frederic Henry very nearly gets himself blown up, Rinaldi comes to the hospital hunting for the words that will make Henry a hero. Henry, however, is "speechless" and cannot describe the event in a way Rinaldi can understand. Then follows the funniest example of this kind of situation in Hemingway's work:

> "Did you do any heroic act?"
> "No. I was blown up while we were eating cheese."

Rinaldi thinks Henry is joking, but he is deadly serious. The old words just won't do, and the Hemingway style is their replacement. Elsewhere, Henry spells out the rationale quite clearly, and quite clearly the war was to blame. "I was always embarrassed by the words sacred, glorious, and sacrifice and the expression in vain," he wrote. He and his generation had heard them until they were numb with the repetition and the irrelevance. In his experience, he "had seen nothing sacred, and the things that were glorious had no glory and the sacrifices were like the stockyards at Chicago if nothing was done with the meat except to bury it." After this riotously irrelevant orgy of abstractions, "only the names of places had dignity. . . . Abstract words such as glory, honor, courage, or hallow were obscene beside the concrete names of villages, the numbers of roads, the names of rivers, the numbers of regiments and the dates." [19]

As a way of exorcising the wounds of war, Hemingway developed two secular rituals that would be objective correlatives of the need for religious ritual in a world where God was dead. The first of these secular rituals was the fishing trip, where the wounded Nick Adams or Jake Barnes could return to nature and gain some peace of soul in response to natural rhythms. The simple style combines with the sim-

---

19 Callaghan, *That Summer,* p. 26; Hemingway, *A Moveable Feast* (New York, 1965, c.1964), p. 12; Fenton, *Apprenticeship,* ch. 2; Young, *Hemingway,* ch. 5; *A Farewell to Arms,* pp. 63, 184–85.

ple acts in the simple woods to refresh a spirit that has been bruised almost beyond repair. When Nick walks in the woods on a hot day, his muscles aching, he is happy: "He felt he had left everything behind, the need for thinking, the need to write, other needs. It was all back of him." He achieves ultimate peace in his tent, which becomes something like a Freudian womb symbol, the antithesis of war-ravaged Italy:

> [The tent] smelled pleasantly of canvas. Already there was something mysterious and homelike. Nick was happy as he crawled inside the tent. He had not been unhappy all day. This was different though. Now things were done. There had been this to do. Now it was done. It had been a hard trip. He was very tired. That was done. He had made his camp. He was settled. Nothing could touch him. It was a good place to camp. He was there, in the good place. He was in his home where he had made it.

Much the same thing occurs in *The Sun Also Rises*, when Bill Gorton and Jake Barnes leave the modern world momentarily to allow nature to refresh them. As Bill says, only slightly drunk, "on your knees, brother. Let no man be ashamed to kneel here in the great out-of-doors. Remember the woods were God's first temples. . . ." [20]

Hemingway's second ritual was the bull fight. Hemingway and his heroes seem to regard the bull fight much the way Poe and his cerebral protagonists regarded mysteries of crime, and for much the same reason: the compulsion about exactitude barely masks a hysterical fear that if one thing goes wrong, the whole world will collapse into madness. "San Fermin is also a religious festival," Jake Barnes points out, and one of the afternoons is given over explicitly to "the big religious procession." In the fiesta the religious elect are those with *afición;* "an aficionado is one who is passionate about the bullfights." These aficionados seem able to recognize each other and to communicate without words. They are amazed that an American like Jake Barnes could have *afición,* and they show their respect by putting their hands on his shoulder. Jake's attitude is precisely the same as Montoya's: "For one who had *afición* he could forgive anything": what could be more post-Christian? Instead of reenacting the Last Supper and the preceding confession of sins, a lapsed Catholic like Hemingway could go to the tragedy of the bull fight and watch the minutely prescribed ritual result in the death of the bull and the cleansing of the sins of the aficionados. With these rituals, Hemingway's style shifts from describing the war to describing the forest and the bull fight in a final attempt

---

20 Ernest Hemingway, "Big Two-Hearted River: Part I," in *The Short Stories of Ernest Hemingway* (New York, 1938), pp. 210, 215; *The Sun Also Rises*, p. 122.

to get some meaning out of a life in which too many people seemed to be like ants trapped on a burning log.[21] In this fashion a whole generation in effect "froze" in the status of late adolescence, unable to enter the "adult" world, or even to speak its language.

VII

Hemingway's adolescents, with their wounds and their air of constantly absorbing adult experiences, in no way exhausted the uses of childhood even among Americans in exile. E. E. Cummings, for example, often wrote about young men of the same age as the Hemingway hero, but he used his young men to give the country some of the most innocent literary creations in its history. Cummings grew up on the streets of Cambridge, almost next door to Harvard Yard, where his Unitarian background had furnished him with the transcendental heritage that so marked his poetry. He studied the classics at Harvard and served in the ambulance corps in France during the war. He also spent time in a prisoner-of-war camp because the French discovered that his traveling companion had written unflattering letters home to America, and so they suspected that Cummings lacked patriotic fervor.

Cummings's work is so rich that it fits into any one of a number of categories. Politically, he belongs to the often vilified group of artists and anarchists who disliked the big state as well as big business. Like Albert Jay Nock, Oswald Garrison Villard, or his friend John Dos Passos, Cummings detested man in the mass, the professional patriot, advertising, and war. Considered historically, his work often resembles that of neoclassicists like Igor Stravinsky and T. S. Eliot. While they revived the forms of Pergolesi or Donne, Cummings turned to the Greeks he had studied at Harvard: from them, he learned such tricks as *syncope* and *apocope,* and drove modern English readers to distraction by using these precedents to separate prefixes and suffixes from the words to which they were normally attached, or to separate adverbs and adjectives from the nouns and verbs they presumably modified. As a modernist, he had affinities with writers like Joyce and Aiken: in his work he frequently presented a stream of consciousness, producing the objects of visual perception and memory without ordering them into obviously artistic forms, and even without translating from the French in *The Enormous Room* or the Russian in *Eimi.* He even opposed science, one of the chief deities of many modern writers, and thus allied himself with the most conservative writers in America: not even Allen Tate hated science and intellectual rationalism more than

---

21 *The Sun Also Rises,* pp. 153, 155, 131–32; Young, *Hemingway,* 96–97; William White, ed., *By-Line: Ernest Hemingway* (New York, 1968, c.1967), p. 84.

Cummings. He regularly mocked the scientific schemes of Freud and Dewey, even as he helped Freud break down the barriers of Victorian prudery, and assisted Dewey by advocating the value of the creative and spontaneous child.

Cummings's greatest contribution to the intellectual history of his time was his fusion of the child and the artist into a viable ideal of human growth. He made his position most intelligible in his brief, early appreciation of the sculptor Gaston Lachaise. "Three things Lachaise, to any one who knows him, is and is beyond the shadow of a doubt: inherently naif, fearlessly intelligent, utterly sincere. It is accurate to say that his two greatest hates are the hate of insincerity and the hate of superficiality." Lachaise's favorite word is "simple": "it means form which completely expresses itself, form that perfectly tactilizes the beholder, as in the case of an electric machine which, being grasped, will not let the hand go." For Cummings, Lachaise was so perfect an artist because he had broken down the walls between the adult and the child; he enabled adults to perceive as if they were children. His work required of the viewer "an intelligent process of the highest order, namely the negation on our part, by thinking, of thinking." Together the artist and viewer must destroy the world: "By this destruction alone we cease to be spectators of a ludicrous and ineffectual striving and, involving ourselves in a new and fundamental kinesis, become protagonists of the child's vision." If he had to analyze child art in one sentence, Cummings said, he would say that "houses, trees, smoke, people, etc., are depicted not as nouns but as verbs." That sentence alone illuminates many of the most difficult passages in his poetry. Children, in short, do not depict the static world the adult sees; they depict the process of perception, and they do it without the encumbrance of vision which years of living inevitably produce. "Consequently to appreciate child art we are compelled to undress one by one the soggy nouns whose agglomeration constitutes the mechanism of Normality, and finally to liberate the actual crisp organic squirm— the IS." [22]

This childlike vision is obviously what Cummings meant when he talked about the child artist as the only really "human" being. The rest of mankind was simply an unindividualized blob, controlled by its leaders and contributing nothing to the sum of beauty and innocence in the world. That was what Cummings had in mind when he was asked by an interviewer: "What do you think happens to people who aren't artists? What do you think people who aren't artists become?" And Cummings replied, like the principal of a child-centered

22 George J. Firmage, ed., *E. E. Cummings: A Miscellany Revised* (New York, 1965), pp. 12–24.

school: "I feel they don't become; I feel nothing happens to them; I feel negation becomes of them." The natural result of this kind of artistic credo was sometimes an emphasis on purity of form and expression, as in Ernest Hemingway; sometimes it was an attempt at a totally private vision and language, as in the French symbolists and surrealists. Cummings shared both these tendencies, as his painstaking attention to typography in his poetry, and his marvelous surrealistic play, *Him*, both indicate. But his chief mode of expressing these private artistic theories is most strikingly represented in the combination of persona and punctuation which he developed early in his career. This combination of child spokesman and "naive" punctuation and typography sometimes suggests the seventeenth-century trick of making the poem resemble typographically the subject of the poem; more often, it recalls Lewis Carroll's experiments in showing how, for a child, the medium and the message are inextricably intertwined. Thus, in the poem beginning "O sweet spontaneous," (Cummings's poems often have no titles) where the "doting fingers of prurient philosophers" are pinching and poking the earth, the only comma in the poem appears at the beginning of a line, and clearly represents the "naughty thumb of science" as it violates the soft earth. Or, in the well-known "here's a little mouse) and" poem, the parentheses that are scattered about the poem, combined with the erratically capitalized letters, are intended to suggest the effect of the little mouse as it scurries about—in the word, "gr(oo)v-ing," he even appears to be looking out at the reader through the middle of the word. For some readers, this playfulness was extremely tiresome, and they found no reason to draw the line between the child-like and the childish in Cummings's work. For others, and they appear to be an increasing majority as time goes on, Cummings established a new persona that changed the way people looked at the world and at words. Like the little girl in "Santa Claus" who was the only character in the play who could tell Santa Claus from the Devil, Cummings's vision has become a permanent part of America's ability to detect sham and experience love.[23]

Cummings's use of childhood did not end with the very young; he also wrote some of his most effective poems using the eyes of a young man and of a young adult in love. Cummings was unabashed in his love for both his parents, in an age when filial love was unfashionable. He also doted on nature, spring, the moon, flowers, and all the other natural phenomena that had so fascinated the transcendentalists, and some of his best work combines images of parenthood with nature.

23 E. E. Cummings, Introduction to *The Enormous Room* (New York, Modern Library ed.); *Poems, 1923–1954* (New York, 1954), esp. pp. 39, 206. Used by permission of Harcourt Brace Jovanovich.

His poems as a young man in love were less successful, if only because he wrote so many of them that failures were bound to be plentiful. Gone are the innocent eye of childhood and the passion of the young adolescent for his parents. Here instead is the young man in the city, often New York or Paris, showing off his skill with argot and profanity, and trying as hard as possible to shock the Cambridge ladies back home with his Rabelaisian immorality. Many of these poems are crude, some are scatalogical, and a few are terribly funny. What they all indicate is that Cummings also had a voice of the same age as authors such as F. Scott Fitzgerald, and that Cummings's young men were considerably more aware of the world than the decadent idealists at Princeton. The best of these poems is the notorious "she being Brand." With its typically adolescent fascination with cars as sexual objects and women as sexual machines, its intentionally bizarre use of punctuation to make people read the poem properly, it provides a proper exit for the man who, all things considered, best summed up in art the spirit of the 1920s.[24]

VIII

For all his experimentation and freshness, however, Cummings did have certain blind spots. Even his portraits of adolescents clearly lacked parts of the adolescent personality that most adults would notice immediately. Cummings's loathing of science, rationality, and precision simply cut him off from one whole aspect of the human personality. He could understand young men who viewed women as machines, but he could not understand young men who loved machines as if they were women. In other areas of the culture during the 1920s artists often felt quite differently. In music, for example, the machine was an integral part of the artists' means of expression, and not the enemy of inspiration that it was to Cummings.

Despite the publication of a number of useful memoirs, and the wide popularity of some of their work, American musicians have never received their due in the cultural history of modern America. In fact, they played a major role, and were of greatest importance during the twenties, when they flocked abroad with the writers and painters, often for the same reasons. They too disliked the cultural poverty of America, the boosterism, the prohibitionism, and the repressive morality. By contrast, musicians loved Paris because Nadia Boulanger was teaching the young American musical generation, because modern work was appreciated there as nowhere else, and because new music was actually played. In America, few orchestras or conductors played any new music,

---

24 *Poems 1923–1954,* esp. pp. 373–75, 253, 178–79.

and if they did, the audience and the critical reaction were both incompetent. The composer never heard how his work sounded, never
received helpful assistance, and had no one with whom he could discuss
his work. Paris was alive, and for all its faults and cliques, it was the
center of musical creativity after the war. Virgil Thomson sat at the
feet of Gertrude Stein just as Hemingway did, and she influenced his
career more lastingly. Aaron Copland experimented with jazz there and
produced works such as his Symphony for Organ and Orchestra and
Piano Concerto that permanently enriched American music. Even so
nationalistic a composer as Roy Harris could find the techniques in
Paris that he needed for his ostentatiously autochthonous works of the
thirties.

Two composers in particular give some idea of the range of the
youthful experimentalism then in vogue in Paris. Both of them found
the machine essential to their work. George Antheil was perhaps the
most flagrantly youthful, both in his age and in his personal and
musical behavior, of all the young men abroad. He had grown up,
appropriately enough, across from a machine shop in Trenton, New
Jersey, where his father was a struggling seller of shoes. The family
eventually moved to a better neighborhood, but the influence of the
machines persisted through Antheil's education, chiefly at the Curtis
Settlement School (later the famous Curtis Institute) and under Ernest
Bloch. This education was musically quite conservative, but Antheil
was too tempestuous and erratic a temperament to follow anyone's
orders for very long. He fell in love with characteristic violence, he
spent some time with Margaret Anderson's bohemian *Little Review*
colony in Bernardsville, New Jersey, and he began to write works that
portended the future: *Airplane Sonata, Sonata Sauvage,* and pieces
called *Death of the Machines* and *Mechanisms.* In a musical context,
he felt an affinity for the cold, hard, and unsentimental pieces of
Stravinsky's postwar neoclassicism, and he disliked anything by Richard
Strauss, Debussy, Ravel, Mahler, or Bruckner.

Characteristically, Antheil went to Europe for the most adolescent
of reasons. He had fallen in love with the teenage daughter of a well-
known eye specialist, and when her parents discovered what was going
on, mother and daughter secretly departed for Europe. Antheil was
frantic and decided that the only way he could follow was to go disguised as a concert pianist. He practiced furiously and when he heard
of an opening he applied, somehow managed to convince the producer
of his abilities and in May 1922 found himself at least on the same
continent as his beloved. His career requirements sent him on a concert
tour, most successfully in Germany, but all the while he wanted to be
a composer and to find his girl. His first success came in Berlin, when
Schultz von Dornberg, a German airplane ace famous for his exploits

all over Germany, decided that he liked Antheil and his First Symphony, and gave the work a successful premier. Only years later did Antheil find his fleeing blonde, and he discovered to his amazement that he no longer really much cared; besides, by then he was deeply involved with a beautiful Hungarian girl.[25]

Soon Antheil was in Paris, sharing with his mistress a tiny apartment upstairs from Sylvia Beach's bookstore, Shakespeare & Co. He was soon deep in the cultural life of the city, and the callers at his apartment included all the rigorously neoclassical leaders of the various disciplines: T. S. Eliot, Wyndham Lewis, Ford Madox Ford, and Hemingway, among others. Antheil was particularly close to James Joyce and was one of the "geniuses" that Ezra Pound specialized in discovering —Pound even went so far as to produce his short book, *Antheil and the Treatise on Harmony.* Among the natives, Erik Satie and Jean Cocteau were soon his champions, and for a time, Antheil became the toast of Paris. Thus, in his exuberant way, Antheil was both a trail-breaking radical and a rule-stressing classicist, in some ways comparable to Eliot or even Cummings. Virgil Thomson recalled him as the "truculent, small boy-genius from Trenton," and spoke of the "brutal charm" of his music. The whole group of aesthetes was "fascinated by Antheil's cheerful lack of modesty." He was, in fact, "the literary mind's idea of a musical genius—bold, bumptious, and self-confident" and, Thomson wrote in a contemporary letter, "the first composer of our generation." Yet this boy-wonder incarnate also stressed formal rules of composition. The "fun" of composing "classical" music, he wrote, "is in the fact that it *does not* contain . . . gorgeous, expanding, all-over-the-place stuff. It rests, rather, in its limiting itself to a certain preindicated sphere of operations, as, for instance, one might call one's shot in a pool game." In other words, the "fun" of classical music consists *"of a strict keeping of the rules, operating to best advantage within them!"* One man's imprisonment was another's liberation.[26]

To his intense regret, Antheil's reputation came to rest on his single most notorious work of this period, the *Ballet Méchanique.* He chose to use his classical principles and to express the machine quality of modern civilization in a work that seems, in retrospect, to have summed up most successfully this side of the twenties' emphasis on youth and experimentation. The noises of industry deserved a high place in an industrial age. Tempi should not be at the whim of individualistic performers, but rather rigidly specified and consistent. Warm instru-

25 George Antheil, *Bad Boy of Music* (New York, 1945), part 1.

26 Ibid., quotation on p. 100, Antheil's emphasis; Virgil Thomson, *Virgil Thomson* (New York, 1966), pp. 75–82.

ments, like the strings, winds, and brass, should give way to percussion, or pseudo-instruments like the player piano. Besides the percussion, the score included eight grand pianos used like percussion, electric bells, and the sound of an airplane propeller. The first performance, directed by Vladimir Golschmann, took place in a Paris salon and simply overwhelmed the friendly modernists of the typical Paris opening night for new music. But when the time came for the New York premier, Antheil unfortunately let publisher Donald Friede make a spectacle of the whole procedure in a city incapable of understanding such things. Antheil was weak from illness, the advertising was in poor taste, a real propeller was imported at the last minute to literally blow the audience over: the whole spectacle became a farce, instead of a breakthrough. Antheil insisted that the *Ballet* "was conceived in a new form, that form specifically being the filling out of a certain time canvas with musical abstractions and sound material composed and contrasted against one another with the thought of time values rather than tonal values." He had, he went on, "used time as Picasso might have used the blank spaces of his canvas," and his "ideas were the most abstract of the abstract." New York thought he was a charlatan in a time that was full of them. "I went back to Paris that 1927 heartsick and broke." His reputation and his ability never recovered.[27]

If George Antheil represented the most flamboyant of the young experimenters, Edgard Varèse represented the most serious, and his music sounds almost as far distant in its effect from Antheil's as it does from the music of the dying post-Romantics. Varèse was devoted to science and technology, and he admired machinery, as did Antheil. He too seemed to place no value on the individual personality: indeed, he had an almost oriental desire to extinguish both his own personality and that of any performer in his musical expressions. He disliked emotions of all kinds, much preferring abstract sound. Yet, rather unlike Antheil and the other less radical neoclassicists, he had a pronounced streak of romanticism in both his ideas and his past. "I dream of instruments obedient to my thought and which with their contribution of a whole new world of unsuspected sounds will lend themselves to the exigencies of my inner rhythm," he wrote in 1917, and if ever musical compositions were expressive of a personality, however austere, Varèse's were. He was drawn to the newest forms of experimental music because he could find no way to express himself in the conventional manner: "When new instruments will allow me to write music as I conceive it, the movement of sound-masses, of shifting planes, will be

---

27 Antheil, *Bad Boy*, esp. pp. 184–85, 197; Gilbert Chase, *America's Music*, 2nd ed., rev. (New York, 1966), pp. 583–84; Randall Thompson, "George Antheil," *Modern Music* 8, no. 4 (May–June 1931), 17–27.

clearly perceived in my work, taking the place of the linear counterpoint." Specifically, such innovations would permit him to write music that delimited one of his favorite concepts, "zones of intensities." Gone would be melody and emotion, and even thematic development as Western music knew it. Only a series of sounds or intensities would remain, pure and undefiled. Soon, he foresaw, all performers would become unnecessary, the composer could put his "intensities" directly on tape, and the mechanization would be complete. Following his own theory to its logical extreme, he eventually ceased composing altogether, so inadequate were the means for realizing his musical ideas.[28]

While Antheil had come from Trenton and gone to Paris, Varèse was born in Paris and came to America only when the world war broke out. Part of his heritage was Italian, since his family came from the Franco-Italian border area of the Piedmont, and his father had business interests in Turin. Varèse was miserably unhappy whenever he was with his parents, since the father was a tyrant over both his wife and his son, and insisted immovably that Edgard pursue an education that would fit him for a business career. When Edgard seemed to be spending too much time at the piano, his father locked it up and forbade any further practicing. Varèse began to sneak off to the local conservatory to receive lessons. His biographer, who is not normally given to psychoanalytic interpretations of his hero, believes that this hatred of his father became in time an inability on Varèse's part ever to tolerate "fatherly" criticism, and thus made all but ungovernable a character that was always strong-minded and original. Certainly, this quality helped cause Varèse's quarrels with his more conservative teachers, most notably Vincent D'Indy. In spite of his father, Varèse went to Paris, received considerable academic training, and soon found himself in the midst of the modernist movement. Although musically he studied with conservatives like D'Indy and Widor, aesthetically he was immersing himself in the ideas of Satie, Picasso, Modigliani, and Apollinaire. He also made an intense study of the Middle Ages, with particular attention to science, physics, alchemy, and astronomy, always trying to relate these ideas to his music. He also studied the works of Hoéne Wronsky and Helmholtz, and heartily approved Wronsky's definition of music as "the corporealization of the intelligence that is

---

28 Elliott Schwartz and Barney Childs, eds., *Contemporary Composers on Contemporary Music* (New York, 1967), pp. 196–208; Chase, *America's Music*, pp. 594–600; Wilfrid Mellers, *Music in a New Found Land* (New York, 1965), pp. 156–68; Chou Wen-chung, "Varèse: A Sketch of the Man and His Music," *Musical Quarterly* 52, no. 2 (April 1966); Henry Cowell, "The Music of Edgard Varèse," *Modern Music*, January–February 1928; Gunther Schuller, "Conversations with Varèse," *Perspectives of New Music* 3, no. 2 (spring–summer 1965); Frederick Waldman, "Edgard Varèse: An Appreciation," *Julliard Review* 1 (Fall 1954); Marc Wilkinson, "An Introduction to the Music of Edgard Varèse," *The Score* (London), no. 19 (March 1957).

in sounds." As for the conservatives in the conservatories, he could only snort, "The teachers were all ruled like music paper." [29]

Yet, when all this has been said, Varèse's incomparable, pioneering iconoclasm remains, and his personality shines through his music. The key to this paradox lies at least in part in his artistic roots. His great hero, Busoni, was a leading experimentalist as well as a noted pianist, and his notes toward a new aesthetic of music were extremely important for Varèse's musical development. Busoni was a romantic idealist, always rhapsodizing about Nature and the Ideal, and how inadequate conventional forms of musical notations were for proper representation of what was really in the artist's mind. Music, he said, is a "child—it *floats on air!* It touches not the earth with its feet. . . . It is—free." All the common musical forms and laws of composition irritated him, and he banished them. He insisted that composers wrote their best music "in preparatory and intermediary passages . . . where they felt at liberty to disregard symmetrical proportions and unconsciously drew free breath." The truly creative artist should be making his own laws from internal necessity, not obeying the tired conventions of the dead. Under the goad of this really adolescent and egocentric experimentalism, Varèse became America's first electronic composer, with music laboratories supplying him with vital sound sources, and allowing his own personality to shine through clearly to the listener, with the irritating middleman of a performer gone forever. "The very basis of creative work is irreverence!" he insisted, much like Cummings. "The very basis of creative work is experimentation, bold experimentation." He even anticipated the spatial music implicit in stereophonic sound, and, in his much delayed *annus mirabillis,* 1957, finally heard his *Poème Electronique* performed as he conceived it, so much earlier, when he was a young man: no fewer than 425 loudspeakers, none of them at a right angle to any other, gave off the atonal equivalents of Le Corbusier's Philips Pavilion at the Brussels World's Fair. No one had ever heard anything—or anyone—like it; experimental youth could never better that.[30]

IX

The fine arts did not, however, always remain at the extremes represented by Cummings and Varèse. Not all young experimentalists hated or loved the machine, even though most of them were

---

29 Fernand Ouellette, *Edgard Varèse,* trans. Derek Coltman (New York, 1968), esp. pp. 1–21; cf. Roger Shattuck, *The Banquet Years* (New York, 1958).

30 Ibid.; see also Ferruccio Busoni, *Sketch of a New Esthetic of Music,* trans. Dr. Th. Baker (New York, 1911), pp. 4, 8; Edgard Varèse, "Freedom for Music," in Gilbert Chase, ed., *The American Composer Speaks* (Baton Rouge, 1966), p. 189.

concerned with it. In painting and the closely related field of photography, for example, America had its clearest examples of a compromise position that used the machine as an instrument to assist creativity and experiment, but also rather mistrusted it, and recognized the possibility that it could constrict freedom and growth. With Alfred Stieglitz and his galleries—the Photo-Secession (later renamed 291), The Intimate Gallery, and An American Place—America finally discovered the most advanced art of the Western world, and did it under the guidance of one of the foremost photographers the country ever produced. In one of Stieglitz's favorite painters, John Marin, America discovered an artist who was really both modern and American, not simply a replica of some European fad; a man who portrayed on canvas a series of examples of what the innocent eye saw in the America of the machine age.

Stieglitz was the son of Edward Stieglitz, a wealthy Jewish woolen merchant who had emigrated to New York from Hanover-Münden in what later became Germany. Edward was something of a bon vivant who loved horses and painting about equally well, and who provided Alfred with quite a different upbringing from that usually accorded to the sons of the Protestant aristocracy. Alfred was educated, chiefly in Berlin, to become an engineer, but while studying chemistry he discovered his life-long fascination with photography. Both in Berlin and later, after he had returned to New York, he devoted all his time and money to experiments with photographical processes and businesses that could use them. His first gallery, the Photo-Secession, and his chief journal, *Camera Work,* were both developments of this infatuation with a science, and he made his contributions to painting and sculpture only after the experiments had been begun with photographs. His gallery opened in 1906, and within two years Stieglitz was displaying the first modern European paintings ever shown in America, first Rodin, and then a few months later, Matisse. Virtually alone, over the years, Stieglitz gave these Europeans and their American counterparts a showing, and far more than the Armory Show, his work made it possible for some kind of creative life to exist in America. As Herbert J. Seligman has written about The Intimate Gallery, Stieglitz's exhibition place from 1925–29: "In this room, perhaps twelve feet by twenty in dimension, was being tested the possibility of the life of the spirit in America." The Intimate Gallery stood for "the relationship of the divinity in men and women as represented by the creative artist, with the entire nation and the life of the world." [31]

---

31 Waldo Frank, et al., eds., *America and Alfred Stieglitz* (New York, 1934), pp. 123–24. For background see especially Milton Brown, *American Painting from the Armory Show to the Depression* (Princeton, 1955), and Barbara Rose, *American Art Since 1900* (New York, 1967).

In addition to his role as exhibitor, agent, propagandist, and father-confessor to a whole series of important American painters, Stieglitz also came to have symbolic significance for the experimental, artistic generation of the twenties. Stieglitz was important "because he integrates the twofold role of the artist and the teacher in one personality," Harold Rugg argued. At a time when it was next to impossible for the artist to achieve an audience or sell his work, Stieglitz not only made a crucial economic difference, he also "maintained his integrity as a creative artist and a teacher of Man-as-Artist." The "very basis of life" at a Stieglitz gallery was "the integrity of each human act—the spoken sentence, the answer to another's question, the production of any craft goods, of a book, a verse, a house, a dramatic scene." Each person found himself accepted as a creative individual without any need for hypocrisy and could become *"what he is."* Stieglitz, in short, became for Rugg the ideal principal of the Child-Centered School-of-the-World, epitomized in this description of An American Place, Stieglitz's last gallery:

> It is such a cultural milieu that I visualize for the ideal school; hence my admiration for Stieglitz's exemplification of the traits needed most in the American teacher. His American Place is a nurturing place; each school in America should become a true American Place. In a great society, "the school," in the broadest sense, would be the culture nurturing place, the true center of the community.[32]

Many students found this school congenial, and they constituted almost an entire generation of American modernists. Arthur Dove, Marsden Hartley, Alfred Maurer, Max Weber, Charles Demuth, Georgia O'Keeffe, and many others received their original recognition and support in Stieglitz's galleries and made careers that might otherwise have been stunted or simply impossible without his aid. But, with the possible exception of Georgia O'Keeffe, who married Stieglitz, the painter who seemed to mean the most to Stieglitz and who became the most important of these modernists was John Marin. With Marin America had still another example of the innocent eye of childhood, this time achieving a more appropriate education than that usually accorded a talented man in America. Indeed, just as Stieglitz became the symbolic principal of the child-centered school, Marin became the perfect pupil, recognized as such even at the time. For Stieglitz, as Herbert J. Seligman has written, "Marin, as he grew, became more and more a symbol." He was in himself "the true, free, joyous, and simple human being, whom it became a necessity to enable to live, as a flower is cared for, or a tree bearing fruit." In addition, Marin represented

32 Frank, *Stieglitz*, pp. 195–97.

all artists in America. "The logic of his situation was clear. If this supreme instance of creative genius and integrity could not survive in America, freed from the degrading and destructive extractions of business, then what chance could there be for lesser strength or for any honest workman?" [33]

Marin was indeed a good example of the creative child in painting. He grew up in a Yankee family that disapproved of his artistic ambitions, and he suffered through four fruitless years in architects' offices when they insisted that he try something useful. When that experiment failed, they shipped him off to the Pennsylvania Academy of Fine Arts, apparently in the hope that he would learn the academic styles well enough to sell his work and make money out of his peculiar obsession. There he studied under Thomas Anshutz, the key transmitter of the Eakins tradition, but apparently learned little from the experience. The next few years, about 1900–1905, were apparently even less rewarding, and finally Marin managed an extended stay in Europe. Yet even here he proved to be a kind of textbook example of Harold Rugg's creative child, growing internally but absorbing very little by way of outside influence. Just as his academic American training marked his style only slightly, so this Paris and European experience seemed to make little difference. Only when Marin returned to New York in 1910 did he see for the first time the pioneering works of European art—at Stieglitz's gallery, of course—and allow himself to absorb slight doses of fauvism and cubism. In fact, as his pictures from this period clearly show, New York and its booming economy affected him far more: two new bridges spanned the East River, the Woolworth Building was under construction, electric cars replaced the horse and cable cars, and the elevated railroad and the subway were operating. The city, as his biographer has rightly pointed out, had speeded up enormously and become disorderly and chaotic, and Marin strongly felt the need to control this raw experience in his art.[34]

Where Stieglitz compromised with the modern world by becoming both an expert in the science of photography and an assiduous cultivator of individual creativity, Marin adjusted rather differently. He was both fascinated with and repelled by the city, and he soon found on the Maine seacoast a kind of objective correlative of peace to use in his art and in his life. His most characteristic city work is full of the jagged edges, the distorted perspectives, and the hysterical quality of New York, while his Maine seascapes soften his techniques and relax the viewer. The use of Marin's most effective medium, watercolor, was a key element in this childlike approach to the city and the country.

33 Ibid., p. 115.

34 E. M. Benson, *John Marin* (Washington, D.C., 1935).

Watercolor made Marin's work seem uncommonly open and innocent, when compared to the oils of a city painter like John Sloan. He approached both his favorite environments like a child on his first visit: overwhelmed by size and noise stimulation in the city and enthralled and delighted by the sea, by boats, and by trees in the country. As his city pictures show very clearly, the central metaphor for Marin in New York is literally warfare, as if the creative child had to fight for his life and seek the protection of a Stieglitz if he were to survive. "I see great forces at work," he wrote in 1913 after he had been home for three years, "great movements; the large buildings and the small buildings; the warring of the great and the small; influences of one mass on another greater or smaller mass. . . ." All things in life "come under the magnetic influence of other things; the bigger assert themselves strongly, the smaller not so much, but they still assert themselves, and though hidden they strive to be seen and in so doing change their bent and direction." As these powers are "pushing, pulling, sideways, downward, upward, I can hear the sound of their strife and there is great music being played." And, he concluded, "Within the frames there must be a balance, a controlling of these warring, pushing, pulling forces. This is what I am trying to realize. . . ." [35]

Given this martial vision of modern life, Marin proved surprisingly insulated from the world war, and was indeed prematurely disillusioned, after the manner of the twenties, about the whole war experience. "Over in Europe they are fighting," he wrote Stieglitz shortly after the war began, "they have all modern appliances, huge guns, great transportation facilities, everything that modern invention and science in the art of warfare can bring to bear and yet, after all, it is the artist who wins out . . . and I guess it'll always be so." A year later, he wrote quite without shame or guilt feelings that, "I am more interested, yea lots more, in me myself and my doings than French wars, German wars, English wars, all other wars, all social doings, social happenings, the trend of the world, all things pertaining thereto." Like his good friend E. E. Cummings, who could pass through the Enormous Room with his innocence intact, Marin (long before it was fashionable) was the perfectly oblivious child interested only in his own creativity. After the war was over, he wrote that "when I put myself into my picture I have created a work of art." Harold Rugg must have liked that.[36]

---

35 Ibid., pp. 65–66.

36 Dorothy Norman, ed., *The Selected Writings of John Marin* (New York, 1949), pp. 18, 20, 45. This collection includes all of Herbert J. Seligman, ed., *Letters of John Marin* (New York, 1931), and the quotes may be found in both books. Marin was also in Mabel Dodge's set, both in New York and, in 1929–30, in New Mexico. See, *inter alia,* Ven Deren Coke, *Taos and Santa Fé* (Albuquerque, 1963).

X

This air of apparent innocence, frivolity, and youth that so permeated the fine arts was not, however, the whole story of the twenties' cult of youth, even in the arts. It certainly predominated in poetry, music, and painting, but competing for a position of equal importance was always the psychoanalytical perspective, with its essentially gloomy and therapeutic view of childhood. Youth was destiny with both groups, but the innocent, creative destiny of one group was rather different from the neurotic destiny of the other. As Freud had pointed out, creative work was often sublimated sexual drive, and could easily work itself out as exhibitionism. In the theater, for example, Freud and his problems appeared in the most predictable and obvious place—where the playwright worked out his personal problems in art, the actors in their performances, and the audience by its identification with the actors.

Like most American artists, the greatest of these dramatists was not directly influenced by Freud, or at least denied that he was; instead, he seems to have come to similar insights through a self-analysis of his own frequently wretched personal life. Eugene O'Neill's father had been a successful popular actor, a great success in *The Count of Monte Cristo,* and a disaster as a husband and father. His mother was a morphine addict most of her life; brother Jamie was a compulsive alcoholic and degenerate whose death wish eventually succeeded in killing him; O'Neill's own eldest son was a successful classics scholar who committed suicide when life became too much for him; and his second son was only a paler version of brother Jamie. Eugene himself, though brought up in rigid Catholic fashion, lost his faith in practically everything but his art and proved no more adept with his own life and his wives than his father. He attempted suicide at least once, lived in the most incredible degradation for many years, and treated his three wives and his children as though he had not the vaguest of ideas about how one decent person could coexist with another.

This background would have prepared even an insensitive man for a pessimistic view of mankind, and O'Neill, for all his personal shortcomings, was hardly insensitive. "If a person is to get at the meaning of life," he once said, "he must learn to like the facts about himself—ugly as they may seem to his sentimental vanity—before he can lay hold on the truth behind the facts; and the truth is never ugly." With an almost obsessive devotion and tenacity, O'Neill searched his own psyche and discovered what any Freudian might have predicted. He did not verbalize these discoveries in any theoretical form but rather allowed them to act themselves out on the stage and thus expose themselves—a kind of therapy, as it were, where the stage became the analyst's couch. It is no wonder that O'Neill could never bring himself to see his own opening nights, or that he was brutally cruel to anyone tampering with his scripts; however degrading the plots were, they were his past, and anyone changing them was trying to reform him. He found in that past a death wish, only natural for a family obsessed with it. He also discovered narcissism, sexual obsessions, subconscious fears, crippling neuroses, sublimations, the influence of parents on the marriage beds of the children, repressions, and an atavism that would owe more to Jung than Freud if it did not come from O'Neill's own emotions.[37]

Psychological themes were present in his work almost from the beginning. In *The Emperor Jones* (1921), for example, the "Little Formless Fears" that Jones sees in his panic are clearly the products of his own heated imagination, yet they take on a real, if indistinct, presence in the woods. Jones's past returns to haunt him, as in his panic the guard over his subconscious fails in its duties and allows the various people Jones had killed earlier to arise and torment him and be killed again. Jones even finds his racial memory playing most un-Freudian tricks on him, and he begins to see Congo witch doctors only his ancestors could possibly have seen in reality.

In *The Hairy Ape* (1922), a class-conscious play with many parallels to Adlerian psychology, the psychology of vocation is the basis for Yank's devotion to his engine room job, and only when he begins to lose faith in his own abilities and self-esteem does he become what society has called him, a hairy ape fit only for the embrace of a gorilla. *All God's Chillun Got Wings* (1923) provides a textbook case of shock causing a reversion to the mental status of childhood, a regression that eliminates the problems of the real world by pretending that they have not yet happened. Finally, in what many critics thought was a blatant dramatization of Freud, *Desire Under the Elms* (1925) presents patently Oedipal themes: Eben Cabot was obviously overdependent on his dead mother, he hated his father, and he fathered a child by his young and passionate stepmother. What O'Neill himself felt about his own invalid mother may or may not have inspired parts of the work, but it seems even more likely that Freud and he had a common source: the Greek tragedy that gave Freud the name for his complex was as common in the O'Neill home as a speller in the homes of other people. With a father who acted Greek tragedy and a son who taught and edited it at Yale, O'Neill scarcely needed Freud to tell him of the theme. When critics insisted, he replied firmly that while he respected

---

37 Arthur and Barbara Gelb, *O'Neill* (New York, 1962); see also Joseph Wood Krutch, *More Lives Than One* (New York, 1962), 137–38, and John Henry Raleigh, *The Plays of Eugene O'Neill* (Carbondale, 1965).

Freud he was no addict, and that any Freudian themes in *Desire* arose from his unconscious; in other words, from his own past experience.[38]

As the twenties wore on, O'Neill became more obsessively psychological. *The Great God Brown* (1926) is a bitter examination of the ways in which people switch on parts of their personality at will, and the use of masks to force this device on the viewer effectively underlines the guises people have for deceiving the world. The rhetoric of the play also makes the girlfriends and the mothers all but interchangeable—O'Neill himself apparently thought that mothering was a vital quality any man sought in sex. But not until *Strange Interlude* did he frankly build an entire play on the basic psychological notion of sexuality as the mainspring for human action. Using a single act of unconsummated sexual desire, he outlined an incredible series of events, all given to the viewer through the unspoken consciousness of the characters. After giving herself to a series of wounded soldiers, as a way of atoning for not giving herself to her dead fiancé, Nina Leeds gradually develops relationships with four men that presumably explore the depths of the female sexual psyche: Marsden, the father substitute who is obviously too attached first to his mother and then his sister; Sam Evans, a harmless young man who needs her like a mother, and whom she marries; Dr. Edmund Darrell, the virile and hard man of science whom she asks to father a child by her and master her as a lover; and finally, her son Gordon—named after the dead pilot who started the whole series of events—a man for whom she has obsessively maternal sentiments and marches through life trying to discourage girls from marrying. *Mourning Becomes Electra* (1931) carries these themes even further. Here again, O'Neill uses Freudian ideas in his own way, and indeed the atmosphere seems more Greek, or even Old Testament than it does Freudian. The world of Eugene O'Neill, in short, was one where personal background and other external influences had at least as much influence as Freud and the other psychologists. Like most of the artists of the era, O'Neill simply added the new material to his arsenal of ideas. He did not replace his old ones, he merely made them more complicated, and spoke them in a language that sophisticated playgoers could recognize. In the course of his work he revolutionized the American theater and became unquestionably the greatest playwright the country had produced.

XI

Freud, and psychology in general, also made a great impact on the criticism of literature. This added dimension of artistic insight

---

38 Gelb, *O'Neill*, p. 577.

was most unpredictable in its fruits. When employed by lesser minds the new techniques meant a cheap psychoanalyzing, with salacious hints about the writer's repressions, Oedipus complex, and sublimations scattered about to intrigue the sort of reader who liked André Tridon. But psychoanalysis in criticism also had its serious practitioners who could use Freud and his fellow theorists with insight and discrimination, and who did not allow meretriciousness to mar their ability to read a text or unravel a complicated artist. One of the best of these critics was the Van Wyck Brooks who wrote *The Ordeal of Mark Twain* (1923). It was a brief book, with no new material to offer from unpublished or even neglected sources. All Brooks did was to read Twain's published writings, a few memoirs by friends, and the recent biography by Albert Bigelow Paine. He neglected any rigorous explication of the texts; he was plainly wrong in his insistence that creativity in America was always opposed to the acquisitive instincts of a business society; he made many statements that later critical spadework has found to need modification on the basis of the unpublished Twain papers. But nonetheless, Brooks materially altered critical opinion of Twain, and his book still offers a welcome critical balance to the overenthusiasm of later writers. Most of all, he dwelt at great length on the relation of the artist to his environment, showing how Twain had been psychically mutilated by the demands of his wife, his literary friends, and his own yearnings for acceptance in a genteel world which was in sharp contrast to the exuberant West of his childhood.

Brooks's assessments of Twain were singularly appropriate for a critic of the 1920s. One need only read "the writer in America," or "sensitive spirit" or "the artist" instead of "Twain" to see what Brooks disliked about American society. Twain, he wrote, had morbid feelings of sin because he had "transgressed some inalienable life-demand" peculiar to his nature. His bitterness "was the effect of a certain miscarriage in his creative life, a balked personality, an arrested development of which he was himself almost wholly unaware, but which for him destroyed the meaning of life." Society had so constricted his ability to grow into his true potential, that his mind "had not fully developed" and his genius "never fully found itself." Sharing as he did the yearning for riches and their conspicuous display that so obsessed other Americans of his day, he felt he had to conform. He went deep into his publishing business and into his disastrous adventures with the Paige typesetter. Even more, he yearned for acceptance in the Eastern society that seemed to him to be the peak of success. Thus he submitted to the fussy, old-maid censorship of his wife, and the almost equally squeamish blue-pencillings of his friend Howells. But his real spirit was bawdy, truthful, and profane, and it resented this submission to the superego of home and publisher. As a result, "Mark Twain was a frustrated spirit, a victim of arrested development, and beyond this fact, as we know from innumerable instances the psychologists have placed before us, we need not look for an explanation of much of the chagrin of his old age." Because of his social environment, "he had been balked, he had been divided, he had even been turned, as we shall see, against himself." The poet and artist had thus "withered into the cynic and the whole man had become a spiritual valetudinarian."

With a sensitive intelligence, Brooks traced his theme through Twain's life, from his mother's influence down to the final furious burlesques and fantasies that he fumed over in his old age. Critics are still arguing about the validity of the picture, and all their attacks have not been able to destroy the book. It still gives an insight into the mind of the twenties, it is still valuable for the way in which the psychoanalytic idea and its symbolic character, the child, worked in the imagination of the intellectuals of the time. For Brooks, the relation of America to the artist was plain: "As we can see now, a sort of unconscious conspiracy actuated all America against the creative spirit." That much was the common if only partially correct opinion of his friends at the *Dial* and the *Freeman*. But for Brooks the key to Twain's personality was childhood: "The real Mark Twain had been arrested in his development, the artist had remained rudimentary; and this is the Mark Twain we have to consider now." Albert Bigelow Paine had exclaimed, "What a child he was, always, to the very end!" and to Brooks, "It was this childlikeness which caused and which explains his lack of spiritual independence as a man and which accounts for the character of his work as a writer." [39] What a change that was from the moralistic criticism of W. C. Brownell or the impressionism of Huneker and Mencken! Suddenly a critic did not try to use literature to examine the style of life. He did not even try to get others to read it through his own enthusiasms. Instead, he saw art as the artifact of the artistic personality, an ink blot to be analyzed for what it said about creativity and neurosis. Through Brooks's work, Mark Twain became a valuable culture hero to the twenties as a kind of casualty of pioneer days. He was the perfect example of the child who had been placed in an unfriendly and uncreative environment. Instead of a Harold Rugg for a teacher, he had to submit to a series of Aunt

39 Van Wyck Brooks, *The Ordeal of Mark Twain* (N.Y., revised edition, 1955, c. 1923), pp. 25, 28, 36, 74, 148. I have purposely used the revised edition as best expressing Brooks's intentions, but most of these quoted passages are also in the first edition. For biography, see Van Wyck Brooks, *An Autobiography* (New York, 1965), incorporating three earlier volumes; and Robert Spiller, ed., *The Van Wyck Brooks–Lewis Mumford Letters* (New York, 1970).

Pollys. Mark Twain's genius was blighted because he had had the bad luck not to have attended a child-centered school.

XII

The general outline of the transition from the progressivism that dominated the view of society before the First World War to the emphasis on the self that predominated during the twenties should by now be clear. In the Progressive Era, the human personality had valuable inherent qualities, but society was at least equally important, and the environment was also crucial to the growing child. Men did not, as a rule, feel estranged from their country or its politics, and often threw themselves into public affairs with an evangelical enthusiasm. However much they might criticize, intellectuals thought themselves a genuine and important part of society, and believed that they could change that society in meaningful ways. Seen in perspective, their most important contribution to the postwar world was the resulting emphasis on *social* science, or how the individual could study society in order to improve it.

The twenties presented a sharp contrast. As an "idea" the twenties began as early as 1909, with Freud's trip to Clark University, and continued to develop through other subsequent events that indicated that small groups were preparing for the twenties: the painting exhibitions, most obviously at the 291 gallery and the Armory Show; the little bohemias that flourished in Davenport, Iowa, Chicago, Provincetown, Massachusetts, and Greenwich Village; the birth control agitation of Margaret Sanger; the host of little magazines. In contrast to the self *in* society, the twenties came to emphasize the self *apart* from society. Society became an environment unfriendly to the growth of art, of the spirit, of freedom, of whatever happened to be the cry of the moment. Instead of reforming society, an individual should cultivate his "self." The result was the emphasis on sex as liberation, on youth, innocence, freedom, cynicism, spontaneity, and the whole new theory of psychoanalysis that seemed to hold everything together. If a youth were not left free to grow and become liberated and artistic, he would develop neuroses, his dreams and his unconscious would torment him, and he would become a psychological cripple. For the typical intellectual of the twenties, the little group of sympathetic friends, either in a city or abroad in exile, was all that was left of "society."

No single person summed up all these typical qualities of the twenties' mentality as well as its designated prose laureate, F. Scott Fitzgerald. Most critics of Fitzgerald focus on his work: the several excellent short stories, *The Great Gatsby* (1925), with its small-scale but well-executed distillation of the American experience, and *Tender Is the Night* (1934), a structurally flawed but moving coda to the themes of the period. But to get at the spirit of the twenties, and the rather disastrous lessons that that spirit has for posterity, a look at Fitzgerald himself, both as he was and as he appeared in his books, is more instructive.

Although Fitzgerald was never in much danger of being an intellectual, he was an acute enough observer of his own fixations and problems to deserve his status as "the" writer of the twenties. His attempts at long works never really succeeded, at least in part because, like his entire generation, Fitzgerald could never really conceive of a large-scale "society" in which to let his imagination roam. Instead, he managed frequently to create scenes that were moving and precise commentaries on his characters, who were, in turn, so much like himself, his wife, and their friends. In his books and stories, the dominating presence is usually either a beautiful child, containing within herself the immature and adolescent ideal that captivated the decade, or else a man of wealth, whose resources and background give him the right to possess what are to other men only dreams. The scenes change, but youthful beauty and great wealth always attract the eyes of all observers, and yet bring with them the inevitable disillusionment that comes with mere possession. Fitzgerald, and many of those who have written about him, like to refer to his disillusion and despair as his tragic sense, but that is too dignified a phrase for what was essentially a tawdry and immature obsession. It was not a tragedy that everyone could not be rich and beautiful. Gatsby and Dick Diver both thought they could be, and so did Fitzgerald, even as he realized the flaws in their characters. It was somewhat pathetic in a grown man to insist on this "tragedy" again and again. Children do not know enough of life to experience tragedy, and it was typical of the postwar years that its most representative author could not distinguish his own lack of self-discipline from the wisdom of the ages.

Like his country, Fitzgerald was fascinated with the upper classes, with social climbing, materialism, drinking and success, and all the conflicting elements that served to separate people into the arrived, the arriving, and the aspiring. "Everybody's youth is a dream, a form of chemical madness," says a character in "The Diamond as Big as the Ritz," and nothing possessed the shabby-genteel Irish boy at Princeton and in New York so much as the young man's dream of making money and becoming himself the object of other adolescent aspirations. Fitzgerald's best embodiment of this dream was of course Jay Gatsby, the slightly disreputable social climber from the Middle West who achieved most of his dreams, captivated the imagination of all around him, and saw it all turn to ashes and violent death. He too had an "incorruptible dream," but the price for it was the one a man had to pay "for living too much with a single dream." His girl Daisy was one of Fitzgerald's glowing flappers, with her promise of being about to do "gay, exciting things." She was all promise and no performance, however, and Daisy's relations with her husband Tom resulted in two deaths and several shattered lives. For the rich were to the masses as the flame is to a moth, destroying them as they did the author. Like Tom and Daisy, the rich were "careless people" who "smashed up things and creatures and then retreated back into their money or their vast carelessness, and whatever it was that kept them together, and let other people clean up the mess they had made. . . ." As for the rewards of materialism, Fitzgerald was equally acute: "desire just cheats you," the hero of *The Beautiful and Damned* (1922) says to his mistress; "It's like a sunbeam skipping here and there about a room. It stops and gilds some inconsequential object, and we poor fools try to grasp it—but when we do the sunbeam moves on to something else, and you've got the inconsequential part, but the glitter that made you want it is gone. . . ." [40]

Yet despite this real insight, Fitzgerald never managed to find enough self-discipline, or even simple maturity, to control his own life or to motivate his characters to find a way out of their debauch with materialism. "There was nothing, it seemed, that grew stale so soon as pleasure," he could write at the end of his longest and most depressing picture of degenerate capitalism, and yet he continued in his private life to drink and party himself into alcoholism, to insist upon marrying a girl who refused him until he had money, and to evoke for his readers one beautiful heroine after another who led men to disaster without educating them, the author, or his readers about the motivations of human behavior. "I'm more beautiful than anybody else," says a character in "Winter Dreams," "why can't I be happy?" Fitzgerald could never answer that question, and neither could many of his contemporaries. Nothing could be more adolescent or materialistic: physical beauty, money, social position, a wild party, all were physical manifestations of the great American desire to get rich and start impressing the neighbors. Money in itself seemed to mean little to Fitzgerald, for he spent wildly whether he had it or not; he was the answer to Madison Avenue's dreams, always consuming in the present and paying up on time. The country could find in all his sad young men, and especially in Gatsby, the embodiment of the success ethic upon which they had been brought up, sheltered in prose that added great charm to the dream and somehow made it seem even more believable.

---

40 Malcolm Cowley, ed., *The Stories of F. Scott Fitzgerald* (New York, 1951), p. 38; Fitzgerald, *The Great Gatsby* (New York, 1953, c.1925), pp. 117, 123, 9, 136; *The Beautiful and Damned* (New York, 1922), 341.

But Gatsby was murdered, and in 1929 the prosperity of the country followed him to the grave. The tendency of any adolescent enjoying himself is to write off conditions outside his immediate presence, and Fitzgerald's first response must have been that which he formulated in "Babylon Revisited": "The snow of twenty-nine wasn't real snow. If you didn't want it to be snow, you just paid some money." It is just the sort of thought Fitzgerald was likely to have, at the precise time that he knew its inadequacy, and even his own inability to act on his insights. For Fitzgerald, like others of his time, shared Amory Blaine's attitude toward those who suffered from lack of material goods: "I detest poor people," Amory once thought to himself. "I hate them for being poor. Poverty may have been beautiful once, but it's rotten now. It's the ugliest thing in the world. It's essentially cleaner to be corrupt and rich than it is to be innocent and poor." Faced with the depression, Fitzgerald's own life took the kind of revenge on him that was the stuff of great novels. His own books did not sell, and his lack of self-discipline refused to allow him to stop spending or drinking. His wife, the incarnation of the rich and beautiful debutante, grew more and more insane, and never recovered to full normality. Still, he gamely worked away on a new novel, dealing with the same old themes but with a new sense of sorrow and death. *Tender Is the Night* (1934) brought together many of the pervasive themes of the twenties: a psychiatrist who is young and handsome; a wealthy young girl of great beauty who captivates him despite—or perhaps because of—her mental instability, and eventually destroys him; alcoholism, sexual perversion and philandering, the power of money, rootless drifting; even a symbol of the era, the bars of gilded metal that Dick Diver uses for paperweights. Like Fitzgerald, something of a victim of his own charm, Diver suffers a fall that is also the fall of the adolescent ideal. It is no longer charming, it is merely disgusting. "But you used to want to create things—now you seem to want to smash them up," his wife tells him late in the book, when she has become more perceptive than he. In 1934 the emotion was scarcely necessary; everything was smashed up already. The rich were indeed different from you and me; there were fewer of them. And in Fitzgerald's case, like that of so many others by 1934, the era of promising if shallow youth was over. The precious psyche of the young was losing out to the demands of society as a whole.[41]

---

41 *Beautiful and Damned,* p. 418; *Stories,* pp. 142, 402; *This Side of Paradise* (New York, 1920), p. 256; *Tender Is the Night* (New York, 1934), p. 286. See also Arthur Mizener, *The Far Side of Paradise* 2nd ed. (Boston, 1965); and Henry Dan Piper, *F. Scott Fitzgerald: A Critical Portrait* (New York, 1965), which seem to me respectively the best biography and the best critical study.

III

SOLIDARITY FOREVER

Whatever their feelings about Freud and the life of art, most of the intellectuals in Mabel Dodge's salon flirted, for one reason or another, with some phase of Marxism. For Walter Lippmann, socialism was only one of his experiments with various elements of social science, and he soon abandoned anything resembling an advocacy of radical social change. Max Eastman, on the other hand, was one of the earliest serious students of Marx in America, and some form of communist sympathy had coexisted peacefully in his mind with Freudianism for many years. But while Lippmann lost many of his illusions in the world war and the resulting debacle of liberal idealism at Versailles, Eastman began to lose his own radicalism after an overexposure to Russia, and the men, led by Stalin, who soon replaced Lenin and Trotsky in power. Just as he had been one of the first Americans to talk about Freud in an intelligent way, so too he was one of the first men of the Left to become disillusioned with the Russian experiment.

But the third key man in Mabel Dodge's circle, Lincoln Steffens, experienced no such disillusion. The more he saw of Russia and the more he compared it to America, the more Steffens found himself becoming even more intransigently radical than he had been in his youth. By the early 1930s, he was one of the best-known and most respected communist sympathizers in America, and his autobiography was one of the most influential leftist books published in the early thirties.

Steffens had long been concerned with public affairs and was inordinately proud of his associations with Progressive Era mayors, governors, and presidents. With his usual modesty, he claimed in his autobiography that he had almost single-handedly stopped Woodrow Wilson from going to war with Mexico. During the war, he entered Russia even before Trotsky, and in the midst of the revolution acted as liaison between Kerensky and Wilson. He helped lead the mysterious Bullitt mission to Russia, in what was supposed to be a semiofficial attempt to set up diplomatic relations between Moscow and Washington. He summed up his attitude to the new regime in one sentence to Bernard Baruch: "I have been over into the future, and it works." Wilson and Lloyd George, for reasons of their own, promptly disowned the mission, but Steffens remained convinced of his own rightness, and slowly became more and more of a fellow traveler. As he studied the events in Russia, he came to accept terror as an inevitable part of revolution; by the 1930s, he thought that even Wisconsin, the most radical state in America, could improve itself enormously by learning from Russian precedents. He had come a long way from the quixotic Christian reformer of the years before the war.

More and more, he expressed his contempt for liberal vacillation. He had several complimentary things to say about Mussolini, apparently because the Italian, like Lenin, was willing to ignore liberal theories and use power to initiate "real" reforms. During the twenties, he participated less in politics, and wrote less, devoting himself instead to a long-delayed family life on the Riviera. He was always willing to admit the wrongs committed by men in Russia and Italy, but he insisted, when he spoke out at all, that parliamentary countries also had many faults, and that all countries and political systems had to be judged impartially, without the habit of prejudgment he thought so common in some of his contemporaries. Liberals, he wrote, were too often unwilling to look at the root of social problems; they were in practice far more concerned with their moral principles than with social action.

The most typical example of Steffens's ambivalence during the early years of the depression was his attitude toward collective movements and group actions. Despite his own individualistic and iconoclastic tendencies, he was fascinated by the spectacle of mass activity. As a good Marxist, he should have denounced big business, but he continued to be attracted as well as repelled by the corporations. The moralist and the intellectual in him had to admit that these huge combines were built through anti-intellectual and even amoral procedures. But they were beautifully efficient, and their very amorality was a sign that they had at least progressed beyond rigid adherence to dogmatic principles like laissez-faire and the moralizing once handed out by the likes of Bishop William Lawrence. For these reasons, Steffens did not view Henry Ford, the most visible industrialist in the country, as some sort of fascist beast or greedy bloodsucker; instead, he praised Ford highly for signs that his head "was working like a Red's." For Steffens, Ford was "a prophet without words, a reformer without politics, a legislator, statesman—a radical. I understood why the Bolshevik leaders of Russia admired, coveted, studied him." [1] Clearly then, if Steffens was at all typical in his line of thought, the key ideas of the next decade or so would not be the obvious themes of communism, fascism, socialism, or capitalism, but rather themes that could unite these tendencies: a concern with large industrial enterprise rather than individual achievement; with security rather than liberty; with cooperative achievement rather than individual self-assertion; with planning rather than spontaneity; with legislative and social achievement rather than with the private and artistic. The cult of the community replaced the cult of the child.

Nothing symbolized this coming change of emphasis like the literary and magazine upheavals of the early and middle 1920s. The chief guru of the bohemian Left during the second decade of the century was undoubtedly Floyd Dell, with his devotion to the life of the child, the artist, and the patient on the psychoanalyst's couch. The chief literary outlet for Dell and his friends at this time was the *Liberator*, the financially impoverished successor to the old *Masses* that had been killed by the Wilson administration during the war. At first, the magazine no more recognized the split between art, revolution, and social science than had the visitors to Mabel Dodge's salon. As Joseph Freeman later recalled, "We fancied ourselves disinterested devotees of art, revolution and psychoanalysis." In Freeman's circle, Dell was the man who made everyone feel at home: "he was father-confessor to dozens of moon calves to whom he opened his house, gave time and energy, literary and material help, to whom he talked with that profusion of ideas, that wealth of information, that brilliance for which he was famous in the prewar Village." He was a remarkable talker, always sympathetic, and absolutely untiring in his willingness to discuss Life

---

1 Lincoln Steffens, *Autobiography* (New York, 1931), pp. 736 ff., esp. pp. 799, 805–6, 832, 852–53.

and Ideas with the men younger than himself. He was, Freeman said, "the brightest exponent" of "art and revolution." As such, he seemed to strike a perfect balance between bohemianism and socialism, between his concern for the child as artist and the adult as revolutionary reformer.[2]

For a while, the *Liberator* reflected all sides of Dell's personality. As Freeman wrote, it "had one foot in bohemia, the other in the revolutionary movement." But the alliance proved increasingly uneasy, as more and more writers seemed to sense that irresponsible bohemianism and social agitation were simply incompatible; that, in fact, the social views expressed by many of the bohemians were merely a kind of symbolic antibourgeois pose which meant little more than that they disliked America and the middle-class values held by its public men. More and more, the die-hard communists seemed to be taking control. The first open sign of the schism was the establishment on the *Liberator* of two separate groups of associate editors, one a chiefly political group, led by Russian-oriented radicals like C. E. Ruthenburg, William Z. Foster, and Jay Lovestone, and the other a chiefly literary group, led by Dell, Claude McKay, and, temporarily, Mike Gold. But even this ad hoc means of channeling disagreements proved inadequate—like the meager supply of money—and the magazine moved briefly to Chicago, grew more and more political, and finally expired in 1924. Dell of course lived on to write several more books on love and himself, but his position of leadership was never again the same. When, in the late twenties and early thirties, he began to defend such bourgeois values as marriage, fatherhood, and the family, he became something of a laughing-stock of the Left. One thing both bohemians and communists agreed on was that such values just would not do.[3]

In a sense, the *Liberator* died from this split between literature and politics, and the magazine that replaced it reflected the new strength of agreement based on a single unifying issue. During 1924 and 1925, plans for financing and shaping the editorial policy of several new magazines made the rounds of the Village, but most of them came to nothing. Finally, a man and a magazine joined to replace Dell and the *Liberator*. Mike Gold and the *New Masses,* following in the tradition of the prewar *Masses,* became symbolic of the new era of group action. Gold did his best to act his part. He was aggressively proletarian, given to wearing dirty shirts, a big, black, and dirty Stetson,

2 Joseph Freeman, *An American Testament* (New York, 1936), pp. 246–48; Daniel Aaron, *Writers on the Left* (New York, 1965, c.1961), pp. 109 ff., 231–36.

3 Freeman, *Testament,* pp. 292 ff.; Aaron, *Writers,* ch. 4 and pp. 231–36; Floyd Dell, *Homecoming* (New York, 1933).

and a stinking, cheap Italian cigar. He liked to spit vigorously on whatever floor he happened to be, and he really did not care whether that floor was covered by an expensive rug and located in plush offices, or was merely bare board like his own office. Despite the naive expression and ironic tone he could assume on occasion, his proletarian pose was no joke. To Gold, the poor and the laborers, the people with whom he had grown up, were the most important people in the world. And his strong proletarian sympathies colored his views on art: the true artist, he insisted, should stop worrying about his precious psyche, his sex life, and his repressions; instead, he should turn to the poor, the ethnic group, the unemployed, and the striker. Bohemian art, he sneered, was merely escapist; it led to little more than café indolence and eccentricity. The new art would be collective, as the artist fulfilled himself by submitting to the rewarding disciplines established by the group wisdom of the revolution. True individuality would come only from a new identification with the mass.[4]

No one outside of leftist circles noticed the passing of leadership status from Dell to Gold, but almost everyone was aware of the first of the great events that led to the American version of the United Front in the 1930s—the execution of Sacco and Vanzetti in 1927. Nicola Sacco and Bartolomeo Vanzetti had been arrested in 1920, in the aftermath of the Red Scare, for the robbery and murder of a shoe-factory paymaster and a guard. Massachusetts at the time was scarcely friendly either to immigrants or to radicals—indeed, it rarely considered the two groups as separate entities—and some circumstantial evidence linked the two men to the crime. At first, the event attracted little attention in the leftist literary world; in fact, for five years or more the majority of radicals gave it little more than passing notice. But as the day of execution neared, and appeals failed again and again, radicals soon discovered the case, the prejudice of the Anglo-Saxon leaders of society and the bar in Massachusetts, the frank bigotry of some of the officials most closely involved, and the usefulness of the case as a weapon for attacking the forces of philistinism and capitalism that were the Enemy. By 1927, the group of protestors, occasionally arrested for their words and picketing, included figures as disparate and well-known as John Dos Passos, Dorothy Parker, Katherine Anne Porter, and Edna St. Vincent Millay, as well as Mike Gold. Even more conventional men were deeply disturbed by the case. Al Smith, for example, said that he did not know what to think about it, since he

---

4 Freeman, *Testament,* p. 257; Aaron, *Writers,* pp. 179–81; Michael Gold, *The Hollow Men* (New York, 1941), p. 21; *The Mike Gold Reader* (New York, 1954), p. 52.

had not studied the case, but that if he had, and if "it left me in such a state of mind that I had to call in a couple of college presidents to tell me what to do, I'd call that a reasonable doubt and let 'em go free." Other figures suddenly discovered a new sense of the proper form of social activity. As the liberal Catholic Shaemas O'Sheel said, "Class consciousness, class struggle, have been summoned from the tomb in which they were composing their reluctant limbs; infused with a new blood of rage. . . ." [5]

What no one seemed to notice about the effect of the case was that the classes that were united in this new consciousness of outrage simply should not have been, at least not according to Marx. The common people were not, on the whole, outraged; if anything, the rich, the middle class, and the poor all seemed to think the men were guilty. As Granville Hicks, already on the road to his 1930s communism, said, the rich and the powerful were certainly not the only people opposed to clemency: "It was also the doctors, the lawyers, the shopkeepers, the farmers, the workers. It was practically all my neighbors in Northampton except for the other members of the college faculty. The battle was between the intellectuals and everybody else." Precisely. Such an event was supposed to unite all the workers with their middle-class leaders; instead, it united most of them, if it united them at all, against their intellectual leaders in the coming revolution. No one seemed to notice the irony. Looking back eight years later, Malcolm Cowley dated from the event not only his own radicalism, but the new sense of solidarity that intellectuals came to feel. Suddenly they were friendly with the communists and unafraid to talk of revolution. Many of them forgot the catalyzing effect of the execution, or emphasized other events. But, Cowley insisted about this new radical alliance, "Almost nobody mentioned the obvious fact that, whatever else it might be, it was also a sequel to the Sacco–Vanzetti case, a return to united political action. This time, however, the intellectuals had learned that they were powerless by themselves and that they could not accomplish anything unless they made an alliance with the working class." By 1928 the intellectuals had found a sense of unity in their opposition to most of American life, and in Mike Gold a leader always ready to speak in their behalf. All they lacked was enough misery in the country to supply them with an audience. [6]

---

5 Aaron, *Writers*, pp. 185–90; G. L. Joughin and E. M. Morgan, *The Legacy of Sacco and Vanzetti* (New York, 1948), p. 331.

6 Aaron, *Writers*, pp. 185–90; Francis Russell, *Tragedy in Dedham* (New York, 1962), p. 332.

II

The shift from concern for the self apart from society during the 1920s to concern for a society that subsumed the self for the good of the masses during the 1930s appeared most sharply in the field of art, and here too the Sacco–Vanzetti case played a key role. Ben Shahn, for example, who became one of the most popular and respected of the social artists, was almost as much a devotee of modernism in its various guises during the early part of his career as any of the modernists of the twenties. He was the son of a carpenter who came from a family of woodcarvers in his native Lithuania. In 1906, when Shahn was eight years old, the family emigrated to the United States, and he was soon apprenticed to a lithographer. But this early experience did not, for a long time, seem to have much influence on his art. He broke from his almost obsessively Orthodox Jewish family, became a Paris expatriate, traveled through Italy and Africa, and painted in the styles that were fashionable in France. He even retained a life-long admiration for Paul Klee. But Shahn could never convince himself that his modernist painting style suited him, and in 1930 he began to move quickly toward the social art that won him his place in American history. He was at work on illustrations about the Dreyfus case when the change began, and he decided that a socially committed realism was more suited to his art. By the next year he had settled on the Sacco–Vanzetti Case, and he produced twenty-three gouache paintings in the space of seven months. As he said later: "Ever since I could remember I'd wished that I'd been lucky enough to be alive at a great time—when something big was going on, like the Crucifixion. And suddenly I realized I was. Here I was living through another crucifixion. Here was something to paint." [7]

Part of Shahn's ability in representational art doubtless came from his training in lithography. Another source was his knowledge of photography, both in his own work and in the work of his friend Walker Evans. Shahn was also something of a genuine collectivist artist, despite his notably individualist temperament. His wife was an active member of the Communist party, and Shahn was a definite fellow traveler who became identified with numerous groups and causes that had a pink tinge to them. He was never able to toe the party line, but he did a series of fifteen gouache paintings in support of the labor leader, Tom Mooney, whose cause during 1932–33 was quite popular on the Left. These works won him his first great collective commission:

---

7 Selden Rodman, *Portrait of the Artist as an American* (New York, 1951); James T. Soby, *Ben Shahn: Paintings* (New York, n.d.), p. 11.

another irascible part-time communist, the Mexican muralist Diego Rivera, admired his work and hired Shahn to help in one of the more improbable commissions of the early depression. Despite Rivera's notorious political views, Nelson A. Rockefeller and a number of other wealthy and influential New Yorkers had been most impressed by Rivera's murals for the Mexican government and for the Ford Motor Company in Detroit, and they asked Rivera and his chosen assistants to portray "Man at the Crossroads Looking with Hope and High Vision to the Choosing of a New and Better Future" on the elevator bank facing the main entrance to the RCA Building in Rockefeller Center. The color red and the face of Lenin that soon dominated the mural infuriated most of New York, and when Rivera refused to make major changes in his work his bosses had the whole scene destroyed.[8]

The "collective" art that came out of Shahn's experiences was only occasionally collective in the sense that he had collaborators. More frequently, it was collective because of the social and political themes apparent in it. Shahn portrayed the depression, the immigrant, the worker, the need for reform, the callousness of the ruling class, and the terror of war, in sharp contrast to those—like himself—who in the previous decades had painted their own consciousness and problems and theories. Sharpest of all was the contrast between the old hatred of government and the new willingness of artists to paint in government buildings and to receive government paychecks for their art. During the early New Deal Shahn worked for the Farm Security Administration in the Special Skills Division, and there he was instrumental in protecting its native folk art activities from the hands of destructive congressmen and other critics. Rexford Tugwell asked him to come to Washington "to explain in posters to the people who need it what is being done for them and to the others what they are paying for." As senior liaison officer Shahn not only soothed politicians, he also painted, designed posters, was chief layout man, and did most of the necessary planning. Also during this period, Shahn and Walker Evans made numerous photographic trips around the country, and these trips provided a wealth of raw material that dominated Shahn's later paintings for years.

As the depression became more serious, the Federal Art Project of the WPA tried to take up some of the slack among artists. For four years, from 1935–39, the government doled out money, about $19,000,-000, to about 5,000 artists. Shahn won out over 375 other artists for the $19,980 job of painting the story of social security on the walls of its new building at Independence and Third streets, and his work

---

8 Rodman, *Portrait of the Artist;* Soby, *Shahn,* pp. 11–12; Bertram Wolfe, *The Fabulous Life of Diego Rivera* (New York, 1963), ch. 26.

there, as elsewhere, became passionately controversial. He also received the commission for the Bronx post office murals, in 1939. During the Second World War, he did some of his most frequently reproduced work, both for the Office of War Information, and for the Congress of Industrial Organization. In the process, he developed theories that made clear how far he had come from the aesthetic individualism of the 1920s and that set him apart from the formalistic conservatism that was soon to dominate in the universities. *"I don't really care that much about art,"* he once said. "I'm interested in life, and only in art in so far as it enables me to express what I feel about life. . . ." For him, "painting had to be a way of arriving at the truth about life—our life here and now." As soon as he found himself putting aesthetic values above the values of reality, "subordinating the end to the means— getting unintelligible, putting too much emphasis on 'shapes' or 'textures'—I drop this lead weight on my foot." [9]

The aesthetic that Shahn evolved from his social art was a straightforward rebuff to other artists. Art, he insisted constantly, took its shape from its content, from the experiences and memories of the artist in real life. No matter what its ostensible form, art had to have this content, and if a painting seemed to have no form at all, then formlessness was its content. When he described the genesis of his Dreyfus paintings, for example, Shahn said that the idea first came to him from reading a history of the case, and in portraying the leading figures he amused himself by consciously deciding to *épater l'avant-garde*, just to reverse the bias of his earlier years, when he preferred to *épater le bourgeois*. France, at the time, was similarly disturbed by America's Sacco–Vanzetti case, and Shahn quickly made the transition in his own work as well. Thus reading and current controversy supplied the kind of content that began to influence the form of Shahn's art. Then, with "as rigorous a simplicity as I could command," he set about creating a spare expression of his emotions that would also appeal to a wider audience than was usually his. By so doing, he apparently hoped to expand the awareness of the democratic mass, improve the environment for the growth of liberal or radical ideas, and cement a community of minds that could work together for the improvement of society and the state. Art, he insisted, had a "unifying power," and he always believed that "the character of a society is largely shaped and unified by its great creative works," that "a society is molded upon its epics, and that it imagines in terms of its created things." With these new works he "had crossed the terrain of the 'social view,'" and he "would not return." He thus not only helped to shape the public mind in support of the New Deal and collective state action, he also

---

9 Rodman, *Portrait*, quotations on pp. 89, 32.

illustrated many of the events of the thirties and forties in work consciously based on a collective, realistic aesthetic emphasizing representational rather than abstract symbolism.[10]

III

A similar emphasis appeared in the social sciences. In education, for example, the new leader was William Heard Kilpatrick, and he soon achieved the status of the most influential teacher of teachers in the country. Kilpatrick had had a conventional childhood, well-adjusted past the point of parody, as a minister's son in Baptist Georgia. He came to his innovative views only slowly, when he was well into his career, and without the normal convulsions and crises common in men of his talent. Darwin, and graduate work at Johns Hopkins, helped deconvert him from the most orthodox of the beliefs of his church, while his school experiences made him a life-long enemy of the orthodox processes of educating the young. In particular, he loathed the report card, because of the inevitable animosities and frustrations it created in the child and between the child and his teachers and parents. After a few years, he had acquired personal experience in the whole range of education, from the elementary to the college level. In time, he even regained some of his lost religion, but he was still unorthodox enough to cause a heresy scandal at his conservative college, and he apparently resigned under pressure.

In 1907, at the age of thirty-six, Kilpatrick finally found his way, to Columbia Teachers College. As a student there, he became very much a disciple of John Dewey, and under Dewey's influence he became a complete relativist, and a present-minded pragmatist. His early books criticized the currently popular Montessori and Froebel systems of education as outmoded and too child-centered to produce appropriately socialized individuals. He agreed with the advocates of the child-centered school that education should not be merely the acquisition of facts, he sympathized with Rugg's emphasis on the cultivation of personality, but his primary goal was to produce socially effective and adjusted members of the community. Finally, in one of the most influential pamphlets in educational history, he hit on his famous innovation: "The Project Method: The Use of the Purposeful Act in the Educative Process." It gave his students a goal, a slogan, and a weapon with which to beat those they disapproved of. What Kilpatrick had finally discovered was a means of injecting the spirit of reform into

---

10 Ben Shahn, *The Shape of Content* (New York, n.d., c.1957), esp. pp. 42–46; Rodman, *Portrait*, pp. 24–25; Selden Rodman, ed., *Conversations with Artists* (New York, 1961, c.1957), pp. 189–93.

the environment of the average school. The "project method," which soon became all but synonymous with his name, stipulated that what each child should learn was not content but rather a means of discovering knowledge. It was a pragmatist's dream, for it was totally operational, open-ended, and capable of unlimited adaptability, unattached as it was to any specific problem or set of social attitudes. As he said in the opening pages, ". . . the unifying idea I sought was to be found in the conception of wholehearted purposeful activity proceeding in a social environment." No longer could students sit and memorize, or indulge endlessly in "artistic" and "creative" behavior; now they attacked one project after another, and each solution presumably taught them a little more about the means of solving still more problems. The emphasis was still child-centered, in that the child usually had to solve the problems on his own; but it was also socially oriented, in that the teacher presumably chose relevant projects, and the results led eventually to the solving of socially meaningful problems.[11]

In his early work, Kilpatrick rarely ventured out of the academic environment into specific social problems, but for any first-rate disciple of Dewey such a trip was all but inevitable. A person who wanted to change the child naturally wanted to change society; presumably, the desire for change was linked to some feeling for what a better society would be like. The "school" thus tended to include all life, since all life at one time or another affected the child, and the child in turn would go out into life when he stopped attending school. "We seem bound to conclude that the proper educational care of the child knows no excluding boundary to shut out any aspect of life which does in fact affect the child's well-being. . . ," Kilpatrick was writing in the early thirties. This widening process "leads on by inevitable steps from this regard for the whole child considered in himself to a new and active regard for the social and economic conditions that affect child welfare," and this naturally included "the welfare of the child's parents. For family conditions certainly affect child welfare." Thus, to reform the child's environment effectively, the educator had to educate adults as well, and in so doing he simply had to discuss social and economic issues. Kilpatrick insisted, however, that such a discussion need not be merely indoctrination, for it ideally would "make the learner an independent judge of such matters." As he pursued this line of thought, he slowly began to sound like an educa-

---

11 Samuel Tenenbaum, *William Heard Kilpatrick* (New York, 1951); Lawrence Cremin, *The Transformation of the School* (New York, 1964), pp. 215 ff.; see also, John L. Childs, *American Pragmatism and Education* (New York, 1956), and Kilpatrick's *Foundations of Method* (New York, 1925).

tional ally of the newer, more political and radical writers and intellectuals. As he summed up the writings of a group of like-minded educators, "the traditional forms and institutions of society and underlying theories no longer fit our technologic society. Even radical reconstruction seems necessary." This situation gave the teacher a moral obligation: "Education as the social process intelligently directing itself cannot be true to itself, cannot be intelligent or act so, except as it knows the social situation and acts accordingly." [12] Clearly, the collective ideal was displacing the creative ideal at Columbia.

What was often muted and hidden in the lumpy rhetoric of Kilpatrick was stated baldly in the work of his Columbia colleague, George S. Counts. Counts stated the new ideas so firmly and so vigorously that he became the leading spokesman, if not the most influential teacher, of the new, socially conscious educational establishment in the 1930s. Counts began his career with highly critical investigations of educational sociology, and he minced no words in denouncing high schools for catering chiefly to the children of the middle class, and boards of education for submitting to their parents. He was also one of the earliest proponents of professional unionism among teachers, and always emphasized the need for teachers to unite in order to increase their ability to resist the pressure groups common in society. Counts even attacked the progressive education movement, the most radical group functioning with views approaching his own, because it elaborated "no theory of social welfare," and because he found it an upper-middle-class variety of progressivism—agnostic, tolerant and benign, composed merely of "romantic sentimentalists" unwilling to do much toward changing the status quo. "If Progressive Education is to be genuinely progressive," he said,

> it must emancipate itself from the influence of this class, face squarely and courageously every social issue, come to grips with life in all of its stark reality, establish an organic relation with the community, develop a realistic and comprehensive theory of welfare, fashion a compelling and challenging vision of human destiny, and become less frightened than it is today at the bogies of *imposition* and *indoctrination*. In a word, Progressive Education cannot place its trust in a child-centered school.

Counts attacked education with all the power consciousness of a Lenin. Education inherently meant telling children what they should believe, he insisted, and the teacher who refused to indoctrinate his students in the truth was simply derelict in his duty. The real argu-

---

12 William H. Kilpatrick, ed., *The Educational Frontier* (New York, 1933), pp. 128, 150, 263.

ment usually came only when people argued over what was true.
Children had to grow up in a meaningful tradition, and the child-
centered school deprived them of this; the older theories ignored society completely, or else taught irrelevancies. Instead, Counts sounded
a call worthy of Mike Gold: "We cannot, by talk about the interests
of children and the sacredness of personality, evade the responsibility
of bringing to the younger generation a vision which will call forth
their active loyalties and challenge them to creative and arduous la-
bors," he insisted. "A generation without such a vision is destined, like
ours, to a life in absorption on self, inferiority complexes, and frustration. The genuinely free man is not the person who spends the day
contemplating his own navel, but rather the one who loses himself in
a great cause or glorious adventure." Teachers have great potential
power, and they should not be bashful about using it to further the
social good. "Education as a force for social regeneration must march
hand in hand with the living and creative forces of the social order.
In their own lives teachers must bridge the gap between school and
society and play some part in the fashioning of those great common
purposes which should bind the two together." By 1939, he was calling
frankly for indoctrination in democratic principles and a curriculum
based on study of the social and economic forces that shaped, and presumably were undermining, American society.[13]

IV

The shift from concentration on the individual to concentration on the group also dominated other social sciences and even
gained a certain institutional foundation. During the second and third
decades of the twentieth century, the Columbia of Franz Boas, John
Dewey, Charles Beard, James Harvey Robinson, Ruth Benedict, and
many others, had been the pioneering and preeminent school for the
various social sciences. Columbia managed to retain this status in the
field of teacher education well past the Second World War, but in
other areas of social science, the University of Chicago slowly became
the most influential trainer of future college professors, especially in
sociology and government. A key figure in this shift of influence was
Harold D. Lasswell, a man whose career not only displays the historical changes of emphasis important for understanding the interwar
years, but whose work has been suggestive to many scholars outside
his own field.

---

13 Cremin, *Transformation,* pp. 224 ff.; George S. Counts, "Dare the School Build
a New Social Order?" (New York, 1932), esp. pp. 7–12, 23, 38–39, 40–42; "The Schools
Can Teach Democracy" (New York, 1939), pp. 17–22.

Lasswell's earliest work was an obvious aftermath of the debacle of Versailles, combined with certain Freudian insights. What interested him most in the early twenties was the way the government had been able to use propaganda to influence its citizens, with no apparent regard for truth, and with no particular rebellion on the part of the majority of people. "Propaganda" he defined as "the control of opinion by significant symbols, or, to speak more concretely and less accurately, by stories, rumors, reports, pictures and other forms of social communication." In his main work on propaganda, as in all his later work, Lasswell exhibited a disturbing tendency to see all communication as some form of symbolic deception, just as Freud had always seen in what his patients told him some other, more important and infinitely misleading form of neurosis or antisocial desire. Ideas, Lasswell seemed to be saying, simply do not exist; they are only the names people use to camouflage their true motives—to trick others into doing what they wish. Despite this unfortunate tendency toward anti-intellectualism, his description of what a government could do was far too obviously true to be dismissed lightly. "The facility with which sincere and dextrous hands may shape cases on either side of a controversy, leaves no doubt that, in the future, the propagandist may count upon a battalion of honest professors to rewrite history, to serve the exigencies of the moment, and to provide the material for him to scatter thither and yon," he wrote, eyeing the men who had prostituted their profession in 1917–18. They were not alone: "The churches of practically every description can be relied upon to bless a popular war, and to see in it an opportunity for the triumph of whatever godly design they choose to further." Of course, some difficulty might arise from the normal Christian condemnation of most war, but this usually posed no problem for the particular war at hand. Such approval "may be expedited by securing suitable interpretations of the war very early in the conflict by conspicuous clericals; the lesser lights will twinkle after." [14]

Lasswell's most influential book in this period was *Psychopathology and Politics* (1930). Here, he began by stressing the importance of studying each individual in a group, as a means of understanding the group itself—saying, in effect, that the psychology of the twenties and the sociology of the thirties needed to work together for proper understanding to result. "Political science without biography is a form of taxidermy," he insisted, and the rest of the book illustrated for historians and political scientists how much value the psychological biography of an individual could have for someone trying to interpret con-

---

14 Harold D. Lasswell, *Propaganda Technique in the World War* (New York, 1938, c.1927), pp. 9, 53, 73.

duct and evaluate ideas. "The purpose of this venture is not to prove that politicians are 'insane,' " he went on, nor is it "to make a hit-or-miss collection of anecdotes about the relation between early experiences and specific political traits and interests." What he wanted was "to discover what developmental experiences are significant for the political traits and interests of the mature." He wanted "to see whether the intensive investigation of life-histories will in any way deepen our understanding of the whole social and political order." He was also careful to show how his work was indebted to several of his predecessors, particularly the students of the Polish peasant in America, W. I. Thomas and Florian Znaniecki, with their autobiographical emphasis, and to Franz Boas, in his studies of primitive man.[15]

But his greatest debt was obviously, and quite consciously, to Freud. For Lasswell, Freud was the man who had brought dream life into the study of human behavior; who had talked about ideas and actions as merely rationalizations for deeper drives; who had shown how all symptoms were unified into the complete personality; and who had been able to show how fantasy life was a means of compensating for earlier deprivations. In using Freud, Lasswell went on to insist that all the education and logical training in the world could not make political leaders capable of operating with complete rationality. In fact, he continued, too much emphasis on logic and reason not only narrowed the mind and cut off necessary conflicting stimuli but was also only a further form of self-deception—surely the man who always stressed his rationality was only overcompensating for his own irrational fears. As a means of beginning a marriage of psychopathology and politics, Lasswell set up categories of political types. Most men, he found, fell into one or more of three categories: the agitator, the administrator, and the theorist. In pursuing these types through a number of detailed case histories, he pointed out how hatred of the government, for example, could come from a hatred for the father during childhood; or, how excessive fear of impotence and shame about sexual involvement could result in crusades against liquor and prostitution, and an attitude of uncompromising fanaticism about reform; or, how a death wish stemming from fears of inadequacy could lead to "heroism" on the battlefield.

Lasswell's conclusions in this book have proved influential for decades. "Political movements derive their vitality from the displacement of private affects upon public objects," he said. The state, as the natural symbol of authority, "is the legatee of attitudes which have been organized in the life of the individual within the intimate interpersonal sphere of the home and friendship group." Politics, then,

---

15 Harold D. Lasswell, *Psychopathology and Politics* (Chicago, 1930), pp. 1, 7–9.

becomes the theater in which all these private emotions and frustrations enact themselves, a kind of theater of the absurd and the irrational: "Politics is the process by which the irrational bases of society are brought out into the open." As long as the lives of a country's citizens are tranquil and secure in an unquestioned moral order, politics *per se* is unnecessary. "Politics seems to be irrational because it is the only phase of collective life in which society tries to be rational. Its very existence shows that the moral order, with all its irrational and nonrational sanctions, is no longer accepted without a challenge. A political difference is the outcome of a moral crisis, and it terminates in a new moral consensus." The only solution for the political scientist was "the politics of prevention": "The problem of politics is less to solve conflicts than to prevent them; less to serve as a safety valve for social protest than to apply social energy to the abolition of recurrent sources of strain in society." [16]

V

Just as Lasswell's work in psychology had led him into the study of group activity in political science, so William F. Ogburn's interest in psychoanalysis led him to the study of the cultural behavior of the group, and thus to the somewhat younger discipline of sociology. Ogburn, who had come of age in the Progressive Era, and had considerable sympathy for reform ideals, but his personal temper was never much attracted by crusading zeal, and he never participated directly in the activities of the period. Instead, as a portent of interests to come, he completed for his Columbia degree a statistics-filled dissertation on all the American child labor legislation he could locate, in an effort to discover which states were pioneers and which were laggards, how the laws differed, and, ultimately, to set up norms for the use of men in state legislatures and thus lead to further reforms in the area. The dissertation, with its emphasis on measurable accuracy and the scientific approach, was an appropriate if virtually unreadable contribution to the current progressive zeal for organizing everything in sight and fixing it immediately. But very shortly afterwards, Ogburn's interests began one of their decisive shifts, and he was soon deep in Freud, in particular *The Interpretation of Dreams*. He found valuable

---

16 *Ibid.*, pp. 173, 184–85, 197. Lasswell usually kept the extraordinarily anti-intellectual implications of this sort of thought well hidden, but a comment in his *Politics: Who Gets What, When, How* (New York, 1950, c.1936), is extremely illuminating. After discussing philosophers and their frequently unhappy sex lives and inhibitions, he writes: "All these men seemed to possess a vigorous impulsive life which they had inhibited by consciences so stern that their efforts to cope with immediate reality were cramped; hence the resort to thought." (p. 204)

the idea that psychosis and neurosis were different in degree rather than kind from whatever constitutes normality, and he saw important implications in Freudian ideas for the treatment of family problems, juvenile delinquency, crime, and insanity. "Indeed, it is perhaps not an exaggeration to say that psychiatry, with its new conception of the genesis of personality and the functioning of motives, has produced a veritable revolution in the approach to the problems of the family, of children, of crime, and of social work." When he looked at history and its interpretation, he saw other uses: the economic interpretation of history, he thought, suddenly took on new luster when seen through Freudian eyes, for then all the other motives normally advanced tend to look like economic motives that had been censured by the superego, and then reformulated to appear altruistic. He even thought it possible that economic motives could play a role in collective behavior parallel to the role sex played in individual behavior, i.e., as the key, basic motivation but appearing in all sorts of disguised ways when the individual went into the world and joined in group action. Yet in all this speculation, Ogburn refused to reduce any sort of behavior to a simplistic formula, and displayed extreme, professional skepticism about those who did. Plainly, he was still testing the value of Freudian ideas, and his progressive love for precision never left him: "It seems to me that the free-association technique is not a very precise instrument of measurement, and is likely to lead to very improbable theories through the influence of suggestion and the desires of the investigator." [17]

The social thought of the late nineteenth century had assumed, largely by intuition and guesswork, that changes in culture were largely dependent on changes in biological make-up; that as man evolved, and only as fast as he evolved, so did his culture as a whole. Increasingly, most social thinkers came to realize that the body of culture, of inherited customs and knowledge, was capable of far-reaching changes even though the biological composition of the men involved did not change at all. They saw, too, that the proper study of the new science of sociology was not the relation of custom to biology, but the study of an entity, culture and its social structure. Culture was the durable

17 Otis Dudley Duncan, ed., *William F. Ogburn, on Culture and Social Change* (Chicago, 1964), pp. vii–xxii, 88; William F. Ogburn, "Progress and Uniformity in Child-Labor Legislation," Columbia Faculty of Political Science, *Studies in History, Economics and Public Law* (New York, 1912), vol. 48; W. F. Ogburn, "The Contributions of Psychiatry to Social Psychology," *Publications of the American Sociological Society* 21 (1927): 82–91; W. F. Ogburn, "The Psychological Basis for the Economic Interpretation of History," *American Economic Review* 9, supplement (March 1919): 291–305.

inheritance which men received when they were born, and to which they could add as they lived. As Ogburn phrased the change, in 1937, "sociology as a study of the group was, *ipso facto,* a study of the group products, that is, culture."

This new realization combined with Ogburn's interest in the new psychology—an interest that extended as far as his own psychoanalysis —to make him a kind of missing link between the progressive students of personality, like Jane Addams or Charles H. Cooley, and the neo-Freudian school which developed late in the 1930s. For the progressives, personality was formed by the groups in which the child grew up, like the home, the school, or the work group; the child developed a personality by imitating the people around him. Cooley called the result the "looking-glass self," because the child saw himself by looking at others. In other words, the child was not born with any personality to speak of, only with the capacity for developing one. For Freud, on the other hand, the biological circumstances of early childhood, the Oedipus complex, the frustrations of toilet training, the repression of polymorphous-perverse sexuality, all meant that the child was doomed to constant warfare with his environment, and his personality developed chiefly, it often seemed, by accretions of scar tissue. The happy individual in the womb became the neurotic adult, and a docile imitation of the men around him seemed highly improbable, or at any rate not really relevant to personality. Using this new concept of the "culture," Ogburn tried to mediate between the two schools with which he had been involved. Personality, he suggested, "is more the outgrowth of group experience and of the culture pattern in which the child is reared," and not a biological inheritance, a product of conflict, or the result of simple imitation. Inheritance, biology, and custom set certain limits on the possible personalities an individual could develop, but within these limits, the key factor was the culture, the set of customs that guided the adults and helped them nurture the child. "Thus the modifiability of original nature, rather than a relatively rigid set of instincts, is a lesson from psychology that offers a basis for describing the different effects of culture on personality." [18]

But about the time Freud was becoming a national craze, Ogburn, in another important change of emphasis, was having second thoughts, and sometime between 1915 and 1922 he worked out his most important contributions to social theory. Shortly after his paper on the economic interpretation of history was published in 1919, Ogburn began to realize that, in discussing social change, the factor of disguise and sublimation on which he had concentrated was really less important

---

18 Duncan, *Ogburn,* pp. 7, 13–15.

than the factor of time. His activity in earlier reform movements had made him an ardent feminist, and he was increasingly impressed with the great lag that separated the modern status of women from the enormous economic and technological changes that were all around them. The idea that the woman's place was in the home was all very well in a society where she was constantly caring for children and relatives, running a large domestic and farm establishment, making clothes, preserving fruit, and so on, but in the twentieth century she no longer had these tasks in most parts of the Western world. Electricity ran the washing machines and lit the house, thus eliminating the worst of cleaning and candle-making; the car and train were diminishing distances and increasing opportunities for people to strike out on their own and set up independent households far from their parents; industry provided employment that drew men from the fields and paid them the money with which to buy what they previously had to make. Yet people still insisted that a woman should stay home and tend the house. Even if she had few children, a couple of maids, and a desire to work, nevertheless she should not work. Ogburn thought this attitude disgraceful, and in his irritation he gave sociology one of its important conceptual tools. The gap between the development of one part of a changing culture and the slower change of another part of that culture, he said, was a "cultural lag": "A cultural lag occurs when one of two parts of a culture which are correlated changes before or in greater degree than the other part does, thereby causing less adjustment between the two parts than existed previously." [19]

The result was Ogburn's most important book, *Social Change* (1922). Here he elaborated his newly developed view of the child, as an entity born into a culture and social heritage, whose character was limited but not determined by biology and environment. Modern culture, the heritage of the child of the twentieth century, was complex and heterogeneous, and one way of discussing this diversity was to describe changes in the culture as "selectively accumulative." In other words, new inventions like the steam engine or the car or a new medicine or a new scientific theory all initiated responses in the culture, and these responses were always uneven. Men might leave home for the factory, and might change all their outer habits, yet still retain the ideas and prejudices of their original environment. Sometimes these outmoded beliefs could be simply quaint, such as a proverb repeated in times of stress; they could become a children's version of an old adult necessity —the bow and arrow displaced by the gun remained in the culture as a game for the young; or they could be simply deadly, as with old medical nostrums that people seemed to prefer to the new-fangled ideas

---

19 Ibid., pp. 86–90.

that might save their lives. As Ogburn noted, ". . . forms of culture such as customs, beliefs, religions, survive because of a utility they possess in meeting psychological needs." These remnants of the past he labeled "cultural inertia," or the impediments to change that caused cultural lag. His affection for social reform then appeared, as he pointed to the need for legislative change as a way of closing the gap left by cultural inertia: workmen's compensation laws were essential to adapt modern life to newer and more dangerous business practices; taxes needed reforming, to cover the enormous amount of new wealth in the forms of intangibles like stock ownership and inheritance, which had previously not existed in times when land was all the wealth that really mattered; state and national legislative bodies should reapportion themselves, to give representation to new cities, and take representation from deserted rural areas; and of course the laws respecting women and the family needed a thorough revision. The material, technological culture had supplied too many inventions for the nonmaterial culture to absorb without pain and difficulty; the elected representatives of the people should try to make up for this cultural lag. While not exactly a ringing call to arms, Ogburn's conclusions were obviously a sociological prelude to the sense of community and group solidarity that later dominated the country in the 1930s.[20]

VI

If Ogburn's career showed how a progressive could become first a Freudian and then a sociologist of cultural change, that of his colleague at Chicago, Robert Park, showed how one could move from progressivism to the study of the masses without apparently ever participating intellectually in the 1920s. Park came to sociology rather late in life, after newspaper work and a period of service as secretary to Booker T. Washington; as a muckraker he exposed the sordid dealings of Leopold II in the Congo, and as Washington's secretary he demonstrated personal and scholarly interest in Negro affairs long before it became the fashionable thing to do. But he had never possessed much interest in man as an individual, psychological entity, and his written work at least shows none of the narcissism so characteristic of the 1920s. Instead, men in groups fascinated him in an almost mystical way. "The will to join with others in collective action is one of the elementary motives that move mankind," he wrote. "The consciousness and the excitement of participation in great events constitutes one of the most exhilarating and satisfying of human experiences." In concerted action with other men, the individual invariably

---

20 William F. Ogburn, *Social Change* (New York, 1950, c.1922), esp. pp. 78, 154.

"acquired a new dignity and a new glory as well as an added moral support." [21]

Like any good progressive, Park had read deeply in Cooley and in W. I. Thomas, the key academic sociologists before the First World War, and his own contributions were clearly built on their work. In looking at men in groups, he insisted that a group was more than merely the sum of the given individuals who composed it. Any culture had what he called a social process, which regulated the affairs of its members by rules which they had had no part in making; a body of tradition and opinion helped to mold the given individual, and even if it failed to regulate his ideas, it forced him to conform at least outwardly to its norms. Thus the student of society need not study the psychology of the child or the neuroses of the adult; rather, he should look on society as a control factor which organized, integrated, and directed the emotions and ideas of the individuals who composed it. The individual, Park argued, grew up to form a conception of himself through his contacts with his associates and a notion of what society considered his proper social role: ". . . the individual is not born human but the character we describe as human is for each of us a personal achievement. Each one of us acquires a personality in his effort to find a place and play a role in some society, and in the various and more or less integrated social groups of which that society is composed. . . ." Neurosis, then, or some such maladaptation to the environment, was not the result of parental mistakes or innate biological inheritance. For Park, individuals often simply could not quite make their inner beings conform totally to the body of culture that was trying to control them, and the result was a kind of permanent *Doppelgänger* motif, a split personality along the lines of Poe's "William Wilson" or Stevenson's "Dr. Jekyll and Mr. Hyde": "We have a private and a public life. In seeking to live up to the role which we have assumed, and which society has imposed upon us, we find ourselves in constant conflict with ourselves." The individual becomes an actor upon the stage of the world, "an actor, with one eye always on the gallery. In the society of other members of the species, he puts on a front, acquires manners and a style and dresses for the part he is expected to play." [22]

Park was one of the most influential teachers in American sociology, and his ideas excited students into dozens of important monographs. A proper assessment of his achievement would have to take into

21 Ralph H. Turner, ed., *Robert E. Park on Social Control and Collective Behavior* (Chicago, 1967), pp. ix–xiv, 250; Robert E. Park, *Race and Culture* (Glencoe, 1950), pp. xi–xiv.

22 Turner, *Park,* pp. ix–xlvi, 14, 190–91; Park, *Race and Culture,* pp. 249–51, 358–61.

account his willingness to generalize, his clear writing style, his influence on his students and sociology as a whole, his near obsession with using the city as a laboratory for cultural study, his work in human ecology, his key ideas ("symbiosis and socialization," "competition, conflict, accommodation, assimilation"), and his studies of newspapers and public opinion. But, Park's greatest achievement was his synthesis of his ideas about general sociology with his experience in race relations. His association with Booker T. Washington prepared him for a lifetime of interest in the Negro, and this interest soon expanded to a concern for all peoples with only a partial membership in the dominant culture of their geographical area. Human ecology, to Park, referred to man's relations to other men, more than to simple geography; and social change depended on the introduction and assimilation of new ideas and cultural groups. The Negro was thus made to order for Park's work, for like the European Jew, the Oriental in California, and other minority groups, the Negro was at best only a partial member of American society: he was an American and a Negro, and thus had a place in two cultures. But this place was an uneasy one, for the Negro often felt no pride in being black, he had little recorded history outside of his own folklore, and at the same time met chiefly with discrimination when he tried to join the dominant social group in his society.

In analyzing this situation, Park pointed out that no one really became upset as long as the Negro "kept his place." That is, society had erected certain moral ideas into a kind of social geography, in which no one became upset as long as no one tried to change his position. A certain amount of upward mobility was essential and permitted, but in practice society demanded that newcomers show no visible signs of their past condition: thus Orientals and Negroes were in the peculiar position of living in a kind of cultural ghetto, since they could not change their skin color and bone structure. To this sense of place and dislike of intrusion, Park gave the name "social distance": on the personal level, it might mean simply, Would you want your daughter to marry one?, or perhaps more realistically, Would your son marry one if he really wanted to? On a more conceptual level, it meant an important insight into the nature of prejudice. Prejudice, Park concluded, "seems to arise when, not our economic interests, but our social status is menaced. Prejudice and race prejudice are by no means to be identified by social distance, but arise when our personal and racial reserves are, or seem to be, invaded." Thus prejudice is not basically aggressive, but conservative, "a sort of spontaneous conservation which tends to preserve the social order and the social distances upon which that order rests." [23]

---

23 Turner, *Park*, pp. 55, 67–68; Park, *Race and Culture*, p. 260.

The normal course of history and migration meant that strangers were forever invading settled cultures, bringing upheavals and change. If skin color or religion did not forbid and impede assimilation—as with, say, most of the European immigrants to America—then three or four generations were usually adequate for the process of acculturation. But where the prevalent mores and the demands of social distance kept the strangers from mingling and intermarrying, the result was what proved to be Park's most influential term: the "marginal man." The marginal man, Park said, was "a cultural hybrid, a man living and sharing intimately in the cultural life and traditions of two distinct peoples; never quite willing to break, even if he were permitted to do so, with his past and his traditions, and not quite accepted, because of racial prejudice, in the new society in which he now sought to find a place." He was a man "on the margin of two cultures and two societies, which never completely interpenetrated and fused." The emancipated Jew, the mulatto in America, the Cape Colored in South Africa, and many other groups of mixed ancestry, all qualified for this status. The marginal man was apparently peculiarly unstable, restless, intelligent, aware, cosmopolitan, and moody. He lacked roots, yet he was the personification of the city; by uniting two cultures he escaped the bounds and restrictions of either, and thus achieved a new detachment, a rationality generally denied to those totally committed to one culture. Yet he was peculiarly prone to psychological instability, since he also lacked the consolation provided by a protecting world. In pointing out these factors, Park was not only enriching the terminological and methodological foundations of sociology, he was also laying a foundation for the more sophisticated work of the post-Second World War world.[24]

VII

The reform bias in social scientists like Lasswell, Ogburn, and Park was almost always muted, hedged about by qualifications and camouflaged by the outward veneer of science and objective research. Yet all these men seemed to think that if people understood the social laws they were uncovering, then changes in political, cultural and racial relations would follow. In the various areas of literature, this reform bias became far more obvious; literary men were normally more temperamental and given to emotion and enthusiasm; they were usually not tied to conservative academic institutions; and the fluidity of their social lives allowed them more contact both with the poor, and with those who wished to abolish poverty by relatively violent means. Of

24 Turner, *Park,* pp. 205–6; Park, *Race and Culture,* pp. 136, 376.

all these men, none had more influence and respect than Edmund Wilson, and few looked less like a Marxist and reformer at first glance.

Wilson was a most improbable revolutionary. He was raised in an upper-middle-class home in New Jersey, and like most people in his class he went to the best private schools, the Hill preparatory school, and Princeton. At Princeton, he was one of F. Scott Fitzgerald's best friends, and he seems to have been much like Fitzgerald in his bohemianism, his belief in literature, and his appreciation of the modern. He was bookish and quiet, while Fitzgerald was noisy and rather foolish, but the point needs emphasizing: Wilson had a distinctive bohemian period, and the unconventional life had considerable appeal for him; he captured this world adequately enough in his novel, *I Thought of Daisy*, which is clearly autobiographical.[25]

Wilson has long been a hard man to categorize, and any generalization about his critical range is bound to be misleading because it has to leave out so much. At times, especially in his shorter pieces, he sounded much like the James Huneker he had read as a boy, full of enthusiasm for literature, given to impressionistic commentary, and with minimal critical judgment. "There are few things I enjoy so much as talking to people about books which I have read and they haven't, and making them wish they had," he once wrote, "preferably a book that is hard to get or in a language that they do not know." At other times, he was the aesthete who believed in art as a kind of substitute religion, who emphasized style, and who seemed perfectly capable of justifying a socially useless life if it produced works of art. This is the Wilson who wrote that one of Eugene O'Neill's worst plays, *Welded*, "failed principally, it seems to me, through not having been well enough written." O'Neill, he went on, "does not pay enough attention to style." That sort of criticism would have irritated any Marxist who read it, and would hardly have been tolerated in a Communist party member, but Wilson cared not at all. In a similar mood he wrote his famous book, *Axel's Castle* (1931), which introduced to American readers one of the most antisocial groups in literary history, the French symbolist poets. On still other occasions, Wilson was as psychologically acute as any critic of the 1920s and able to produce work which has influenced world critical opinion about certain writers. When Wilson produced his analysis of Charles Dickens, for example, he demonstrated how Dickens's childhood trauma, produced by his months in a blacking warehouse, resulted in certain obsessional themes which permeated his novels—hatred of father figures and bourgeois Victorianism, identification with thieves and criminals, especially murderers. A generation of

---

25 Sherman Paul, *Edmund Wilson* (Urbana, 1967). See also Burton Rascoe, *A Bookman's Daybook*, ed. C. Hartley Grattan (New York, 1929), pp. 28–29.

academics has made a minor industry of embroidering on Wilson's insights.[26]

Yet none of these approaches are really basic to an understanding of Wilson's historical importance in American criticism and history. Of more importance are his growing social commitment and his increasing emphasis upon, and labor over, the work of Karl Marx. Even as Wilson was alternating between his guises as impressionist, psychologist, and aesthete, he was developing this fourth guise as a socially concerned man who thought history and politics were vital weapons for a literary critic. Even in the 1920s, for example, he could write that what was wrong with the younger American poets was that they had "no real stake in society. One does not want them to succumb to society; but one *would* like to see them, at least, have some sort of relation to it." But the key document for this phase in Wilson's career is the essay, "An Appeal to Progressives," first published in the *New Republic* on January 14, 1931. The old progressives, like the magazine's recently deceased editor, Herbert Croly, Wilson thought, no longer had a viable, relevant position. Whether called Fabianism, gradualism, liberalism, or progressivism, the slow encroachment of government over the control of the economy was obviously inadequate as a method of reform during the depression. Capitalism in 1930 was not benevolent enough to accept even stop-gap reforms, let alone real socialism, and it was obviously impotent in its own efforts to restore prosperity. Wilson strongly suggested that capitalism as a system was breaking down, and that henceforth it may not be able "to guarantee not merely social justice but even security and order."

The depression, he continued, "may be nothing less than one of the turning-points in our history, our first real crisis since the Civil War." Yet the response to date of liberals had been woefully inadequate. Apparently liberals had really been betting on capitalism, as a reasonably domesticable animal that only needed the proper leashing to take the country where it wanted to go. Our liberalism, Wilson snorted,

> seems to have little to offer beyond a discreet recommendation of public ownership of water power and certain other public utilities, a cordial feeling that labor ought to organize in a non-social-revolutionary way and a protest, invariably ineffective, against a few of the more obviously atrocious of the jailings, beatings-up and murders with which the industrialists have been trying to keep the working class docile.

At the very least, what society required was a firm commitment to socialism, and Wilson thought liberals ought to say so, firmly. In his

---

26 Edmund Wilson, *The Shores of Light* (New York, 1952), pp. 376, 104; *The Wound and the Bow* (New York, 1965, c.1941), pp. 3–85.

final paragraph, he stated what proved to be a liberal–intellectual rallying position for the whole decade: American radicals and progressives who repudiate much of Marx and much of the dogma of Russia, yet who still "hope to accomplish anything valuable," must "take communism away from the communists, and take it without ambiguities, asserting that their ultimate goal is the ownership by the government of the means of production." Americans were in the rather peculiar position of seeing an ex-bohemian literary critic raise a banner to unite the democratic Left, at a time when most politicians were helplessly impotent and many intellectuals were falling into despair or advocating totalitarianism.[27]

VIII

As it turned out, none of the important novelists of the thirties could restrict himself sufficiently to be a purely Marxist writer any more than Edmund Wilson could. Steinbeck often turned out to be sentimental and usually without a political ideology beyond an indiscriminate pity. Dos Passos soon became disillusioned and grew increasingly anti-Communist in the books that followed. But in many ways the most instructive case among proletarian writers was that of James T. Farrell. In his stubborn insistence on his own vision and integrity, his refusal to write something he did not believe in, and his essentially middle-class analysis of the common man, Farrell demonstrated again and again that good novelists in America simply could not commit themselves wholly to ideology in the way that a Louis Aragon could in France or a Mikhail Sholokov in Russia. Like Freeman, Farrell thought that art had to arise from the normal functioning of society, but he simply could not see society as a functioning example of the dialectic. Leftists, Farrell wrote, tended toward a "revolutionary sentimentalism," like Mike Gold, or else toward a "mechanically deterministic" Marxism, like Granville Hicks. Farrell, who was something of a self-taught intellectual, took his aesthetics from Dewey and George H. Mead as well as from Marx, and he insisted that Gold and Hicks and their followers had perverted Marx. Terms like "bourgeois" and "proletarian," he argued, were merely labels when applied to art, not standards of judgment. True art was never propaganda or name-calling. Farrell classified himself as a naturalist and a realist, instead of a proletarian or Marxist. By "naturalism," he meant "that whatever happens in this world must be ultimately explainable in terms of the events in this world." He believed that "all events are explainable in terms of natural origins rather than of extranatural or supernatural

---

27 Wilson, *Shores*, pp. 203–4, 522, 528–29, 532.

origins"; yet even with this belief, he did not write novels to prove it; he wrote novels "as part of an attempt to explore the nature of experience." Realism he saw as basically the same thing: "to present life as it is, in so far as I can see it, to present it in terms of the patterns of destiny, the patterns of language, and the patterns of thought and consciousness, which I can grasp and open, or which I imagine with the conviction that this is the way it is." [28]

The communists never really knew what to do with the books Farrell wrote, because they outwardly looked so much like what they wanted, yet proved so exasperatingly idiosyncratic when read. Farrell was obviously deeply concerned with the social and economic history of his time: the characters in *Studs Lonigan* worry about their jobs and their stocks, about the First World War and the effects of the depression. Studs's life is symbolically parallel to the course of American history, hopeful when the country is, patriotic or complacent or poor when appropriate, and dying in the depths of the depression along with American capitalism. Farrell obviously hated the Catholic church in which he was raised, and his hatred was an added attraction. His books really had no hero, centering instead on a Studs Lonigan or a Danny O'Neill as a kind of Everyman in the constricted social environment of his family, school, church, and job. Paddy Lonigan was an obvious attack on the success myth, with his dreams of prosperity changing into the disastrous reality of the depression. Yet Farrell refused to follow the party line. Studs does not reach his hospital deathbed because he is a member of the oppressed masses or because he struck a capitalistic plant and slowly starved; he gets there because he is too inarticulate to express his emotions, especially to girls, and so has to swear and fight and rebel to establish his identity. He is also lazy and full of bad habits, the result of what appears to be an unresolved identity crisis. His was thus a purely personal tragedy in a social environment—but that was not what Mike Gold wanted at all.

The society Farrell portrayed was even worse from the doctrinaire communist viewpoint. Instead of heroic workers and devoted proletarian mistresses, the family of Danny O'Neill, the central autobiographical figure in Farrell's next group of novels, is a collection of cursing, drunken, sexually repressed bigots with scarcely the vestige of a social conscience among them. They want a lover, or a priest, or business success, and their chief feeling for the neighbors is fear that they may get ahead of the O'Neills in financial or social security. The O'Neill and O'Flaherty homes, where Danny lives, have no proletarian solidarity and no ideology, and they produce in Danny only anger, rebel-

---

28 James T. Farrell, *A Note on Literary Criticism* (New York, 1936), pp. 29–31; *Reflections at Fifty* (New York, n.d.), pp. 150–51, 195.

lion, and a desire to escape. Al O'Flaherty is their chief representative —the middle class salesman who uses Lord Chesterfield instead of Marx for his guide, and thinks bad grammar and atheism the chief evils a boy can experience. As Danny grows older, he does in fact escape, but while he becomes an atheist and a University of Chicago student and holds part-time jobs like that of gas station attendant, he never acquires anything much that is usable for propaganda, and nothing that resembles a true social conscience. At times, he looks more like Horatio Alger on the way up than Joe Stevedore out to uplift his class. This may not have been communism, but it was real life as Farrell had experienced it, and Gold and his cohorts never forgave him for it. Except for occasional critical retorts, Farrell successfully ignored them and became in time probably the most popular, if not the most critically admired, of the writers labeled "proletarian."

IX

A writer who had a more serious flirtation with communism, but who was also too stubbornly individualistic to conform for long, was Richard Wright. Several of the intellectual currents of the period come together in Wright: he was poor, he was black, he was communist, he was a protester, and he believed in solidarity. For a while the Negro novel seemed likely to achieve cultural maturity in his work. Of all the marginal men that Robert Park had described as a group, surely Richard Wright was the most articulate, the writer who best expressed the frustrations entailed by a "marginal" status. His position, he wrote afterwards, was divided: "I'm black. I'm a man of the West." These two facts were bound to condition his outlook. He could understand the West because of his birth and upbringing, but because he was never really a part of Western life, and had ethnic roots in Africa, he also had an outside perspective. "Being a Negro living in a white Western Christian society, I've never been allowed to blend, in a natural and healthy manner, with the culture and civilization of the West." Therefore, as both a Westerner and a Negro, Wright felt "a psychological distance, so to speak, between me and my environment. I'm self-conscious. I admit it." This feeling that he was an outsider, a marginal man, created in Wright the need to find some group that could give him a place, a ready-made history, and a hope for the future. In the Communist party he found, for the first time, a group of white men who treated him as their equal, and who could supply him with an intellectually respectable ideology that had nothing to do with color. "It was not the economics of communism, nor the great power of trade unions, nor the excitement of underground politics that claimed me," Wright remembered after his break with the party; "my attention was caught by the similarity of the experiences of workers in other lands, by the possibility of uniting scattered but kindred peoples into a whole." This, he thought, would be a valuable way to formulate and organize Negro experience, because it transcended blackness and made for one large group. The party did not say, Wright recalled, that you had to conform to it; rather it said, "If you possess enough courage to speak out what you are, you will find that you are not alone." [29]

In his attempt to analyze his own psychology, Wright borrowed from Nietzsche the term "frog perspectives" to describe the Negro's view of the white world. He saw himself as "someone looking from below upward, a sense of someone who feels himself lower than others." The phrase was descriptive of psychological rather than physical distance, and the distance was always vertical rather than horizontal. "A certain degree of hate combined with love (ambivalence) is always involved in this looking from below upward and the object against which the subject is measuring himself undergoes constant change." The Negro "loves the object because he would like to resemble it; he hates the object because his chances of resembling it are remote, slight." Wright gave a good example of this feeling in his autobiography. He was working in an optical goods store when a Northern white man asked him if he were hungry, and offered him a dollar. The more the man talked and insisted, the more frightened and uneasy Wright felt, and he repeatedly refused the money even though he really was hungry. Southerners simply would never talk that way to a Negro, and Wright was terrified at this man's breach of custom. When the man finally left, Wright was much relieved. He explained his confused emotional reaction to the man's act of kindness and concern: "I avoided him after that. Whenever I saw him I felt in a queer way that he was my enemy, for he knew how I felt and the safety of my life in the South depended upon how well I concealed from all whites what I felt." [30] Wright, as a Negro, had to "keep his place"; he could not do so if white men refused to treat him as a marginal man.

Native Son, Wright's best-known work in this period, and still one of the best Negro novels written in America, is about this same psychological distance and the psychology of the marginal man. It is the story of how Bigger Thomas, a poor unemployed Negro, gets a job as chauffeur for a wealthy liberal family, murders their daughter, and is hunted down by white society. As a story the book is successful enough, at least until the tedious trial speeches toward the end, but its real

---

29 Richard Wright, *White Man, Listen!* (New York, 1964, c.1957), p. 47; Richard Crossman, ed., *The God That Failed* (New York, 1959, c.1950), p. 106.

30 Wright, *White Man*, p. 6; *Black Boy* (New York, 1966, c.1945), pp. 253–55.

achievement is in its description of what it is like to exist on the margin
of a culture and then suddenly find all one's preconceptions and taboos
violated. Bigger is used to being treated badly by whites; the Daltons
treat him kindly. Their daughter Mary is a white girl and should be
terrified of young black men; she turns out to be a communist sym-
pathizer who wants to sit next to Bigger, eat with him, and treat him
as an equal. The result is a conflict of stereotypes. To the Daltons,
Bigger is a poor boy whom they want to raise to middle-class self-
respect; their intentions are so noble they simply know he could not
disappoint them. To Bigger, all white folks are oppressive; therefore
Mary, her communist boyfriend Jan, and the Daltons must be trying
to trick him somehow. Their inappropriate kindness upsets him, just
as the kindness of the Northern white man in the optical goods store
upset Wright himself: marginal men fear the unexpected. For their
part, Jan and Mary are just as much the victims of stereotyping: to
them, Negroes are so musical, they have so much emotion, and so on
—they are the equals of white men or better. The result is that by
treating Bigger as a man Jan and Mary confuse him so much that he
acts like a beast—in fact, like the stereotypical Negro of the white night-
mare. He murders Mary by accident; he tries to frame Jan for the crime
as a way of taking revenge on those who do the unexpected; he murders
his mistress, Bessie; and he is hunted down like a dog by white men
who really think he is one. In the entire book, no one actually knows
what it is like to see a man as he genuinely is and to treat him in a
way that is appropriate to his psychological situation. Even at the end,
Bigger is still the Wronged Victim of Society or The Animal, depend-
ing on one's point of view. For a decade that thought in stereotypes,
and even gloried in treating men as parts of a group rather than as
individuals, he stands as a perfect example of man's fate.[31]

X

The habit of looking at men less as individuals than as
parts of a mass was not confined to fiction; all the arts became involved to some extent. The most vivid and permanent examples of
this new view were in architecture, and many individualistic Americans found themselves living and working in buildings that seemed
somehow opposed to their own deepest feelings. Many of the more
belligerent suspected foreigners and ideologists for this invasion, and
for once they were at least partially correct. American architecture

31 Richard Wright, *Native Son* (New York, 1966, c.1940), esp. pp. 58, 60, 65, 67,
70, 76; see also Robert A. Bone, *The Negro Novel in America* (New Haven, 1965,
c.1958).

during the twenties was at its lowest level since the period after the Civil War. The heritage of H. H. Richardson, Louis Sullivan, and Frank Lloyd Wright seemed scarcely visible anywhere, and Wright himself was in disgrace for his personal life. Instead of experimentation and originality, American architects had turned to the imitation of Europe, stirred and corrupted as they were by the phony classicism of the 1893 Chicago World's Fair and the influence of the now sterile École des Beaux-Arts. They ignored the precedents of the Chicago architects, who had shown how the use of glass and iron did away with the need for great masses of supporting columns and demonstrated conclusively that buildings could remain erect while unsupported by Greek columns or burdened with buttresses flown in from some distant cathedral. Businessmen were more comfortable with what became known as "mercantile classicism," a style which made their banks and office buildings look vaguely like a Greek ruins; or with "Woolworth Gothic," which gave them instead a religious aura, rather appropriate for a time when men worshiped money and business. In Europe, Le Corbusier, J. J. P. Oud, Mies van der Rohe, and Walter Gropius were leading a movement away from all this nonsense, but to America they remained unknown or scorned, and the imitative ruled supreme. As two young proponents of the newer European styles noted sardonically, "So bad in every way have been the facades of most American commercial edifices that their rear elevations, which are at best merely sound building, seem by contrast to possess architectural quality." [32]

Oddly enough, these Europeans did owe at least one debt to America—many of their key ideas came from, or at least were stimulated by, the early work of Frank Lloyd Wright. Despite his individualism and romanticism, Wright had appealed enormously to Europe and its most socially conscious architects, and the first real appreciation of his work came from Europe in 1910 and the years following. This influence was, however, all but invisible to anyone outside of architectural circles and seemed increasingly improbable in view of the wide disparity in living habits, teaching methods, types of buildings normally built, and even political opinions later displayed by Wright and the major Europeans. Instead of Wright's houses, built for individuals, modeled precisely to the natural site, decorated where appropriate, and utterly unadapted to the lives of the mass of men who lived in cities, the Europeans tended to build factories, schools, hospitals, and apartments, all of them rigorously plain and austere in appearance, and absolutely unmistakable as to function. Wright's larger buildings,

---

32 John Burchard and Albert Bush-Brown, *The Architecture of America* (Boston, 1961), parts 4–5; Henry-Russell Hitchcock and Philip Johnson, *The International Style* (New York, 1966, c.1932), p. 79.

no matter how beautiful, often seemed like his favorite house plan, one large room with adjoining smaller areas, grown to huge proportions, as if he were subconsciously trying to put business in a home and somehow domesticate it. In contrast, the new European work not only looked totally unlike a home (even, at times, when it was supposed to be a home), it also in no way resembled Greek temples or Gothic churches. The buildings were unmistakeably the products of modern industry and an aesthetic that approved of and used modern industry.

These innovations came publicly to America in 1931 when the Museum of Modern Art planned its first architectural exhibition and centered it on this new work. Some forty architects, several of them American, were represented. One key book summed up what they had in common, enabling the whole profession to learn, for the first time in some cases, what the innovators were doing. Philip Johnson and Henry-Russell Hitchcock called their book *The International Style: Architecture Since 1922,* and their title gave both a name and a creed to the new movement.

The creed of the international style made a sharp, self-conscious break with the past: buildings should be functional not monumental, and architecture should draw its inspiration from function, not from an abstract idea like classicism or the Gothic style. A building should display the "true character" of its construction, and express clearly the architect's "provision for function." Three principles followed from this new emphasis on function. The first stressed a new concept of space in architecture: "The effect of mass, of static solidity, hitherto the prime quality of architecture, has all but disappeared; in its place there is an effect of volume. The prime architectural symbol is no longer the dense brick but the open box." The surfaces should be "unbroken in effect, like a skin tightly stretched over the supporting skeleton," and the windows should be the most prominent element in the exterior. The second principle concerned regularity: Good modern architecture should express in its design a "characteristic orderliness of structure" and a "similarity of parts" which reveals the "underlying regularity," and the main task of the architect is "to adjust the irregular and unequal demands of function to regular construction and the use of standardized parts." Both principles were based not on any abstract idea of regularity but on the demands of function and modern technology. "Just as the aesthetic principle of surface of volume has been derived from the fact that architecture no longer has solid supporting walls, the second principle, that of regularity, depends on the regularity typical of the underlying skeleton of modern construction." Given these two principles, the third followed automatically: avoid applied decoration. The aesthetic effect should come from the total building constructed appropriately for its function and additional decoration was an unnecessary detraction from this effect.[33]

But America did not really adopt the international style until Hitler and his reactionary artistic policy forced the breakup of the Bauhaus, the chief school for the origination and dissemination of these new ideas. Because of Hitler, America received German musicians, physicists, novelists, and men of culture and learning in virtually every field. In architecture, the influence of these German ex-patriates was decisive. The key figure was the founder of the Bauhaus, Walter Gropius, a deep believer in architecture as a contributor to social progress, a lover of the machine and modern technology, a devotee of standardization and mass production, and a firm believer that teams, and not single architects, were the originators of true modern buildings. In all these views he went counter to American tradition, and by introducing them to American soil he brought a sense of social solidarity into American architecture. After spending the years 1934–37 in England, he came permanently to America and an extremely influential post at Harvard, where he remained until 1952. He then formed the famous company, The Architects Collaborative (TAC), as a living and functioning example of his principles, a company of architects who worked as a group to produce industrial and technological architecture.[34]

Gropius's principles and practice indicate how far social ideas had permeated architecture. He was concerned with remaking the total environment of man as well as with architecture, as his phrase "total architecture" indicates. He deeply wished to see each man able to govern himself democratically, and part of this governance was the freedom to allow each man's creative spirit to grow. At first glance his attitude has much in common with the creative individualism of the 1920s, but Gropius was never a supporter of the individualism of Cummings, Rugg, or even Frank Lloyd Wright. Instead, he believed that men would realize themselves best if they worked as teams and lived in large groups, each with a minimum competence and no one with too much. In such an environment the architect would concern himself with present economic conditions, the needs of the majority of the population, of industry, and of the modern man's habitat, the city that Wright hated so violently. In Gropius's vision of society, the machine, the bane of many American artists and intellectuals at least since the time of Hawthorne and Thoreau, became the handmaiden

---

33 Hitchcock and Johnson, *International Style*, pp. 41–45, 56–58, 69 ff.

34 Burchard and Bush-Brown, *The Architecture of America*, part 5, section 12; Sigfried Giedion, *Space, Time and Architecture*, 5th ed., rev. (Cambridge, 1967), pp. 477 ff.

of art, "an instrument which is to relieve man of the most oppressive physical labor and serve to strengthen his hand so as to enable him to give form to his creative impulse." Art, appropriately symbolized by The Architects Collaborative, became a social act to improve society: the commission at hand would grow "gradually above the individual, who finally hardly remembers who initiated this or that part of the idea, as all their thoughts resulted from mutual stimulation." Just as democracy "obviously hinges on our ability to co-operate, I want the architect, as a co-ordinator by vocation, to lead the way toward developing the new technique of collaboration in teams." He then put into italics the goal shared by all social artists: *"Synchronizing all individual efforts the team can raise its integrated work to higher potentials than is represented by the sum of the work of just so many individuals."* [35]

XI

Similar ideas permeated the theater. Nothing illustrates the pervasiveness of the social ideal quite so well as the marked parallels between artistic fields so disparate as architecture and drama—even if, admittedly, the results on the stage were considerably inferior to the results on the landscape. The American theater was the most politically committed field in American culture. At times its commitment took the form of a well-tempered unionism, about as harmful to most American ideals as Sam Gompers had been. The well-known stanza from the International Ladies' Garment Workers' satiric review, *Pins and Needles* is typical:

> Sing us a song with social significance
> Or you can sing until you're blue
> Let meaning shine from every line
> Or we won't love you.

At other times, it was explicitly Marxist. "The Theater Union Manifesto" promised to "produce plays that deal boldly with the deep social conflicts, the economic, emotional, and cultural problems that confront the majority of the people," and its authors proclaimed their work "a new kind of professional theatre, based on the interests and

---

35 Walter Gropius, *Scope of Total Architecture* (New York, 1962), pp. 22, 80. See also Sigfried Giedion, *Walter Gropius: Work and Teamwork* (New York, 1954); Walter Gropius, *The New Architecture and the Bauhaus* (Cambridge, 1965); Herbert Bayer, et al., *The Bauhaus, 1919–1928* (Boston, 1952, c.1938); and the article by William Jordy in Donald Fleming and Bernard Bailyn, eds., *The Intellectual Migration: Europe and America 1930–1960* (Cambridge, 1969).

hopes of the great mass of working people." Most often, the new drama remained rather self-consciously political, dragging in earnest statements of concern even when the plays did not really warrant them. The results of their efforts were mixed, and the much-publicized Federal Theater of Hallie Flanagan was a typical example. Even as the new plays put many unemployed actors to work, and gave new outlets for creative imaginations, they also excited fear and resentment in the people and their congressmen. Even a politician without a vestige of culture could sense that the social ideals of these new theater groups threatened traditional American ideals even when they were not explicitly communist or pro-Russian.[36]

Perhaps the most important of these new groups was the aptly named Group Theatre, whose vitality spanned the 1930s and brought to public attention important works by William Saroyan, Tennessee Williams, Maxwell Anderson, and others. It was not an explicitly political organization, and in no sense another Theatre Union or a purveyor of agitation-propaganda (agit-prop). It was a group of theater people who shared a bias in favor of reform rather than revolution, but whose interests were almost entirely cultural. As Harold Clurman, their guiding spirit and principal historian has pointed out, the presence of actors on a stage "was the very flower of large social contact, even when the occasion for this contact, in terms of literature, was a silly anecdote." At every performance "something happened between contemporaries that was a deep pleasure for those who loved the human vibration of people in their common play and enthusiasm." Clurman, like Gropius, was a moralist of the social group: "We must help one another find our common ground; we must build our house on it, arrange it as a dwelling place for the whole family of decent humanity," he insisted. "For life, though it be individual to the end, cannot be lived except in terms of people together, sure and strong in their togetherness." His Group Theatre was, in a sense, the theatrical counterpart of The Architects Collaborative. It allowed no member to be a star or to have billing precedence over any other actor; as a matter of principle the actors were listed in alphabetical order in all advertisements. Again and again, Clurman insisted that the Group was more than merely a collection of individuals; by joining together, they had created something new and worthwhile where individual idiosyncrasy had no place. "What I wanted for the Group, what all these people wanted, was the chance to tie sporadic individual work into units of

---

36 Gerald Rabkin, *Drama and Commitment Politics in the American Theatre of the Thirties* (Bloomington, 1964), pp. 33, 45. See also Joseph Wood Krutch, *The American Drama Since 1918* (New York, 1957); and Morgan Y. Himelstein, *Drama Was a Weapon* (New Brunswick, 1963).

collective endeavor," he said. "This would not only strengthen them individually but would serve to make their values objectively effective, forceful, permanent." [37]

The most successful, and even notorious, playwright in the Group was Clifford Odets. Like other self-conscious writers of the period, he was a typical bourgeois proletarian. The son of a Jewish peddler who rose to the middle class, Odets had had a rather desultory acting career during the 1920s. Success for him was a role like Abie in *Abie's Irish Rose* or similar parts in stock company productions. By 1930, he was a charter member of the Group, but as an actor more than as a playwright. The depression moved him to join the Communist party in 1934, but he left after only eight months, refusing to let the party dictate his art to him. He became instead a socialist-leaning liberal. But his politics are not really particularly interesting. His lack of much political commitment seems more significant than what little commitment there was. Odets was a middle-class Jewish boy thoroughly conscious of, even corrupted by, American dreams of success, and he was no more capable of being an earnest party member than his Irish Catholic counterpart, James T. Farrell. He was also devoted to the Group, and he shared its need for a feeling of solidarity. "He wanted comradeship," Harold Clurman wrote. "He wanted to belong to the largest possible group of humble, struggling men prepared to make a great common effort to build a better world. Without this, life for him would be lonely and hopeless." [38]

Like the novels of Farrell, the plays of Odets dealt with the lower middle class, with its pioneer generation full of dreams for their children, and the children full of frustration because the depression has prevented them from realizing any of these dreams. Their goals presented in these plays constitute the American ideal—success in business, happiness in love—and only rarely strike the note of class warfare, even obliquely. Their problems are personal and familial, not simply reflections of a larger class struggle, and perhaps that is why Odets appealed to many theatergoers who were hardly of the working class. His greatest success and his most obviously proletarian effort was a play that he wrote for the Group in three days. In *Waiting for Lefty* a group of cab drivers is trying to decide on whether to strike, and the play gives a series of brief flashbacks to indicate why each man comes to vote for the strike. A few of the men, it turns out, are really career drivers, but many of them are middle-class and even professional men who have lost their jobs. One is a Jewish surgeon, fired from a

---

37 Harold Clurman, *The Fervent Years* (New York, 1957, c.1945), pp. 11, 28, 89.
38 R. Baird Shuman, *Clifford Odets* (New York, 1962); Clurman, *Fervent Years*, p. 133.

hospital on account of his race; another is a chemist who refuses to work on poison gas even for a big raise in pay. For only one character is poverty the primary motivation; for the others, the key to motivation lies in the lost dreams of success, and in love. The greatest tragedy that can befall an Odets character is that his wife may walk out on him, or that he may not be able to marry his girl—all because of a lack of money. Perhaps because of these themes, *Lefty* was an instant success, and the nature of the success was a perfect embodiment of the new social ethic of the 1930s. On the opening night of the play, Clurman wrote, scarcely minutes had gone by "when a shock of delighted recognition struck the audience like a tidal wave. Deep laughter, hot assent, a kind of joyous fervor seemed to sweep the audience toward the stage." The actors did not act before the audience, but with it, "carried along as if by an exultancy of communication such as I had never witnessed in the theatre before. Audience and actors had become one. . . ." For a brief moment, middle-class theatergoers could feel themselves part of the great world, friend to every man, and estranged only from the unnamed profiteers. The social goal had received its ultimate embodiment in art, for all were on the stage and no one was left alone. The creative individual of the 1920s had been replaced by the reforming group of the 1930s.[39]

XII

For all the enthusiasm they were capable of generating, however, the creative artists who shared the communitarian ideals of the 1930s were only on the periphery of effective political action. At the time, such action was more important and more central than art, and ideas that told men how to act were obviously more relevant. In a time of depression, economics was of course at the core of these ideas. One of the paradoxical aspects of this period is that so important a field as economics should present such a picture of chaos. While the professional economists were disagreeing among themselves, President Roosevelt was initiating a modern economic policy without understanding the reasons for its success or discarding the older economic ideas responsible for the failures of his predecessors.

The vogue of individualism and self-indulgence in the 1920s, it now seems clear, was a great help in reinforcing the older economic ideas of Herbert Spencer and William Graham Sumner. In the older view, ultimately derived from Adam Smith, each economic atom, each man, acting out of his own self-interest for his own gain, contributed

---

39 *Six Plays of Clifford Odets* (New York, 1939); Clurman, *Fervent Years,* p. 138.

in some mysterious way to some sort of hidden world equilibrium, while an "invisible hand" made sure that everything worked out all right in the long run. Indirectly, each man's greed worked for the economic benefit of society as a whole. Politically, this meant that government should leave businessmen to do as they wished; in practice, businessmen wanted tariff protection and friendly judges who would prevent laborers from doing as *they* wished. The Freudians and the artists of the 1920s frequently had great scorn for this sort of business activity, but in most instances, they responded not with demands for reform but with demands to be left alone. Business society soiled the hand that touched it, and the creative children wanted none of it. They were content to leave businessmen alone, and did little to keep men like Coolidge out of office.

But during the 1920s, the economic imbalances of the country were slowly building up pressures that a weakened society could not long withstand. The intellectuals and artists frequently lived on money sent from bourgeois parents at home, or on inheritances from bourgeois parents who had died. It never occurred to most of them that while their parents had such money, a great many other parents did not, and the reasonably stable prosperity of the years after the brief postwar depression kept conditions attractive enough so that the inherent inequalities in the country did not become severe enough to show. But farmers faced declines in real income and were increasingly pressuring Congress for relief. More significant for the future, profits from increases in worker productivity were not passed on to the laboring classes either by raises in wages or decreases in prices. Instead, due to the tax climate created by Treasury Secretary Andrew Mellon and the credit practices of the Federal Reserve Board, banks, and stock exchanges, the new money generated by the prosperous years went more and more into a complex pyramid of debt; too many people went into speculation to make money with money, rather than with investments in factories or similar hard industries. Because a surplus of money was chasing the relatively stable supply of land and securities, prices naturally began to rise. As prices rose, people began to make large profits with minimal effort, thereby attracting more people with more lazy money. The two chief areas of speculation were Florida land, which went through the first boom and bust; and the stock markets, which detonated with a shock big enough to set off the depression. The privilege of buying land or stock with a small down payment meant that people bought far more than they intended to keep or use. If they sold out, they made a profit far in excess of what they would have made if they had paid cash for the entire amount—if they sold out in time, that is. Most of the speculators did not sell in time, and when prices broke they found themselves without land or securities enough to pay their debts.[40]

Every crisis produces a hundred saviors, and the depression was no exception. Many of the ideas were foolish—the Technocracy of Howard Scott, Upton Sinclair's or Dr. Francis Townsend's easy ways to end poverty in California, Social Credit, and so on—but with few exceptions most people had trouble separating the fools from the innovators. The economically orthodox, led by Herbert Hoover and most of the bankers in the country, moaned predictably at every opportunity about the need for fiscal restraint, for a balanced budget, for moral vigor, for faith, hope, and sometimes a little charity, but the worsening crisis indicated clearly that they did not know what to do, and many of them admitted as much. They had taken credit for prosperity, and they received blame for the depression. But other men, some of them economic critics of long standing, had ideas that seemed worth a try. These critics in effect denied that men working only for their own self-interest produced prosperity for society as a whole. The practical results of this theory had become all too evident. In its place they insisted that men had to work together for the common good in both public and private life, and that government planning and action had to intervene when individual initiative and private action had failed.

The idea was not entirely new. For years, Simon Patten, to take just one example, had emphasized cooperation, the use of government planning, the need for spending rather than thrift, and the need for economic plenty as a social rather than an individual goal. But Patten was a figure out of the Progressive Era, and he could only triumph posthumously, as it were, in the New Deal, through his students and the students of those who agreed with him. Of these, the most brilliant was probably Rexford Guy Tugwell, who studied under Patten at the Wharton School of the University of Pennsylvania. Tugwell came from rural New York, and he retained an interest in agriculture throughout his career. In addition to teaching at the University of Washington and at Columbia, he also served a term as special investigator for a state milk commission. His colleagues at Columbia, men like Wesley Mitchell and John Dewey, encouraged him in this activist tendency, and Tugwell was never afraid to leave the academy and dive into "real life" with his theories. He had been a Republican, but he switched to Al Smith in 1928 for an extremely significant reason: he wanted to give his allegiance to the men and parties that seemed most likely to restrict the states' rights and expand the power of the nation as a whole. He made a trip to Russia to see how the opposition was doing, but he was in no sense a communist and apparently did not even favor

---

40 John K. Galbraith, *The Great Crash: 1929* (Boston, 1961, c.1954), passim.

government ownership of the means of production. Instead, he seemed to prefer government spending and activity to reconstruct industries that were in trouble.

Unlike many reformers, Tugwell did not have any overwhelming faith that human nature could be improved. He did not think people had changed much over the course of history, but he did insist that men had been able to mold their environment, and that this progress had been in the direction of increasingly complex social units. The city, to take an obvious example, was a new unit formed from inventions in transportation, sewers, schools, hospitals, communications, etc. His concept of the problem owed much to the work of his former teacher, William F. Ogburn. In comparison with the physical sciences, he thought, the social sciences suffered from a form of cultural lag, which Tugwell called an "institutional lag." Man's tendency was always to form theories based on his own past and his personal problems, but what he needed was to base these theories on the present needs of his social environment. The field of economics was a perfect example of Ogburn's and Tugwell's theories. Their opponents, the men old enough to be running the country in 1930, had been brought up in the world of Spencer and Sumner, of Say's Law and inevitable progress, when thrift and free trade were somewhat more important than cleanliness in achieving godliness, and their minds suffered from cultural or intellectual lag. The job of the new generation of economists was to diagnose current problems and then devise cures that ignored the mythology—as well as the demonology—of the past. In doing his part of the job Tugwell pointed out, for example, that excess profits did not really reward the worker who earned them: they went into speculation and expansion rather than into active purchasing power and thus drained funds that were needed for the public welfare. As the depression demonstrated with unmistakable clarity, the wealth of the rich depended ultimately on the survival and viability of the poor, for without the purchases of the man on the street, the product of the man in the mansion could not return him a profit. For Tugwell, Adam Smith's invisible hand, which supposedly regulated the old economic regime, was a hoary myth that precluded constructive thinking about current problems. Like other "institutionalist" economists, Tugwell wanted to change all this by remaking the institutions of society in such a way as to channel men as much as possible toward socially valuable behavior. He wanted to make it difficult to be greedy, to exploit the poor, to hoard and speculate with profit, and easy to be a socially useful citizen, paying decent wages and making useful goods.

Tugwell's favorite device was government regulation of business in order to make it function in a socially useful way. He suspected that businessmen's emphasis on profit was part of the reason for the depression, and he wanted to teach them to change the emphasis to production. More and more, business in modern times was coming to exercise the function of government, he thought, and he hoped laws could be framed that would encourage business to plan its work and take care of its men in the same long-range fashion that government took care of its citizens. One way to do this, he suggested, was to halt the custom of plowing all profits into reserves, plant expansion, and dividends. In the long run this policy actually harmed the businessman. Instead, he should pay at least part of this money out in the form of higher wages and thus expand worker purchasing power. Otherwise, business would face again the problems of 1930—overexpanded production and lack of purchasing power to buy the resulting goods. By 1932, Tugwell was doing more than just theorizing. Dating the exact beginning of Tugwell's influence is difficult, but about this time Franklin D. Roosevelt began to sound occasionally like Tugwell in some of his speeches, and he soon included Tugwell in the inner circle of his advisers, the so-called "brain(s) trust." In time, the ideas of Tugwell, and others like him—Marriner Eccles, Adolph Berle, Gardiner Means —did in fact change the economic face of the country. The new emphasis on the needs of the present, on experimentation, on the sense of men working together for community solidarity and mutual benefit, helped lead to many of the New Deal reforms in agriculture, business, finance, and conservation.[41]

As they slowly worked their ideas into New Deal policy, these men inadvertently prepared the way for the economic doctrine that was to become one of the main contributions of New Deal practice to intellectual life. The conditions of the time required emergency spending to help farmers, workers, and businessmen, and the money required could not be raised by taxes because the economy was not functioning well enough to create taxable income in any large amount. Roosevelt, an orthodox budget-balancer at heart, spent only with the unhappy feeling that he was temporarily violating good theory for the sake of a great emergency. But, contrary to theory, it soon became clear that somehow spending did increase prosperity, giving workers money to buy and businessmen money to invest again. Apparently Tugwell and his friends had some insight into what was happening. As a result, New Deal practice had opened the door to the theories of John Maynard Keynes.

---

41 Bernard Sternsher, *Rexford Tugwell and the New Deal* (New Brunswick, 1964); Arthur M. Schlesinger, Jr. *The Age of Roosevelt,* including *The Crisis of the Old Order* (Boston, 1957), *The Coming of the New Deal* (Boston, 1958), and *The Politics of Upheaval* (Boston, 1960).

All his life, Keynes had been telling governments how to run their business. After the First World War, he wrote a book so critical of the victorious Allied leaders that it turned them all against him and prevented him from ever again enjoying the high government position he held during the war. Nevertheless, his prediction of what the Versailles Treaty would do to Europe proved so accurate that the book achieved permanent status both as an economic guide, and as a warning to future makers of treaties. Roosevelt never quite forgave the treatment that Keynes gave to Woodrow Wilson, but his administration broke ground for the Keynesian economic ideas that swept the academic world in the 1940s and 1950s and the political world in the 1960s.

Briefly, Keynes destroyed the old idea that supply created its own demand (Say's Law). If the depression proved little else, it proved unquestionably that a society could in fact produce mountains of goods that no one had the money to buy. He had little faith in laissez-faire, unregulated capitalism, or its excessively dreary opposite, socialism. He favored a managed capitalism that would enable government to step in when supply and demand were too far out of balance, when too much money was in the hands of a small, under-consuming group, and not enough in the hands of the majority. Concentrating on employment, rather than the excessively theoretical concerns of his predecessors, he saw that the government could restore full employment in a time of depression by spending at a deficit to prime the pump of the economy and increase the flow of funds in economic life by increasing the money in circulation. In addition, government spending would build the schools, roads, and hospitals that the country desperately needed. The money paid to the workers, to suppliers of materials, and others involved, would get into circulation immediately by what Keynes called the "multiplier"—money given to a worker would immediately be spent by him for groceries, or a car, or clothes; the grocer, carmaker, or clothier would immediately spend most of this money in buying farm goods, steel, or raw cotton, and so on the cycle would go, in ever-widening circles, and economic health would return. Deficit spending would inflate the economy slightly, and the government would have more control than in the past, but Keynes was convinced that this was a small price to pay for prosperity. Careful circumscription of the governmental sphere, and a timely rise in taxes, could redress the balance when the time came. Increasingly, such ideas came to dominate the thought of many of the New Deal economists; at times they were attractive even to Roosevelt himself. But Keynes, it seems likely in retrospect, did not really influence American politics directly until the Kennedy administration in the 1960s. As far as the

New Deal was concerned, he was an underground influence that provided influential support for the inevitable and respectability for ideas
that seemed distressingly unorthodox when voiced by lesser men.[42]

XIII

The support Roosevelt and the New Deal received from
economic liberals and radicals, however, did not mean that the American Left was united behind the president. In fact, many liberals and
radicals were furious and bitter about certain New Deal policies. The
origins of one school of liberal dissent were clearly in the frustrations
felt by progressives during the First World War and the subsequent
disclosures by historians and journalists of the shoddy motives that
had apparently been at the base of American intervention. Some were
pacifists who felt vindicated by the failure of the Versailles Treaty.
Others had supported the war and apparently felt guilty at the results
of their action. Still others examined the quickly opened diplomatic
documents of Russia and the Central Powers and discovered evidence
that Germany, the chief object of hatred during the war, was probably
less guilty, all things considered, than her ally Austria or, for that
matter, America's allies Russia and France. The moral and religious
fervor with which the war had been conducted contrasted painfully
with the slowly appearing story of sordid imperialistic intrigue, diplomatic conniving, deceitful secret treaties, peace initiatives squashed by
America's allies, undemocratic methods used by leaders even as they
mouthed Wilson's pieties—the influential issues were many. But regardless of the particular issue that influenced any one man, a recog-
nizable school and attitude grew up that swept through much of intellectual America. "Revisionism" was the name normally given to
the reassessment of the causes of the war and of American entrance
into it; "isolationism" was the term, often used synonymously with
the term "continentalism," for the resulting attitude toward American
foreign policy. Combined with the 1920s' love of beating its ancestors
over the head and its general contempt and irreverence for the past,
these new ideas gave intellectual support for the general scorn of politics in the period. In the 1930s, when social-reform goals were again of
great importance, men had only to look over their shoulders at the
fate of the last age of reform to become belligerent critics of any move

---

42 Schlesinger, *The Politics of Upheaval,* esp. pp. 400–408; Robert Lekachman,
The Age of Keynes (New York, 1966); Seymour Harris, "The New Economics," in
A. M. Schlesinger, Jr., and Morton White, eds., *Paths of American Thought* (Boston,
1963); R. F. Harrod, *The Life of John Maynard Keynes* (New York, 1969, c.1951),
445–67.

likely to cause events to repeat themselves. Congress conducted spectacular investigations into the banking and munitions industries and cast a suspicious eye on a president known for his passion for naval affairs.

Many men participated actively in the revisionist and isolationist movements. They did so for a variety of reasons, often of wildly conflicting origin, but a few generalities can stand so long as they are not pushed too far. A great many Americans felt that America entered the First World War naïvely, even incompetently, because Wilson and his advisers let events or their own pro-British sentiments lead them to war; that the Versailles Treaty had been overly vindictive against Germany, and economically disastrous in its terms for reparations; and that, all things considered, America was better off minding its own hemisphere and leaving Europeans to fight their battles out among themselves. A large number saw war as economically and politically disastrous, destructive of what they felt was valuable in America and in democracy generally. They felt that legislation was needed to keep events from entangling America in European quarrels.

No one person was really typical among the revisionists, and all the important members of the group had careers in other fields. C. Hartley Grattan, for example, already had a solid career as journalist, historian, and literary critic when he became a revisionist, and he never gave up these other interests. He had been influenced by books like *Three Soldiers* and *The Enormous Room* at least as much as by the reports of the guilt of the Allied governments. His book, *Why We Fought* (1929), did not really display his critical interests or his own personal disillusionment. Instead, like several of the other influential revisionist works, it was carefully unsensational, full of extended documentation, and without any obvious reformist intention. In a sense, that was the point: America entered the war not for any stirring, moral reasons, but because of a long chain of complex business, banking, and diplomatic decisions that carefully wove strand after strand of alliance between America and England and that every day left fewer ways of avoiding a declaration of war. He painted a picture in which no country was to blame, where the worst that could be said of Germany was that her methods were "crude and spectacular." The claim that the invasion of Belgium was a violation of a sacred commitment was only a phony pretext for British intervention. Sir Edward Grey, far from being the devoted liberal man of peace of American propaganda, was really an extremely insular man, unable to understand foreign affairs and frequently thwarting peace initiatives. American diplomats were often even worse, with Colonel House, Secretary of State Lansing, and Ambassador to London Walter Hines Page the most openly pro-British. Grattan also pointed out in careful detail how the British had used propaganda and censorship to shape American opinion to suit their purposes. But primarily he emphasized the role of economics, the countless ties between business and banks that made America and Britain virtual Siamese twins, each unable to survive without the other. Every reputable historian who dealt with the war, Grattan insisted,

> no matter how great his preoccupation with the diplomacy of its precipitation, regards the diplomacy, the propaganda, the alleged aims and objects for fighting, as mere secondary structures reared on the foundation of money and trade. The flag follows trade, the politicians follow the flag, the propagandists follow the politicians, and the people follow the propagandists.[43]

In his subsequent books on foreign policy, Grattan indicated more clearly his reform bias. He viewed participation in the war as the villain that would destroy a truly democratic community. He paid considerable attention to the condition of poor people under capitalism, and thought that the war he saw coming would generate a number of revolutions, in which these poor would choose some sort of communism. For him, pacifism was no solution: pacifists were only trying to expand a personal morality into a national morality, and they totally ignored the immoral or amoral business entanglements that lay behind war. Businessmen, he insisted, could act in what appeared to be a completely moral, Christian, and peaceful way, and yet still have the sum of their various innocent activities add up to war. Roosevelt, he said, was trying to restore capitalism, not replace it, and thus the New Deal, like every other government under capitalism, "must, in the final analysis, evolve and execute policies which are in harmony with the fundamental drives of capitalism." Once again, he repeated his position on the First World War, as a prelude to his position on the coming Second World War: "Economic entanglements with the Allied powers in the First World War made the participation of the United States in it on the side of the Allies possible, logical, and in the end, necessary to the health of private capitalism; the wartime policies of the United States Government made participation inevitable."

In the face of this, Grattan, as a continentalist, preferred to work for domestic reform and a rise in basic living standards; he was "isolationist" (a word Grattan disliked) only in that he wished to stay out of Europe's quarrels and not force upon her the surplus of unconsumed American goods. "If Americans want a better world they must build

---

43 Warren I. Cohen, *The American Revisionists* (Chicago, 1967); C. Hartley Grattan, *Why We Fought* (New York, 1929), pp. 9, 127.

it in America. It is no contribution to the building to fight abroad. Americans will suffer far less from a policy of abstention with regard to Europe's muddle than by plunging into war with starry-eyed phony idealism, an idealism corrupted at the heart by its appeal to force." If, on the other hand, the country did go to war, the future was clearly marked: "A major war for the United States will mean fascism in this country. That is inescapable." [44]

XIV

The appeal of isolationist-revisionist ideas reached even men who now would seem to be unlikely prospects for conversion. One improbable example of this appeal was the most notable figure in American religion in this period, Reinhold Niebuhr. The son of a pastor in the Evangelical Synod, Niebuhr had attended a small, unknown college, and an equally obscure divinity school, before gaining the chance to study at the Yale Divinity School. His small-town Missouri origins, and his small sect, with its strict rule that each student serve immediately in a pastorate after proper education, seemed to condemn Niebuhr to the life of a preacher and organizer of church socials. Even his two years at Yale were considered extraordinary at the time, and Niebuhr did not protest when his church sent him to the Bethel Evangelical Church in Detroit, where eighteen families needed a pastor. He remained there throughout the First World War and the twenties, formulating his social, economic, and theoretical ideas in the process of instructing others. He had supported the war without particular enthusiasm, and the Versailles Treaty and the literature of revisionism had a marked effect on him. He was soon a reasonably strong advocate of peace, opposed to force in international affairs, and skeptical about the goodness or badness of any one power in the war or subsequent diplomacy. But while this same feeling drove many other disillusioned Americans to pious moralizing, to advocate treatymaking, and to the pursuit of their own private concerns, it set Niebuhr to thinking about power, about the qualities that separated man as an individual from man as a part of a crowd, and about the relation of all these basically social concerns to Christian doctrine.

Detroit at the time when Niebuhr took up his duties was the perfect social laboratory for testing ideas and developing new ones. Niebuhr had in his congregation many employees of Henry Ford, and many Americans assumed that Henry Ford was an enlightened capitalist who paid his workers more than he needed to, both because he was gen-

---

44 C. Hartley Grattan, *Preface to Chaos* (New York, 1936), pp. 6, 66; *The Deadly Parallel* (New York, 1939), pp. 51–52, 154.

erous and because he wanted his men comfortable enough to buy his cheap Ford cars. In fact, Niebuhr found, Ford often did not use men for more than a few days out of a week, or for more than a few months out of a year; he fired old men exhausted by assembly line work, and hired fresh young men to take their places; and as a result, Ford workers generally were as underpaid, as insecure, and as miserable as workers anywhere, sometimes even more so, while Ford himself kept enormous sums for his own profit.

In philosophy, Niebuhr heard again and again from fellow reform-minded individuals about the enlightened ideas of John Dewey. If men attacked social problems without preconceptions, if they worked rationally and scientifically, they could solve these problems amicably and in the process slowly remake the human personality. An enlightened society, in short, would change human nature through legal and educational reforms and apparently make capitalism and religion obsolete. In religion, Niebuhr was told that he should preach a personal salvation. If benevolent Christians worked at converting others to their own exalted state, then businessmen would cease to exploit the masses, nations would cease to wage war, and all the unrest of the times would dissipate. Social reform on a mass level was unnecessary; rather than stir up the wealthy businessman whose contributions might pay for the minister's salary, the minister should instead work to enlighten the man's heart and open his purse for charity. Working to encourage unions or raise wage rates or institute pensions was un-Amercian; the poor were always with you, and charity was a means to the kingdom of heaven.[45]

Niebuhr frequently displayed a tendency to oversimplify the positions of his opponents, setting up straw men so that the tough-minded master of power and politics could then demolish them. This stated, there is still considerable truth in the systematization Niebuhr made in 1936 of the basic ideas held by those liberals who had been affected by Dewey and those religious thinkers whose thought resembled his. Certainly many men in the street, if they verbalized their ideas at all, did subscribe to much of this "liberal" faith:

1. That injustice is caused by ignorance and will yield to education and greater intelligence.
2. That civilization is becoming gradually more moral and that it is a sin to challenge either the inevitability or the efficacy of gradualness.

45 Reinhold Niebuhr, *Does Civilization Need Religion?* (New York, 1927); *Leaves from the Notebook of a Tamed Cynic* (Cleveland, 1957, c.1929); Paul A. Carter, *The Decline and Revival of the Social Gospel* (Ithaca, 1954); Donald B. Meyer, *The Protestant Search for Political Realism, 1919–1941* (Berkeley and Los Angeles, 1960).

3. That the character of individuals rather than social systems and arrangements is the guarantee of justice in society.
4. That appeals to love, justice, good will, and brotherhood are bound to be efficacious in the end. If they have not been so to date we must have more appeals to love, justice, good will, and brotherhood.
5. That goodness makes for happiness and that the increasing knowledge of this fact will overcome human selfishness and greed.
6. That wars are stupid and can therefore only be caused by people who are more stupid than those who recognize the stupidity of war.[46]

As Niebuhr heard these ideas repeated in various forms day after day, he began to test them against the facts: the greed of Henry Ford and the misery of his workers; the First World War and the revisionist case against it; the overwhelming ascendancy of businessmen and material values in America; the union-busting of management; and the obvious decline of any real religious faith. He disliked what he saw. By the time the country reached the depths of the depression, he was ready for a major blast at the enemy.

"The thesis to be elaborated in these pages," Niebuhr began in *Moral Man and Immoral Society* (1932), "is that a sharp distinction must be drawn between the moral and social behavior of individuals and of social groups, national, racial, and economic; and that this distinction justifies and necessitates political policies which a purely individualistic ethic must always find embarrassing." The subsequent argument went something like this: the natural tendency of people of good will is to work out for themselves some kind of commonsense ethics. They believe in loving their neighbor, in doing unto others as they would have others do unto them, in taking care of the unfortunate, and so on. This tendency, Niebuhr argued, was in many ways admirable, and the people who practiced it were frequently worthy of the emulation of anyone. But it had two serious flaws: it neglected the element of original sin in man, which made it necessary at times to resort to force and violence in order to further the social good; and it neglected the fact that men of good intentions, when they act as a group, often seem to do more damage, and have meaner and more cynical motives, than any one individual would have if he acted alone. In other words, man was not only prone to original sin, he became

---

46 Quoted in D. B. Robertson, ed., *Love and Justice: Selections from the Shorter Writings of Reinhold Niebuhr* (Cleveland, 1967, c.1957), p. 12, from Niebuhr, "The Blindness of Liberalism," *Radical Religion*, Autumn 1936.

more prone with every friend he found to act with him: "In every human group there is less reason to guide and to check impulse, less capacity for self-transcendence, less ability to comprehend the needs of others and therefore more unrestrained egoism than the individuals, who compose the group, reveal in their personal relationships." The social gospel had come a long way from the progressive years, when men working as a group for approved social goals could expect utopia to come with Christian socialism.[47]

With this animus, Niebuhr then went after the enemy. He attacked common notions of patriotism by insisting that loyalty to the nation was a force that tended to soak up the altruistic feelings of a people, and convince them that this was a sacred emotion, a source of all good. Patriotism was never subjected to the kind of criticism that other emotions and ideas received, and therefore most people cheerfully allowed their governments to act as they wished, even though the presidents and premiers might be greedy, tyrannical, or imperialistic. "Thus the unselfishness of individuals makes for the selfishness of nations." In other words, men saw in their government a symbol of their own good will toward other men and were blind to the fact that in international relations their good will produced war, imperialism, and economic domination.

Next, Niebuhr turned to that doctrine most irritating to Americans, Marxism, to produce one of the more unusual hybrids of American intellectual history. Despite his conservative theology, his insistence on original sin and man's impotence, Niebuhr acted politically at times as if he thought men could remake the world. He voted for the Socialist party candidate, Norman Thomas, for president several times, and regularly defended the good ideas he found in Marx and in pre-Stalinist Russia. For what Niebuhr saw in Marx was another religious vision, in its way as valid as the Christian one. In Marxism, "political hopes achieve religious proportions by overleaping the bounds of rationally verifiable possibilities, just as, in the soul of the true Christian, moral hopes achieve religious verification." But he could be just as critical of the Marxists as he could be of the utopians of any other faith, and he insisted that notions like the withering away of the state after the dictatorship of the proletariat were just as sentimental as anything in John Dewey. Human nature, by which he generally meant original sin, would defeat any such hopes.

---

47 Reinhold Niebuhr, *Moral Man and Immoral Society* (New York, 1932), pp. xi–xii; see also the essays by Arthur Schlesinger, Jr., and John C. Bennett in C. W. Kegley and R. W. Bretall, eds., *Reinhold Niebuhr: His Religious, Social and Political Thought* (New York, 1956).

Finally, Niebuhr turned to the topic of violence, a theme associated with his name from that time on and one that contrasted sharply with his postwar pacifism. On the subject of violence he was frankly a philosopher of power. The middle classes and the rationalistic moralizers, he insisted, "are wrong in their assumption that violence is intrinsically immoral. Nothing is intrinsically immoral except ill will and nothing intrinsically good except goodwill."

But although he could defend violence, his primary concern at this time was equality. His main theme was that, for the sake of human progress toward equality, men must attack false virtues like sentimentalism and rationalism. In other words, while he shared the goals and communitarian ideals of men like Dewey, he felt compelled to defend the use of power and even war as a means to achieve these ends. "If a season of violence can establish a just social system and can create the possibilities of its preservation, there is no purely ethical ground upon which violence and revolution can be ruled out. . . . The real question is: what are the political possibilities of establishing justice through violence?" [48]

The question reveals Niebuhr's doubts about the possibility of creating a just society and the deepening of the depression only made him more pessimistic. Capitalism, he proclaimed, was a dying system and the New Deal nothing but an inadequate remedy. The course of events in Russia and Germany made him gloomier still and more certain that a revolution was coming. Increasingly, he insisted on the value of Christ and Marx as sources of inspiration for social ideals. At the same time he warned that both men had been talking about utopias that could never be experienced by human beings; their words expressed men's yearnings and guided men's ideas, but they should never be regarded as norms for human society. Guided by this dualism, Niebuhr became the most eminent Christian champion of social revolution, military opposition to nazism and fascism, and pragmatism in political action. For the pacifism he had once shared, he had only scorn. This position, adopted by so many Christians who shared Niebuhr's social-reform goals, seemed to him to amount to the simple statement that war was worse than totalitarianism, that life under Hitler was preferable to death opposing him. He would rather die fighting. As if to symbolize the split in Christian ranks which he created, almost single-handedly, Christian magazine readers found themselves with two choices. The old *Christian Century* became the voice of the isolationist and pacifist liberals. The new *Christianity and Crisis* was the organ of Niebuhr and his friends, gloomy, indignant, and militant,

---

48 Niebuhr, *Moral Man,* pp. 91, 155–56, 170, 179–80.

hurling the anathemas of the 1930s against those who were, in essence, the lingering voices of social-gospel progressivism.[49]

XV

Meanwhile, the man who shared with liberal Christians the burden of Niebuhr's disapproval, John Dewey, outwardly paid almost no attention to the challenge. Dewey never had had much use for theologians, and his own book on religion, *A Common Faith* (1934), was a secular and pragmatic substitute for religion that could only have irritated convinced Christians. Instead of noticing critics like Niebuhr, Dewey spent most of his time in what in retrospect seems like the most productive old age in American intellectual history. Just sixty when he produced *Reconstruction in Philosophy* (1920), he then proceeded to revolutionize the more technical aspects of philosophy— logic, aesthetics, metaphysics. Each year seemed to produce a new book that could not be ignored by any professional philosopher. Many of these books were too technical to have much effect in intellectual history. Others were public lectures that popularized Dewey's newest ideas on politics, religion and education. But at least one had the lucidity, the originality and the historical importance to make it an influence in areas far from technical philosophy. In *Human Nature and Conduct* (1922), Dewey produced a key work in the history of psychology, uniting the insights of progressivism with post-Freudian developments without ever using specifically Freudian ideas.

The progressive psychology that lay behind Dewey's educational ideas had assumed that the child formed his personality by imitating people around him. No longer did liberals assume with an earlier generation that men were just born one way or another, headed for heaven or hell by some sort of divine election, and able only by cease- less striving and noble character to mitigate or improve a fate that seemed to proclaim some wicked and therefore poor, and others virtu- ous and therefore rich. Freud, in his own way, had reinforced the laissez-faire fatalism of this older psychology; instead of God, the traumas of childhood determined which way the person would grow. Either philosophy made human action seem only minimally helpful, a way of easing the pain rather than making true happiness possible. Dewey, however, carried on the progressive traditions without ever

49 See Carter, Meyer, and Schlesinger citations, notes 47 and 49 above; Niebuhr, *Reflections on the End of an Era* (New York, 1934), *An Interpretation of Christian Ethics* (New York, 1935), and *Christianity and Power Politics* (New York, 1940); and Robertson, ed., *Love and Justice*, pp. 25–46.

seeing much in Freud; even his critical remarks are oblique and made in passing, as if he did not want to draw attention to Freud even negatively. This anti-Freudian bias was of great importance to American reform, because most people saw, rightly enough, that if Freud were correct in his theories, meaningful social reform was doomed from the start. If people acted as they did because of inevitable complications involved in their childhood, society and its schools could do little but try to channel malice and frustration into socially harmless areas. If, on the other hand, progressives like Cooley, Addams, and Dewey were right, and people formed their personalities from imitating other people in their immediate environment, reform had a chance: change the environment, make it admirable, and children would grow up more democratic and more responsible. Their children, in turn, would have even more ideal models to form their characters upon, and so progress would be assured.

Dewey's child psychology provided a theoretical basis for this view. Instead of viewing the child in Freud's terms as an isolated soul by nature in conflict with society, Dewey saw the child as a social organism composed chiefly of habitual reactions to stimuli. For Dewey the child was a part of society from birth and developed through the experience of interacting with society. Apart from this experience, the child had no standards of its own, no innate sense of the difference between what is, and what ought to be. A child simply acted, received pleasure or pain, and formed habits based on those actions that bring pleasure. These habits, for Dewey, were "good" if they enabled the child to "grow" (whatever "grow" meant) and bad if they did not. The child's personality was the sum of its habits. "Personal traits are functions of social situations," Dewey wrote, so "we change character from worse to better only by changing conditions. . . ." What most people called "principles" were only firmly entrenched habits based on their reactions to past experience. Reformers, then, should ignore abstract principles and fixed goals for human behavior and concentrate instead on controlling the social situations that influence the growth of the child. As Dewey saw it, the task of the educator, who governs the child's immediate social environment, was to distinguish between "routine, unintelligent habit" and "intelligent habit, or art" and not to worry about the fusty moral baggage of society's past or the personal traumas of the child. Human nature was thus at least partially malleable, and the chief impediment to change was not the individual's unconscious but the inertia of society. "People" were often stolid, inert, conservative; a "child" was adaptable, able to become almost anything. From this point of view, Dewey too had a place in the cult of the child in the 1920s, since he saw reform as a kind of product of the growth of the uncorrupted child. Freud and his followers looked at the child and saw the source of neurosis and repression; Dewey saw an infinitely renewable source of social change.[50]

Dewey's emphasis on the present, his belief in social reforms, and his insistence that an individual could change his character given the proper environment prepared American intellectuals for the movement that was the most fruitful attempt to unify American social thought between the wars. It is one of the ironies of the period that Karen Horney, the first figure in this movement to gain popularity and acceptance in America for her ideas, was unaware of Dewey or her other American predecessors when she formulated the theories that unified their social ideas so well. An immigrant from Germany, she received her training in the most rigidly Freudian sort of intellectual environment. But by the 1930s, when she was writing her best-known works, she had found too many problems in Freud's theories to remain an orthodox Freudian. Profiting from the anthropology that had developed since Freud had worked through the sketchy literature of his own time, she pointed out how the work of Ruth Benedict, Margaret Mead, Bronislaw Malinowski, and their coworkers invalidated Freud's belief in the universality of the neurotic symptoms he encountered in his wealthy bourgeois female patients in Vienna. Many of the anthropologists' newly discovered cultures, for example, had family structures that did not seem to produce the Oedipal frictions Freud had always insisted were universal and basic to human nature.

Her criticisms of Freud ranged beyond the field of anthropology and penetrated to some of his most fundamental assumptions. She disliked Freud's bias toward scientific and mechanical models for his ideas on personality, and the way he persistently cast his discussions in the form of mechanical dualisms—the ego *vs.* the id, the sex instinct *vs.* the death wish. Freud, in her opinion, was too much in the habit of letting his early medical and scientific training restrict his focus. As a result, he was too pessimistic about human nature, too willing to see problems and conflicts as inevitable and thus incurable, and too ready to disregard the social environment and its influence. She found his emphasis on childhood trauma as the primary influence on the problems of the adult more of a hindrance than a help to the therapist; frequently the most important influence lay in the immediate environment where it could be dealt with directly. Finally, she disliked Freud's image of the analyst as the imperturbable scientist who made no moral judgments. Analysts were deluding themselves if they thought they could avoid making moral judgments or even avoid revealing their moral values to

---

50 John Dewey, *Human Nature and Conduct* (Modern Library ed., 1930, c.1922), pp. 20, 77.

their patient as they discussed his problems. They should therefore make their own values clear as they explained the patient to himself.

In all of her criticisms, the main issue on which Karen Horney differed from Freud was the relative force of biological and sociological influences in shaping the personality. Freud's diagnosis of the causes of female neurosis was a case in point. She obviously resented Freud's insistence that the root cause of much female neurosis, if not all of it, was penis-envy. In her view the so-called castration complex was not nearly so important in determining female attitudes as the social environment, the cultural conditioning that made women act submissively and denied them equal opportunity and treatment with men. As a result of her emphasis on the importance of society, she was also far more politically conscious than Freud. Although Freud was a liberal in a sense, he was conservative by temperament and did not in general concern himself with politics. Karen Horney was on the political left, not perhaps as firm or as deep a student of Marxism as her fellow neo-Freudian Erich Fromm, but still dedicated to the goals of social equality that were common in Europe through the days of the Popular Front. For Freud, so many of man's problems were of biological origin that attempting to solve them through passing laws and political means was irrelevant and sentimental. For Horney, so many of man's problems were of social and cultural origin that changing society through political means seemed to be an integral part of psychotherapy.

Mrs. Horney spoke with an authority too great to ignore. She had published many technical papers and had spent over fifteen years in Berlin as a member of the Berlin Psychoanalytic Institute. In America, she first received a wide audience for her views in 1937, when *The Neurotic Personality of Our Time* became something of a cult volume for people suffering from anxiety. The book was a perfect do-it-yourself kit for the literate, dissatisfied housewife with a good education and nothing but children and laundry on her hands. Although Mrs. Horney may not have intended anything of the kind, her ideas soon achieved almost as much circulation, and often in as debased a form, as Freudian ideas had in the 1920s. A neurosis, as she defined it succinctly, was "a psychic disturbance brought about by fears and defenses against these fears, and by attempts to find compromise solutions for conflicting tendencies." It was not inevitable in an adult, and if it did occur, it had been present only in embryonic form in the child. It developed from childhood, but it did not necessarily, or even often, repeat childhood experience, as Freud had insisted. She firmly pointed out that Protestant Christian capitalism, the chief cultural heritage of much of Western Europe and America, demanded that men compete against one another even as they were commanded to love one another: "The isolated individual has to fight with other individuals of the same group, has to surpass them and, frequently, thrust them aside. The advantage of the one is frequently the disadvantage of the other. The psychic result of this situation is a diffuse hostile tension between individuals." The chain of events became clear: culture, not biology, determines conflicts and anxiety; the individual finds he is always competing and is frequently unsure of himself or his ability or position; he cannot count on the affection he needs, because he is always afraid someone may be getting ahead of him; he becomes fearful and anxious, and feels increasingly isolated; he thus seeks love in one form or another, and cannot always find it. The neurosis is his involuntary attempt at psychic self-protection.[51]

This new concept of the neurotic personality and its origins naturally led Mrs. Horney to revise her ideas of psychoanalysis, and here her modifications of Freud were equally extreme and important. She criticized free association as a therapeutic device because she thought that the memories it called up were often irrelevant, and she noticed that frequently her patients preferred to dwell in their childhood world as a means of escaping the pressure of present society. Dreams and repressions also became less important, again because the past was less important than the present. The meaning of sexual maladjustment became quite different: instead of the psychic trauma due to childhood problems, it became simply the way some neurotics expressed their needs for affection, reassurance and comfort in a coldly competitive world. In short, *New Ways in Psychoanalysis* (1939) marched straight through all the key Freudian concepts and found Oedipal conflicts, penis-envy, the death wish, and the rest to be the result of competitive pressures on weak individuals. Mrs. Horney gave Freud credit again and again for opening up the whole subject of the unconscious, of dreams, of psychotherapy, and for putting forth many fruitful hypotheses that had regrettably been found inadequate. In so phrasing her praise and her revision, she remained clearly a follower of Freud, even as she tried to destroy all of the emphases that were dearest to him. But just as both Dewey and Freud, incompatible though they were, had appealed to the twenties, so this new synthesis appealed to the depression- and war-worried thirties. As an ending to the thought of a decade full of intellectual schisms, it was a welcome attempt to reintegrate the mind as well as the spirit of the country.

---

51 Karen Horney, *The Neurotic Personality of Our Time* (New York, 1937), pp. 28–29, 284. For background see J. A. C. Brown, *Freud and the Post-Freudians* (London, 1961), esp. ch. 7; Nigel Walker, *A Short History of Psychotherapy in Theory and practice* (New York, 1960, c.1957), esp. pp. 106–11; Karen Horney, *New Ways in Psychoanalysis* (New York, 1939); and Clara Thompson, *Psychoanalysis: Evolution and Development* (New York, 1957, c.1950).

Unfortunately for their ultimate effect, however, Karen Horney's ideas suffered from the same fate that John Dewey's had during the First World War. They postulated an environment that was fixable, one in which people of good will, education and effort could become socially better adjusted to themselves and their culture. Her theory could no more cope with Hitler than Dewey's could cope with the Kaiser. Faced with nazism, which appeared to be an absolute evil, deeply rooted in human nature, neo-Freudian thought found itself counseling individuals about their troubles. Karen Horney had no Randolph Bourne to write a scathing farewell, but the fate of her ideas was much the same: faced with the Second World War and then the Cold War, Americans proved ripe for far more pessimistic and rigidly scientific doctrines.

IV

"RID OUR MINDS OF CANT"

Clearly time did not deal at all kindly with the men and ideas that had ruled in Mabel Dodge's prewar salon. The schisms that led individualistic bohemians to abandon their hopes of social reform in order to concentrate on the cult of the child and drove social reformers to scorn individuality made any worthwhile social intercourse between the two groups impossible. Only the most perverse imagination can picture Mike Gold and E. E. Cummings sitting down together in mutual respect over cocktails and trying to reach some viable compromise between their positions. In the twenties, civilities between partisans of different ideologies were strained. During the thirties, even friends and allies could become personally estranged over what now seem absurdly petty points of abstract doctrine. This splintering of thought also produced one result which many intellectuals probably never recognized at the time: it made some men into conservatives. These were the men who were repelled by the bigoted ideologues proclaiming heresy and anathema; who decided that if intellectual life produced so little civility, then something must be wrong with intellectuals and their pet ideas; and who insisted that, despite the claims of Freudians and Marxists, human behavior was not determined entirely by Oedipus complexes, traumas of toilet training, social class, or some foggy idea called the dialectic of history. For the conservatives, ideas—of God, religion, art, morality, intellectual life, myth, nature—were far more important.

Unless he came from the South or from Europe, the postwar conservative did not usually call himself by that name; to him, "conservatism" suggested something faintly un-American. After the war it was no longer possible to continue the tradition of American conservatism represented by Charles Eliot Norton and Henry Adams. The postwar conservative could not share Norton's nostalgia for medieval Italy or Adams's affection for medieval France. Instead, with an apparent perversity all too typical of the confusions of American thought, the newer conservatives usually called themselves liberals. They identified themselves with the liberal humanism of John Stuart Mill in England or Thomas Jefferson in America. Their "liberalism" had little to do with the Social Darwinism of the later nineteenth century. For them the word evoked something like the Jeffersonian ideal, a world of educated gentlemen who could afford to tolerate ideological differences among friends who shared a civilized dinner and a bottle of port. In their ranks, these "liberals" could find people like Robert Frost, Abraham Flexner, Joseph Wood Krutch, and Hendrik Willem van Loon. Gradually loosening the definition to include people of a more traditionally conservative type, they could find figures who belonged at times in other categories, yet who had distinctively conservative qualities, like Albert Jay Nock, E. E. Cummings, John Dos Passos and Harlan Fiske Stone. Finally, they might meet obvious conservative types, individuals of temperament that any age would recognize as conservative: the Southern Agrarians, poets like T. S. Eliot and Wallace Stevens, judges like Taft, Holmes or Hughes, novelists like Thornton Wilder or Willa Cather. As these lists imply, only the most perverse commentator on the period could identify "conservatism" with politics alone. It was not merely a political stance but a habit of mind, like individualism or communitarianism, that affected attitudes in many fields.

The conservative between the wars, then, must be judged as a representative figure for a large part of American culture and not in the common narrow stereotype merely as a tired Republican in Washington. In so far as a composite picture of any group is accurate, he was more likely than most people to be legalistic, skeptical, and cynical in his temperament. He greatly preferred mental to physical pleasures and was far more likely to be home reading a book than out in the world trying to change people and their institutions. Often he believed in God and practiced some sort of religion. Even when he did not believe in any formal religion, his assumptions reflected the religious concepts of original sin and the superiority of man's spiritual to his physical nature: men were flawed and human institutions fallible; worldly success was a vulgar and demeaning measure of human aspiration. Inevitable progress, another worldly idea, was a preposterous dream foisted on the West by scientists who were carried away by their own discoveries. The conservative looked to the past, not the future, for his ideals. The older culture of Europe had much to offer America, and the civilization of the past as a whole had ideas of importance for the present. As one man, conservatives shared a definite if unspoken agreement that the most valuable things in life were not gained through political or economic means, that change did not necessarily mean progress, and that ideas did have consequences.

Conservatism also demonstrated a quality that became obvious only after the Second World War—an ability to pick up the disillusioned drop-outs from the majority position. Of the three representative men in Mabel Dodge's salon, for example, Walter Lippmann was obviously a conservative by some time in the early twenties, and Max Eastman was a convert certainly by some time in the early thirties. Only Lincoln Steffens grew more radical as he aged, and he died in the middle thirties, apparently a communist. By the time of the Moscow trials and the Hitler–Stalin pact, the rate of conversion to conservatism increased daily. Unfortunately the new converts frequently brought with them all the bigoted ideological intolerance that had originally made them so unpleasant, as well as their old habit of seeking change through political and economic, rather than through cultural and intellectual, channels. Excluding these converts, most of the genuine conservatives of the period may be organized into two groups—secular and religious. The secular conservatives were often older progressives from the years before the war, who saw reform largely as a matter of administrative efficiency and who were unfriendly to the expansion of federal government activity. Often, too, they were men trained chiefly in the arts and letters but without religion, who brought to what political writing they did a bias toward humane learning and the artistic personality, rather than social engineering. The religious conservatives were even more likely to avoid politics. They had no progressive background at all, and were much less likely to have a secular cultural ideal that guided their lives. Religion came first in their lives, and everything else came later.

Walter Lippmann was the best known and most prolific of the secular conservatives. By 1914, Lippmann had already come under the influence of William James and George Santayana, and the political writing of Harold Laski and Graham Wallas. He had even tried out his peculiar combination of pragmatism and socialism in a few discouraging months as an adviser to a new socialist mayor of Schenectady, New York. During the war he had been active on the *New Republic* and had been an adviser behind the scenes at Versailles. This wide range of experience left Lippmann disillusioned, but without the bitterness of his fellow intellectuals. Unlike them, he did not reject politics altogether in the twenties. Although he rarely wrote directly on political topics at any length until the thirties, political problems were always lurking behind his books about newspapers, public opinion, and morals. Like most conservatives, he did not confuse an interest in politics with a faith in its infinite ability to change men. He tended to concentrate on how to make government at least minimally effective in sustaining the conditions vital to the development of humanism, and he had no faith whatever in the benevolence of a government subject to the whim of the majority.

Lippmann's work immediately after the war reflects his pained response to the disaster of Versailles. There he had observed the leading statesmen in the world deciding its destiny with only the sketchiest information about what they were doing and with a constant fear that they would be repudiated at the polls if they did not do as their countries wished. As a journalist, Lippmann naturally tended to see the world's mistakes as the result of the failures of his own profession. "The present crisis of western democracy," he said, "is a crisis in journalism." All that the worst critics of democracy have said about it is true, "if there is no steady supply of trustworthy and relevant news." His experience at Versailles had demonstrated to him all the many problems involved in enlightening the voting public—the confusion, censorship, cost of cables, the official news handouts—and naturally enough the rulers often found themselves handicapped by this popular misinformation. Lippmann saw a real threat not only to the democratic form of government but to the ideal of liberty itself. "There can be no liberty for a community which lacks the information by which to detect lies," he insisted. "Liberty is the name we give to measures by which we protect and increase the veracity of the information upon which we act." [1] For Lippmann, there could be no liberty without an informed public and this belief was the basis for his detailed analysis of public opinion, *Liberty and the News* (1920).

The problem as he saw it was that the average citizen has his head full of a "pseudo-environment," a collection of half-baked and often misleading ideas, symbols, and impressions that have little resemblance

---

1 Walter Lippmann, *Liberty and the News* (New York, 1920), pp. 5, 11, 64, 68.

to reality. Because "the real environment is altogether too big, too complex, and too fleeting for direct acquaintance," the real world that important men have to deal with politically "is out of reach, out of sight, out of mind. It has to be explored, reported, and imagined." The natural result is that leaders have to play up to popular misconceptions and manipulate the commonly accepted symbols or else face the possibility of no longer being in a position to do anything at all. What most fervid democrats failed to see, Lippmann argued, was that neither the self-sufficient individual, nor some kind of democratic Oversoul, could explain the workings of public opinion. Men did not spontaneously generate rational ideas that suddenly became majority opinion, nor was there a special angel for democrats who enabled the state to function autonomously in accordance with some supposed mutual agreement of the masses. A people could judge an action already done, and vote yes or no; or, they could choose a man to do their judging for them, and then vote yes or no. It was simply fatuous to expect the representative to remain totally responsible to his electorate. Democracy, he insisted, needed two professional elites in order to function properly: disinterested journalists and capable administrators. The journalists should offer independent, objective reports of the news, without the distortions so obvious in the 1920 newspapers. The administrators, a "specialized class whose personal interests reach beyond the locality," should be a politically independent class who would do the work now performed by elected officials and who would be largely immune to the passing whims of public fancy. "It is on the men inside, working under conditions that are sound, that the daily administrations of society must rest." In order to function, democracy had to reduce itself to the reasoned choice of men the people trusted to judge for them about the unknown events to come. "The members of the public, who are the spectators of action, cannot successfully intervene in a controversy on the merits of the case. They must judge externally, and they can act only by supporting one of the interests directly involved." In Lippmann's view, a public issue was a course of action that someone challenged. The voter judged not from an infinite number of ideal solutions, but for or against a specific man or issue. Either way, the majority vote was decisive. That was all you could expect of a democracy. In the 1920s, Lippmann was the very model of a Jamesian pragmatist, made somewhat skeptical by time, but still untrammeled by rigid rules or outworn dogmas.[2]

As Lippmann continued to study the public, he began to find more problems. In particular, he was impressed by the quality of rebellion

---

2 Walter Lippmann, *Public Opinion* (New York, 1965, c.1922), pp. 10, 11, 18, 150, 146–47, 19, 195, 250–51; *The Phantom Public* (New York, 1925), pp. 103–4.

in the twenties. People were presumably enlightened by the advance of science and the decline of dogmatic religion, yet they found no happiness in their new freedom. Modern man was "haunted by a realization, which it becomes constantly less easy to ignore, that it is impossible to reconstruct an enduring orthodoxy, and impossible to live well without the satisfactions which an orthodoxy would provide." He saw the twenties as the first time in which large numbers of people could experience the results of a successful rebellion against established values. Once the act of revolt was over and the excitement gone, people had to face up to "their disillusionment with their own rebellion." Popular religion was no help at all. The preaching of a theological liberal like Harry Emerson Fosdick, Lippmann said, left out "the most abiding of all the experiences of religion, namely, the conviction that the religion comes from God." Men could no longer picture a God, and the religion of their fathers no longer seemed to be relevant to the concerns and pressures of modern life. Lippmann's modern man was in no sense a crusading atheist or devotee of science, but a man who wants very much to believe, yet who finds himself not quite believing." At every turn, he is confronted "with radical novelties about which his inherited dogma teaches him something which is plainly unworkable, or, as is even more often the case, teaches him nothing at all." He finds himself merely a point in the flux of time, and his reality is only a sampling of immediate present desires. To him, "experience has no underlying significance, man himself has no station in the universe, and the universe has no plan which is more than a drift of circumstances, illuminated here and there by flashes of self-consciousness." [3]

Unlike the religious conservatives, Lippmann offered no encouragement for a return to orthodoxy. Instead he advocated a humanist attitude, largely inspired by ancient Greece and somewhat modified by his Harvard teacher, Santayana. Lippmann pointed out that virtually all the great religions "taught that one of the conditions of happiness is to renounce some of the satisfactions which men normally crave." What he wanted was "a sane and civilized asceticism" that gave men "a discipline of the mind and body" in order to fit them "for the service of an ideal." Instead of giving in to the selfish whims of the moment, men should learn to "abandon all private aims and to find their happiness in an appreciation of a perfectly ordered commonwealth." All virtues, he said, "have disinterestedness as their inner principle," and his favorite virtues were "courage, honor, faithfulness, veracity, justice, temperance, magnanimity, and love."

In contrast to the child-centered educators, Lippmann made "ma-

---

3 Walter Lippmann, *A Preface to Morals* (Boston, 1960, c.1929), pp. 20, 17, 47, 56–57, 106.

turity" the goal of the continuing moral effort he called "progress": "If we knew all the stages in the development to maturity, and how to control them, we should have an adequate science of education, we could deal successfully with functional disorders, we should have a very great mastery of the art of life." This vision of ordered progress to maturity, defined as a mean between extremes, he called "the matrix of humanism." In place of the creative child or the group-oriented social reformer, he placed his own conservative, humanistic ideal, the man of moderation in all things. In place of the heaven that religion provided, which he defined as "a prophecy and an anticipation of what life is like when desire is in perfect harmony with reality," Lippmann simply created an earthly substitute with the same definition, leaving out God and eternity. His new humanism replaced a no longer credible orthodoxy with the "discovery that men can enter into the realm of the spirit when they have outgrown all childishness." Virtue would be its own reward.[4] For some reason, no one at the time pointed out that what Lippmann was apparently doing was setting up his own personal qualities as the goal for all democratic citizens. In some ways attractive, his ideal rather ignored the fact that most men had passions and compulsions foreign to the character of Walter Lippmann, and that all the education in the world would have trouble changing their nature.

Lippmann's view of the depression was also typical of the secular conservative. He acknowledged the misery around him but he tended to keep his distance from the people and concentrate instead on what he knew best: financial affairs and diplomacy. He praised Herbert Hoover for his attempts at budget balancing, and agreed with the president that foreign causes, particularly war debts and monetary problems, were largely responsible for the depression. He even shared Hoover's tendencies toward platitudes, the repetition of the refrain that many of the problems lay in people's attitudes, and the idea that a change in mental climate was vital for a change in the economic one. He recommended experiments in cooperation between business and government and devoted his attention to technical matters like money, credit, and tariffs, in preference to the bread-and-butter measures of immediate relief like public works. Unlike other conservatives, however, Lippmann was willing to try direct public assistance on an emergency and self-sustaining basis. And, although he could see faults in some of Hoover's programs, he could work up little enthusiasm for his opponent in the 1932 elections. Franklin D. Roosevelt apparently did not have a very clear mind: "His purposes are not simple, and his methods are not direct." He appeared to be "a highly impressionable person, without a firm grasp of public affairs and without very strong

---

4 Ibid., pp. 156, 159–61, 175, 221, 193.

convictions." He was far too eager to please, and his vacillations about the Mayor Walker scandal in New York City did him no credit. "Franklin D. Roosevelt is no crusader. He is no tribune of the people. He is no enemy of entrenched privilege. He is a pleasant man who, without any important qualifications for the office, would very much like to be President." [5]

Despite his reservations about Roosevelt, Lippmann readily tolerated the early experiments of the New Deal. He approved of what he called "free collectivism," apparently because the state would assume some responsibility for a minimum standard of living for all its citizens. But his own ideal state would not so much direct private enterprise as keep itself ready to right things when some part of the economy became unbalanced. He even anticipated the Keynesian theory of the more advanced New Dealers later on in the decade when he suggested that the government raise taxes in good times, lower taxes in bad times, and sponsor public works when unemployment became serious. [6] As the New Deal became older, Lippmann grew more critical. He loathed the "midsummer madness" of the NRA, and thought tax proposals that would soak the rich and ignore the poor were intolerable class legislation. By 1935, he was complaining more and more about the increase in executive power, the currency manipulation, and the dole. The emergency was growing far less serious, yet the lack of planning, the vagueness, and the executive irresponsibility seemed likely to go on forever. [7] As if to call a halt, he began writing *The Good Society,* which gave the conservatives as good a statement of their principles as they had ever had from an American. But most conservatives were in such a state of confusion that they continued to denounce the course of history, largely ignored the book, and probably would have condemned it for vacillation had they read it at all.

Little in the book is particularly original. Lippmann gave a caustic analysis of the collectivist tendencies in the world and a useful summation of the growth and doctrines of liberalism. Like the old liberals and the newer secular conservatives, he tended to begin his analyses from the "given" of the market economy, and he insisted that anyone who did not do so was asking for trouble. In particular, he thought that the collectivists did not do so, and he regarded their attempts to make a country, its economy and its citizens, fit into some preconceived mold a prelude to regimentation and, ultimately, to war. Lippmann

---

5 Walter Lippmann, *Interpretations, 1931–1932,* ed. Allan Nevins (New York, 1932), esp. pp. 251–62.

6 Walter Lippmann, *The Method of Freedom* (New York, 1934), pp. 46, 54.

7 Walter Lippmann, *Interpretations, 1933–1935,* ed. Allan Nevins (New York, 1936), p. 113.

valued rational order at least as much as the collectivists did, but in this book he clearly differentiated between their sort of order and his. Unstated but clearly present in *The Good Society* were the concerns of his earlier books, especially the man of moderation that had emerged as the new ideal in *A Preface to Morals*. In his new book, the man is a judge, Lippmann's replacement for the collectivist planner. In a truly free and liberal society, Lippmann insisted, "the state does not administer the affairs of men. It administers justice among men who conduct their own affairs." Speaking broadly, "we may then say that liberalism seeks to govern primarily by applying and perfecting reciprocal obligations, whereas authoritarianism governs primarily by the handing down of decrees." As a secular conservative, Lippmann believed that men would be able to achieve their goals outside of politics if the government kept procedural and administrative lines clear and just.[8]

II

Lippman's ideas revealed certain elitist tendencies, but on the whole, he subordinated them to greater challenges and more pressing concerns. Abraham Flexner, the most influential secular conservative in educational theory, had no such need to water down his message. The son of a Bohemian immigrant, he grew up in Louisville, Kentucky, in a Jewish family fully aware of the value of education and culture. Flexner early demonstrated his remarkable abilities: he managed to teach himself Greek with only minimal outside help, and he worked his way through the difficult curriculum at Johns Hopkins in two years, under the pressure of his family's poverty. He returned to Louisville to teach high school and then founded his own private school. In the process of gaining an education, he fell in love with the classics, and developed a great hatred for the instrumental, utilitarian education popular with his uncultured fellow citizens. He was soon firmly convinced that too many people were attending college, and that they not only failed to learn anything of value to themselves but also watered down college curricula and standards so that the really talented students suffered. A poor Jewish immigrant's son was unlikely to turn this insight into a demand for an aristocratic education; instead, in what proved to be a pattern for secular American conservatism, he insisted that Americans should follow the lessons of Matthew Arnold; they should acknowledge the existence of a "saving remnant" of intelligent men and create a meritocracy by cultivating this remnant to the best of its ability, leaving the rest of the people with whatever

---

8 Walter Lippmann, *The Good Society* (New York, 1943, c.1937), pp. 267, 289.

vocational or present-minded knowledge they proved capable of assimilating. His own private school did so well in following this course that it excited Harvard president Charles Eliot to ask what Flexner did to prepare students for Harvard fully three years before most of his competitors.[9]

But Flexner soon became restless at the thought of confining himself to life in a Louisville private school, and he determined to strike out on his own. He studied briefly in the East and then in Europe, and the first fruit of his travels was a book criticizing some of the modern practices he saw, especially at Harvard—the electives, the lectures, and the system of assistantships. The Carnegie Foundation was impressed and commissioned him to examine the nation's medical schools, assess their value, and recommend changes. Using Johns Hopkins as a model, Flexner toured all the 155 medical schools in the United States and Canada, and found skeletons rattling in the closets of virtually all of them. The training methods he discovered were lethal: men were admitted without a college degree or sometimes even high school training, teaching standards were sloppy, exams meaningless, professors only local doctors moonlighting for the lecture fees, and laboratory and clinical facilities ludicrously bad. The carnage was terrific, and the schools, exposed as they were by name, frequently folded on the spot, or else consolidated into more respectable institutions. He then went on to Europe and performed similar research there. In 1913, he finally joined the General Education Board, probably the most influential foundation then working in the field of education. Supported as he now was by Rockefeller money, Flexner was in a position to put his ideas into practice. The result was a career that did more to revolutionize American education than all but a handful of his predecessors. Just as Charles W. Eliot and Daniel Coit Gilman had remade the American college and university in the late nineteenth century, and as John Dewey had remade the elementary and secondary schools during the Progressive Era, so Flexner and his Board totally changed the teaching methods in American medical schools and greatly strengthened the entire university system in America.

He began his written comments on general education rather unobtrusively in the early twenties, commenting mildly on some of the mindless democratic excesses that he observed. Yet he did not insist on a wholesale return to the classics, however much he believed in them for people like himself. Although he was critical of some tendencies of the twenties, he supported many of Dewey's emphases on modern, relevant, useful topics. But he always insisted that "an aristocracy of excellence is the truest form of democracy," and that schools were

---

9 *Abraham Flexner: An Autobiography* (New York, 1960), pp. 1–57.

wrongheaded to ignore their brightest students and keep learning keyed to the least common denominator. "It is of undeniable and overwhelming importance that American boys and girls should be honorable, high-minded, courageous, comradely," he said. But, he then added, "let us cease to suppose that these qualities are a substitute for, or in any wise inconsistent with, intellectual interests and intellectual training." Flexner admitted that the American people did value education, but they seemed to have perverted the word into some sort of indefinite prolongation of youth, and few citizens associated the schools with anything intellectual. What America really valued was "happiness, at an easy, unproductive, non-energized level." Instead, the schools should emphasize merit, campaign for public realization of the values of humane learning, and raise the salaries of educated men and teachers to the point where they were the economic equals of businessmen. But in the 1920s, few listened.[10]

By the end of the decade, however, Flexner's distaste for the American educational stewpot had grown to the point where he felt he had to place himself on record, just as he had about medical schooling during the first decade of the century. His book, and the chief institutional result of his work, were in the best tradition of American conservatism. *Universities: American, English, German* is a strong defense of the value of a detached intelligence in the modern world. Flexner argued that even when considered on utilitarian grounds, the current emphasis on vocational technique was misguided. What modern democracies needed most was a group of highly educated and cultured intelligences, trained to be detached and objective in what they saw about them. He did not condemn vocational schools; in fact, he approved of them. What he did condemn was the vocationalizing of all humane learning, and the watering down of content to suit the dullards in a given class. A true university was, like Johns Hopkins, "an institution consciously devoted to the pursuit of knowledge, the solution of problems, the critical appreciation of achievement, and the training of men at a really high level." But Americans had not kept up this standard: "a sound sense of values has not been preserved within American universities." Flexner freely admitted that many American universities offered facilities for "scholarly and scientific work of the highest quality such as not even the most sanguine could have predicted a generation ago." Unfortunately they have also "thoughtlessly and excessively catered to fleeting, transient, and immediate demands; they have mistaken the relative importance to civilization of things and ideas; they have failed, and they are, in

---

10 Ibid., p. 67; *A Modern College and a Modern School* (New York, 1923), p. 72; *Do Americans Really Value Education?* (Cambridge, 1927), p. 8.

my opinion, more and more failing to distinguish between ripples and waves." Many of them, especially in the West and South, "are hotbeds of reaction in politics, industry, and religion, ambitious in pretension, meagre in performance, doubtful contributors, when they are not actual obstacles, to the culture of the nation." [11]

Formerly, the high school had sorted out students into the worthy and the unworthy, but American democracy objected to this. "Would not selection and distribution of students on the basis of industry, ability, and capacity to go forward on intellectual lines be democratic?" Of course it would; yet in practice, the high school found it could not do this. "It is, on the contrary, a kind of bargain-counter on which a generous public and an overworked and underpaid teaching staff display every variety of merchandise—Latin, Greek, science, agriculture, business, stenography, domestic arts. . . ." When these students reached college, they brought with them a kind of intellectual contamination, infecting the B.A. requirements and lowering the whole tone of the university. Athletics, cooking, business courses, anything with a popular lobby behind it, had its place in all but a handful of Ivy League and Seven Sisters schools, thus making an academic degree meaningless in practice, since it did not necessarily include any academic learning. On the other hand, Flexner did approve of certain recent innovations, like the Harvard tutorial system and the Swarthmore honors program, and he found many of the graduate schools "by far the most meritorious part of the American university." Yet even here, in certain areas, learning and culture had no place, while idiotic theses and meaningless courses predominated:

> A very large part of the literature now emanating from departments of sociology, departments of education, social science committees, and educational commissions is absolutely without significance and without inspirational value. It is mainly superficial; its subjects are trivial; as a rule nothing is added to the results reached by the rule of thumb or the conclusions which would be reached by ordinary common sense.[12]

The book was influential enough among college administrators, although rather impotent in the face of the democratic, anti-intellectual legislators who controlled the public institutions. But it did lead to a kind of symbolic fulfillment for Flexner. He became the moving spirit behind the Institute for Advanced Study, set up near Princeton University, a post-graduate school, research retreat, and haven for

---

[11] Abraham Flexner, *Universities: American, English, German* (New York, 1930), pp. 42–45.

[12] Ibid., pp. 47–48, 73, 127.

some of the most brilliant men in the world and a few selected students. In conscious rebellion against the overorganized bureaucracy in other schools, administration was kept to a minimum, faculty meetings all but abolished, salaries and tenure made secure. The structure was kept purposely loose, to permit change and prompt innovation of new techniques. The goal, in terms of men and the institution, was clear:

> There should be complete academic freedom as there is in England, France, and as there once was in Germany. We are, let it be remembered, dealing with seasoned and, I hope, eminent scholars, who must not be diverted from creative work. These men presumably know their own minds; they have their own individual ways; the men who have, throughout human history, meant most to themselves and to human progress have usually followed their own inner light; no organizer, no administrator, no institution, can do more than furnish conditions favorable to the restless prowling of an enlightened and informed human spirit seeking its intellectual and spiritual prey. Standardization, organization, making trifles seem important, do not aid: they are simply irksome and wasteful.

With the early support of Albert Einstein, Flexner got his intellectual Abbey of Thélème off to an ideal start.[13]

III

Given Lippmann's disillusionment with politics and Flexner's disillusionment with much of modern education, the secular conservative naturally found himself in need of positive statements of value. The answer was almost inevitable: their very disillusionment implied a positive emphasis on the value of art, of philosophy, of what Albert Jay Nock was fond of calling "useless knowledge," knowledge that made a man more humane without in any way making him more directly useful to society. The perfect embodiment of this ideal would be a man familiar with the failures of the cult of the child and the cult of the social group, who was able to show how art and the cultivated mind could supply answers to problems these more popular fads left unsolved. That man was Joseph Wood Krutch. Growing up in bucolic Tennessee, Krutch had originally wanted to become a scientist; he had been something of a local iconoclast, active in writing about the changes in American morals in the twenties, and convinced that the only thing wrong with this change was that it was not coming fast enough. He had never been of an especially religious temperament, and he found the new ideas of Freud and his popularizers a

---

13 Flexner, *Autobiography*, p. 239.

handy and valid way of criticizing the flaws of the society in which
he had grown up. In his first important book addressed to a general
audience, he produced a study of Edgar Allan Poe that asked questions
about Poe's character and suggested answers that were both important
for Poe scholarship and a symptom of the concerns of the 1920s. But
for the image of Poe himself the effect was not flattering: there is no
reason, Krutch proclaimed, to think that "Poe would have written at
all except as the result of a complete maladjustment to life. . . ." Poe's
stories were totally sexless, many of them obvious outlets for his own
severely repressed sexuality. The stories of ratiocination were likewise
desperate psychological ploys constructed in order for Poe to keep
from going mad. The ultimate picture of Poe was of a narrow neurotic
belonging to no tradition and having little influence outside France.
"We have, then, traced Poe's art to an abnormal condition of the
nerves and his critical ideas to a rationalized defense of the limitations
of his own taste." [14]

But Krutch was incapable of joining for long with any popular fad.
Having sown his intellectual wild oats, he realized that he had little
in common with the child-worshipers and word therapists. He was
too pessimistic by temperament, too ready to expect the worst, and
too skeptical about the opinions of those around him. Finally, he
decided that people often acted as they did more because of innate
ideas and basic traits of character than because of any accident of
childhood. The obvious result of this change in intellectual orientation
was a new pessimism: if character were determined at birth, then reform was futile. Utopianism was impossible, and intellectual fads offered no hope of real change. As an expression of these new attitudes
and disillusionments, Krutch turned to a study of contemporary America, and in *The Modern Temper* he produced a book that diagnosed
what was wrong with the country. He discovered people who had lost
faith in the old religion, but who could find small comfort in the
newer science. People desperately wanted to believe "that right and
wrong are real, that Love is more than a biological function, that the
human mind is capable of reason rather than merely of rationalization,
and that it has the power to will and to choose instead of being compelled merely to react in the fashion predetermined by its conditioning." Yet science refused to let people believe what they needed to
believe, and the mass of mankind seemed in danger of losing any desire for a rewarding life. Even in his darkest moments, man could
once believe "that the universe was rational if he could only grasp
its rationality," but now he was slowly realizing "that rationality is

---

14 Joseph Wood Krutch, *More Lives than One* (New York, 1962); *Edgar Allan Poe*
(New York, 1926), pp. 18, 234.

an attribute of himself alone and that there is no reason to suppose that his own life has any more meaning than the life of the humblest insect." Man was an ethical animal who yearned for standards and objects worthy of belief, yet all the best minds of his time told him standards were relative, and nothing was really worth believing in. "What man knows is everywhere at war with what he wants." [15]

In his examinations of humanism, love, tragedy, and art, Krutch found himself always coming back to the notion that "civilization," as he understood the term, was artificial, that it separated man from his environment, and that it thus weakened man when he came to face the brute facts of survival and propagation. Unthinking man, caught in his primitive activities and beliefs, was best able to cope with life; thinking man was least able, and most prone to depression. Krutch's own answer to this dilemma was the perfectly predictable response of a drama critic and university professor. *Experience and Art* (1932), the book that followed *The Modern Temper* as a kind of comment upon it, summed up quite well the solution that many intellectuals apparently found. Even if the universe is essentially meaningless, Krutch argued, people need a meaningful universe to live in; their only solution is to create their own. The artist—and by that term he apparently included philosophers, theologians, and anyone who created a logical mental world—could locate his own peculiar order in the world, find meaning in the order he created, and give the reader or viewer a brief moment in which he could share the insight and the order. Watching a great play took the place of watching the celebration of holy communion, and viewing a painting replaced looking at the inspirational stained-glass window. The art critic became the modern theologian, and the artist the modern equivalent of God. The catharsis of participating in a work of art may not have been inherently satisfying in the way participation in communion was satisfying, but it was the best modern man could do without consciously believing in lies and denying the knowledge he had available.[16]

IV

Joseph Wood Krutch wrote primarily about the drama, and it is not clear from his published work whether he paid much

---

15 Krutch, *More Lives*, pp. 17–20, 210–11; *The Modern Temper* (New York, 1956, c.1929), pp. xi (written in 1956), 7, 10; *The Autobiography of Mark Van Doren* (New York, 1958), p. 82.

16 *More Lives*, p. 227; *Experience and Art* (New York, 1962, c.1932).

attention to contemporary poetry. Nevertheless, the poetry of Wallace Stevens often reveals ideas and attitudes that have much in common with Krutch's philosophy of art. At times Stevens appears to be acting on Krutch's view that the function of the artist is to create art out of the meaningless flux, and enable his audience to share briefly in what earlier ages called a religious experience. On the surface, Stevens was a singularly improbable choice for such a place in the history of American thought. He had attended Harvard and a New York law school around the turn of the century, but had not been notably successful in his attempts at careers in journalism or law. He finally joined the legal staff of an insurance company, and for the rest of his life he was a reasonably successful businessman, chiefly in Hartford, Connecticut. He was not an entrepreneur, however, and he readily admitted privately to a physical indolence and a Sybaritic delight in the sensuous pleasures. As he wrote to Witter Bynner in 1904, "My idea of life is a fine evening, an orchestra and a crowd *at a distance,* a medium dinner, a glass of something cool and at the same time wholesome, and a soft, full Panatella." His business life, predictably enough, was not rewarding. As he wrote to his future wife, "I certainly do not exist from nine to six when I am at the office."

But even this early in his life, Stevens had reached the position Krutch formulated years later. His attitude shows through most clearly when he is discussing churches and religion. Churches, he wrote, "are beautiful and full of comfort and moral help. One can get a thousand benefits from churches that one cannot get outside them. They purify a man, they soften Life." Few in America would have argued with him so far. But he then continued, addressing his future wife: "Don't *care* about the Truth. There are other things in Life besides the Truth upon which everybody of any experience agrees, while no two people agree about the Truth." He was very eager to have her join a church, he said, yet he readily admitted, "I am not in the least religious." At the time, this attitude toward religion might have appeared ambiguous, but as his later career made clear, he believed that the emotional responses evoked by religion had a value quite independent of the truth of the dogmas involved. He was a believer in belief, a kind of dilettante of the religious sublime.[17]

Family responsibilities kept Stevens earning money in the office during the day, but elsewhere he was something of a solipsist. Life, he soon determined, "is as meaningless as dew," and he retreated behind the notion that ". . . the imaginative world is the only real world,

---

[17] Holly Stevens, ed., *Letters of Wallace Stevens* (New York, 1966), pp. 44–45, 74, 121, 96.

after all." He took occasional notice of political events, finding a few things to praise in Mussolini and feeling an aesthetic revulsion against much that was associated with Marxism, but the contempt of the poet for the affairs of lesser men makes his politics largely irrelevant to his career. His real interest, like Krutch's, was in finding a psychological substitute for religion. "I ought to say that it is a habit of mind with me to be thinking of some substitute for religion," he wrote a friend in 1940. "I don't necessarily mean some substitute for the church, because no one believes in the church as an institution more than I do." His trouble, and the trouble of many other people, "is the loss of belief in the sort of God in whom we are all brought up to believe." Humanism should have been a logical substitute, but somehow he disliked it. Two years later, he was toying with his basic philosophical insight: "I said that I thought that we had reached a point at which we could no longer really believe in anything unless we recognized that it was a fiction," he wrote another friend. "Of course, in the long run, poetry would be the supreme fiction; the essence of poetry is change and the essence of change is that it gives pleasure." The poem had replaced the religious text as the source of religious regeneration, the poet was the priest, and the people reading his poetry experienced a sublime feeling from the experience that was as close as they could come to heaven.[18]

What most people called "reality" Stevens found boring and drab. "Disillusionment of Ten O'Clock," to take one of his most accessible poems, uses the possible colors of ladies' nightgowns to indicate that the lives of average people lack anything of the imagination. To make life worth living, people had to be imaginative exotics, wearing strange colors, and capable of dreaming "of baboons and periwinkles." But the only people capable of such dreams were those half-gone in alcohol, like the old sailor, who, "Drunk and asleep in his boots, catches tigers in red weather." The natural response of the poet to this bourgeois drabness was a retreat into the imagination, his function was to imagine reality into an ordered and satisfying stimulation to the mind. The poem that embodies this act for the early Stevens is, naturally enough, the voyage of Crispin, "The Comedian as the Letter C." Crispin's imaginary voyage, with its overtones of exoticism, its irony and detachment, was clearly something of a psychological autobiography for Stevens, as if he found it difficult to take seriously his own attempt to state that which he thought important. Here are all the qualities that bother and entrance his readers: the poem is an ode to

---

18 Ibid., pp. 250–52, 289–95, 348, 430. See also *Opus Posthumous* (New York, 1957), pp. 157–62, 206.

the individual imagination, tending toward solipsism, lushness and exoticism, wryly commenting on the separation of man and the nature he needs to give life to his mind and to save what is left of his soul. Crispin's eye "hung on porpoises, instead of apricots," for "Crispin was too destitute to find in any commonplace the sought-for aid." Instead, "what counted was mythology of self," and so Crispin, like Stevens and many other conservatives, "Became an introspective voyager." He too found in the imagination a substitute for faith, as he "knelt in the cathedral with the rest, this connoisseur of elemental fate, aware of exquisite thought." But, since he was an artistic personality who had no real faith, "he gripped more closely the essential prose as being, in a world so falsified, the one integrity for him." The resulting doctrine was Stevens' poetic vision of what the drunken man saw: "Crispin concocted doctrine from the rout. The world . . . came reproduced in purple, family font, the same insoluble lump." Reality worked on the imagination; the imagination worked on reality; and the resulting process kept the mind working so that the poet could find a satisfaction in a world otherwise devoid of meaning.[19]

The age demanded that Stevens think in terms of groups, that he respond to social needs. He denied that the poet had any social obligation whatever and asserted that the poet, in being true to his own imagination, did perform a valuable function by making his imagination public by showing a way of ordering and controlling reality. Stevens's finest statement of this doctrine was "The Idea of Order at Key West," where the female singer represents the creative process, or what once was called God. The sky became "acutest" only when her voice so willed it. "She was the single artificer of the world in which she sang." When she sang, "the sea, whatever self it had, became the self that was her song, for she was the maker." The implication is that the world exists fully only when it is in the mind of a creative personality. The observers "knew that there never was a world for her except the one she sang and, singing, made." Plato, Bishop Berkeley, Santayana, the stray bits and pieces of Stevens's philosophical readings all combined in "Key West" to proclaim that the world that so obsessed the social reformers of the world did not really exist. Only art, and artistic creation, really mattered. Politics could give people material benefits, but it could never order their lives like the singer at Key West.[20]

19 Wallace Stevens, *The Collected Poems of Wallace Stevens* (New York, 1954), pp. 66, 27–46. Reprinted by permission of Alfred A. Knopf, Inc.

20 Wallace Stevens, *The Necessary Angel* (New York, 1965), pp. 3–36; *Collected Poems*, pp. 128–30. Reprinted by permission of Alfred A. Knopf, Inc.

V

The gulf between these secular conservatives, like Krutch and Stevens, and the religious conservatives, like John Crowe Ransom or Allen Tate, does not in practice seem very great. One group sought to find a substitute for a lost faith, while the other tried to revive it; both groups were concerned with ethics and human conduct in general, and both shared many philosophical enemies. The parallel seems even closer when the chief ancestor of the religious conservatives, Irving Babbitt, receives the amount of critical attention he deserves. Despite his later identification with Harvard and the genteel tradition, Babbitt was a child of the Midwest, an Ohio boy who had seen rugged living in his career and taught at the University of Montana as well as Williams College. At Harvard, for many years he was far from popular, and his position was frequently precarious. His first love was the classics, but departmental politics denied him a position in the field, so he joined the Department of French, working his way to the rank of assistant professor by 1902, and professor by 1912. This change of field was regrettable; as his friend Paul Elmer More once mused, Babbitt in a congenial atmosphere might well have been an entirely different person from the moral scourge he became. As it was, he soon established himself as an astonishingly erudite authority, and the most outspoken member of a faculty that normally disliked contentiousness. Certainly Babbitt never made much effort to hide his true feelings on any subject. "I am not thin-skinned, and I do not readily adjust myself to people who are," he once said. As if to prove his point, he once declared to his departmental chairman that, after all, French was only a cheap and nasty substitute for Latin.[21]

Babbitt began his full-scale campaign for his own peculiar standards by an attack on the philological methods dominant in the Harvard English department and its imitators. Steeped in German footnotes, and smelling a bit musty, the philologists insisted that literature be treated as a science; they demanded concentration on language, especially languages like Old High German and Old Norse, and they derived a perverse pleasure from writing learned dissertations on the roots of English words. Literature for them was merely an artifact, to be examined like an old rock or a piece of cave art, for the facts it would yield. Irving Babbitt had to control more temper in a month than most men had to control in their lives, and for several years he became infuriated by the absurdity of this method. What he desired

---

21 Frederick Manchester and Odell Shepard, eds., *Irving Babbitt: Man and Teacher* (New York, 1941), p. 4, passim.

above all was to cultivate men's minds, to develop their moral sense, and thus give them a genuine opportunity to lead an ethical life. To him, the Germanic philology was not only stupefying, it was immoral because it neglected the very purpose through which literature was worthy to survive. He particularly admired teachers like Charles Eliot Norton and writers like Matthew Arnold; even more, he loved the religious teachings of Buddhism. His whole temperament was anti-clerical, and while he approved of much of Christianity for others, he never had much use for it for himself. This peculiar combination of vigor, ethics, and the moral interpretation of literature formed the mind of the man who directly or indirectly taught many of the conservatives of the 1920s, and who came to worldwide prominence during the decade as the most learned and vigorous defender of what became known as "humanism."

Babbitt early demonstrated that most progressive thought inspired him chiefly by revulsion. What a typical progressive thinker like Jane Addams would view as a life devoted to service was for Babbitt "promiscuous benevolence." If, he wrote, "we are told that we should give no thought to ourselves, but live entirely for others," we should have to reply with Dr. Johnson "that our first endeavor should be to rid our minds of cant, of which every age has its own special variety." This being a philanthropic age, "it behooves us to rid our minds of the cant of philanthropy." Babbitt, in his way, was one of the deepest-dyed individualists in the history of American thought. In his view, reform began at home and withered upon export; philanthropy and social reform were the flabby expressions of slack ethics and self-indulgent behavior, based on a moral materialism that could lead only to social decay. His ideal, like Lippmann's, was the humanist who knew the golden mean of human behavior, who could exercise an "inner check," a *"frein vital,"* over his capricious wishes. "The humanist, then, as opposed to the humanitarian, is interested in the perfecting of the individual rather than in schemes for the elevation of mankind as a whole; and although he allows largely for sympathy, he insists that it be disciplined and tempered by judgment." [22]

As a scholar, Babbitt naturally expressed his ideas in the guise of literary criticism, and in the process he often transformed criticism into a species of disembowelment. The area for combat was romanticism, and the victims were chiefly Rousseau and Bacon. Something is "romantic," he stated flatly, when "it is wonderful rather than probable; in other words, when it violates the normal sequence of cause and effect in favor of adventure." It is romantic "when it is strange,

---

22 Ibid., Irving Babbitt, *Literature and the American College* (Chicago, 1956, c. 1908), pp. 4, 47, 5.

unexpected, intense, superlative, extreme, unique, etc. A thing is classical, on the other hand, when it is not unique, but representative of a class." With these standards, Babbitt attacked the villainous tendencies he saw in his own time, when he saw everywhere the baneful influence of the romantics. The "Rousseauist" was his chief target. He was a "specialist" who specializes "in his own sensations," seeking emotional thrills for their own sake. His program "amounts in practice to the indulgence of infinite indeterminate desire, to an endless and aimless vagabondage of the emotions with the imagination as their free accomplice." For the chief offender, he had only contempt: "Perhaps no one has ever surpassed Rousseau himself in the art of which I have already spoken—that of giving to moral indolence a semblance of profound philosophy." Compared to him, Bacon was merely a "scientific naturalist," a man who used human reason the way Rousseau used human emotion. For Babbitt, men like Bacon were merely misguided victims of their own curiosity, trying to reshape the world with their new knowledge and never bothering to ask whether the moral quality of life was improved. Change to Babbitt was not reform, and most industrial and scientific progress was ethically meaningless and even harmful. Anything that made men more moral, more self-controlled, he favored; but science, like naturalism, merely gave men additional tools for their own self-destruction.[23]

Babbitt did not normally deal directly with current affairs, preferring wisely to concentrate on those elements in classicism which best expressed his views. But in the twenties, things looked so unpromising that he entered the fray briefly. As far as he was concerned, "we are living in a world that in certain important respects has gone wrong on first principles; which will be found to be only another way of saying that we are living in a world that has been betrayed by its leaders." One of these delusions, held by the majority of intellectuals, was that economics and politics were the proper spheres in which to attempt social progress. That view, Babbitt snorted, was "superficial. When studied with any degree of thoroughness, the economic problem will be found to run into the political problem, the political problem in turn into the philosophical problem, and the philosophical problem itself to be almost indissolubly bound up at last with the religious problem." Politics, in his view, became a kind of moral battleground: Rousseau and the forces of darkness against Burke and the forces of light; romanticism and unchecked, self-indulgent sensualism against classicism, the "inner check," and moral responsibility. As Babbitt saw it, the dark forces of romanticism were winning and the fruits of their

---

23 Irving Babbitt, *Rousseau and Romanticism* (New York, 1955, c.1919), pp. 18, 58, 74, 168, passim.

victory were imperialism, dictatorship, communism and the fiasco of the First World War. Unfortunately, while his criticisms of the enemy were often savagely accurate, he had nothing positive to offer the conservatives who might be in power, short of despair and meditation. Politically, he was in the same deep rut that the Social Darwinists had plowed—totally irrelevant to a world that was in serious trouble. "The remedy for the evils of competition is found in the moderation and magnanimity of the strong and successful, and not in any sickly sentimentalizing over the lot of the underdog. The mood of unrest and insurgency is so rife today as to suggest that our leaders, instead of thus controlling themselves, are guilty of an extreme psychic unrestraint." That mad sensualist, President Calvin Coolidge, comes immediately to mind.[24]

VI

However much Babbitt tended to extremes, or seemed simply irrelevant in the context of modern America, he was still a popular and gifted teacher, even among those who were not, strictly speaking, his intellectual disciples. Some of Babbitt's better-known students, like Walter Lippmann, wandered far from his first principles and doubtless received their teacher's private condemnation with each successive book. Others, while rarely devout in their attitude toward their teacher's ideas, were still obviously his intellectual offspring, and proud to admit it. T. S. Eliot was the most prominent and one of the most grateful of these students. He quite willingly acknowledged that once a man had been his student, Babbitt "remains permanently an active influence; his ideas are permanently with one, as a measurement and test of one's own." It was a visit from his former teacher in the middle twenties that inspired Eliot's formulation of his creed as "classicist in literature, royalist in politics, and anglo-catholic in religion." Babbitt recognized that Eliot had developed a largely independent position, and thought he should make his new views known. In fact, as Eliot spelled out pointedly in two articles, he had gone into territory where Babbitt was temperamentally unfit to live. While Babbitt saw humanism as a substitute for religion and a bulwark against naturalism, Eliot insisted that humanism without religion inevitably slipped into naturalism whether it wanted to or not. For Eliot, Christianity was historically durable and absolutely

---

24 Irving Babbitt, *Democracy and Leadership* (Boston, 1924), pp. 26, 1, 205. On Babbitt's and the humanists' feud with the school of Mencken, which I have not discussed, see especially C. Hartley Grattan, ed., *The Critique of Humanism* (New York, 1930); and Alfred Kazin, *On Native Grounds* (New York, 1942), ch. 14.

essential for the life of Western man. Humanism was little more than a parasitic doctrine, critical of religion, and could have no truly independent life. If it destroyed religion it would destroy itself, for it was essentially a negative criticism and not an affirmation of anything intrinsically worthwhile. What, Eliot asked, were all these people "going to control themselves *for?*" [25] Without God and the religious world view, that was an extremely difficult question for anyone in Babbitt's position to answer.

As critics, the two men produced similar results in their respective fields. While Babbitt was marooned in his French department cursing Rousseau, Eliot was a student of the classics and English literature, and thus had the more promising task of sorting out writers worthy of praise that others had neglected, only occasionally finding it necessary to deflate or rearrange reputations that other critics had erected without adequate justification. In his theoretical formulations, Eliot proved a more effective warrior than Babbitt against naturalism. His chief contribution was an attack on the cult of personality, the romantic egotism so obvious in both Europe and America in the years after the First World War. "No poet, no artist of any art," he insisted, "has his complete meaning alone." An artist is born into a past as well as a present, and his art is destined to be only an isolated spectacle briefly marking the course of history if he does not discover his cultural roots, discern his own proper place, and then use this tradition to make his own small contribution to the sum of his culture's art. "What happens is a continual surrender of himself as he is at the moment to something which is more valuable. The progress of an artist is a continual self-sacrifice, a continual extinction of personality." For Eliot, the poet was more of a mediator than an originator; he took what his culture gave him, by way of language, religion, memory and tradition, and added his own experiences in the world. His genius, if he had one, came out not as pure originality but as a new synthesis of what his culture had already given him, a work of art distinct from the character of the poet. A writer was not a true poet if he could not transcend his own ego and embody his culture in his art. Nothing could be further from the cult of the child. [26]

Eliot's discussion of tradition and the individual talent was only a necessary prelude to his work on culture, religion and education. Culture, he stated flatly, "may even be described simply as that which makes life worth living," and "no culture can appear or develop except

25 Manchester and Shepard, eds., *Irving Babbitt*, pp. 103–4; T. S. Eliot, *For Lancelot Andrewes* (New York, 1929), p. vii; *Selected Essays*, new edition (New York, 1950), pp. 419–38; esp. p. 424.

26 Eliot, "Tradition and the Individual Talent," *Selected Essays*, pp. 4–7.

in relation to a religion." He would go still further, "and ask whether what we call the culture, and what we call the religion, of a people are not different aspects of the same thing. . . ." At this point, Eliot became even more controversial than usual. His ideal Christian society was possible only if the great mass of people shared a common family, religious, and social life, and if the rulers of the country found that they had to work within a Christian context: "Such a society can only be realized when the great majority of the sheep belong to one fold." Not only did everyone need a common religion, they also needed a common racial background. Therefore, "any large number of free-thinking Jews" was "undesirable," and "a spirit of excessive tolerance" was "to be deprecated." A "right tradition" must be a "Christian tradition" and "orthodoxy." "However bigoted the announcement may sound, the Christian can be satisfied with nothing less than a Christian organisation of society . . . in which the natural end of man—virtue and well-being in community—is acknowledged for all, and the supernatural end—beatitude—for those who have the eyes to see it." [27]

In the course of developing these arguments, Eliot seemed almost to be making schoolmasterly jokes about his profession and his deeply held beliefs—as for example, when he talked about modern mass political movements as "very bad for the English language," and grumped that "good prose cannot be written by a people without convictions." But for a man in his position such a stance was true and important. For Eliot was in many ways the most important and respected voice during this period to be raised against the majority liberalisms of Western man. His work on education summarized his position as a whole. He attacked the accepted notions that more education was always better, that schools were the place for everyone regardless of ability, and that individualism in the choice of course material was always the best policy. In place of the liberal ideal, which saw all study as equally rewarding, and the radical ideal, which indoctrinated students on the assumption that they should be prepared to enter the material and egalitarian world mechanically trained for their roles, Eliot put his own orthodox view: If the Christian religious and ethical teachings were true, then all children should be brought up to assent to them, and the elite should be put through a stiff regimen of the classics, especially the Latin and Greek languages, to prepare their minds to resist the heresies of modernism. All of Eliot's views come together in the notion of an elite, educated, homogeneous, Christian society. This was his way of establishing a third point from which to challenge those who believed in creative individualism on the one

---

27 T. S. Eliot, *Christianity and Culture* (New York, 1940, 1949), pp. 100–101, 37, 27; *After Strange Gods* (London, 1934), pp. 20–21.

hand, and the mass of men working in harness together on the other. "There should always be a small vanguard of people, appreciative of poetry, who are independent and somewhat in advance of their time or ready to assimilate novelty more quickly." The mass of men do not need to be up in front all at once; the culture need only maintain "such an *elite*, with the main, and more passive body of readers not lagging more than a generation or so behind." The reader of poetry, the teacher of Christian ethics, the statesman who tried to be true to his religion—Eliot wanted a small group that would guide the mass toward heaven and make them give up childish things—like Marxism, fascism, nazism, materialism, and the bitch goddess, success. In many ways it was indeed a poet's politics, often socially irrelevant in its own context in England, let alone in America, yet it captured the imagination of at least a few Americans and contributed to the values of a few more.[28]

VII

The essentially religious and ethical biases of Babbitt and Eliot were obvious ancestors of the conservative American criticism that developed in the 1920s, but they shared paternal responsibility with a singularly improbable source. In England during this period I. A. Richards and his students, especially William Empson, were working out what proved to be some of the most influential syntheses of critical and scientific ideas in the century. The philosophical and psychological bases of these ideas and the elaborate new terminology developed to express them are the province of the history of philosophy and literary criticism and not of American intellectual history. Yet, technical as the material is, its effect on American thought was considerable, and its influence on criticism was decisive. Richards and his disciples attacked most of their older competitors in the field: Croce's expressionism, Roger Fry's theories of pure form, Tolstoy's bigoted moralism, and other positions which Richards regarded as aberrations went down under the impact of his logic. In his search for a more comprehensive and philosophically valid theory, he turned to some of the new insights of science and psychology and developed an "affective" criticism. While the older critics had depended on some preconceived ideal—beauty, religious truth, social significance—against which to measure the work of art, Richards insisted that literary criticism should abandon such preconceived ideals and take as the point of departure the reader's response. The critic should spend his time

---

28 *Christianity and Culture*, p. 15; *Selected Essays*, pp. 452–60; *On Poetry and Poets* (New York, 1961), p. 11.

distinguishing between the art object and the way the reader perceived the art object. The object presumably conveyed certain paraphrase-able truths, which Richards called "scientific," or objectively verifiable. The reader, however, often perceived a good deal more (and sometimes far less) than the paraphraseable content of the art object. This extra baggage Richards called the "emotive" meaning of the words. In other words, he was elaborating on the common distinction between the denotative and the connotative meanings of words. Poetry, because it used words with many connotations, frequently attached emotive meaning to a simply scientific statement. This emotive meaning was to Richards "a pseudo-statement," a phrase that offended those who thought poetry superior to the indecent language of science.

Richards's ideas and terminology evolved considerably over the years between the wars, but his impact was largely of a piece. No longer could reputable critics proceed without challenge along the older critical paths: they could not simply effuse about the glories of the work or measure it against some ethical norm or assess its social impact or talk of its relations to the Divine. They had to analyze the text itself for the scientific statement, and then analyze the reader's re-sponse to discover the emotive pseudo-statements, the many extra mean-ings that the writer evoked indirectly in his art. A whole generation of critics suddenly found itself discarding its commentaries on the artist's biography, his social milieu and the unique emotions his work excited in their own psyches. A new precision entered criticism, all the more effective for the new generation in its sophisticated use of scientific terminology, made especially popular by Freud.

Critically, the chief consequence of this new critical outlook was an often obsessive search for multiple meanings in words. A poem, for example, now became "great" in direct proportion to its semantic complexity. The more an imaginative critic could read into a poet's words, the greater the poem seemed to be. Even if none of the mean-ings were consciously intended by the author, the critic could continue; the ambiguities were simply a sign that the writer's unconscious was at work as he wrote, and like other members of the new generation, critics were obsessed with the workings of the unconscious. This doc-trine was readily accepted by American conservatives; if they concen-trated only on the text, and only on problems of meaning and am-biguity, they could safely ignore social concerns. The artist did not need to feel that he had a social function; he did not have to have political views that seemed to work for the betterment of society; he needed only to practice his art and have a complex unconscious, fertile in the production of pseudostatements. This gave both a new freedom and a new rigor to critical analysis that was of incalculable importance in the sophistication of the modern mind, and only the most churlish would deny the value of these ideas. But like any new ideas, these could be debased and distorted in the hands of lesser men, and Richards lived to see whole generations of young scholars mindlessly searching for intricacies in a text about which they knew virtually nothing in any solid historical or biographical sense.[29]

VIII

Given these three disparate ancestors, American critics still had to make such ideas their own. Babbitt was a student of the classics and romance languages, Eliot an emigré to England, and Richards an immigrant to America only in the 1930s. The key men in the process of domestication proved to be the central figures in three successive groups of Southern American artists and critics, desperately in search of new weapons in their fight to retain their cultural roots in the face of an increasingly urban, industrialized, and flagrantly Northern nation. The first of these groups was a small number of poets who had gathered at Vanderbilt University just after the First World War. The leading figures included both students and faculty: John Crowe Ransom was the acknowledged first among equals, Allen Tate and Donald Davidson were prominent, and a younger and in some ways a more brilliant colleague, Robert Penn Warren, completed the core of the movement. These "Fugitives," as they called themselves, began by rebelling against two Southern traditions which they thought were destroying life as civilized men wished to lead it. They loathed the legend of the Old South, with its magnolia blossoms, happy darkies, sighing belles, and sweet songs at sunset. At the same time, they refused to adopt what the period called the ideas of the New South, the business ethic of Southern leaders like Henry Grady or Walter Hines Page. These poets saw their enemies as a false nostalgia and a false faith in business and progress. At first they had little else in common besides their love for poetry. They had developed no particular cult of the South or of rural life, both of which came later, and no real agreement on what poetry should be. Ransom, for example, favored old-fashioned and ironical poetry; Tate, in contrast, was a passionate experimentalist who preferred the new forms of poets like T. S. Eliot.[30]

---

29 See especially I. A. Richards, *Principles of Literary Criticism, Practical Criticism*, and *The Philosophy of Rhetoric*. See also W. K. Wimsatt and C. Brooks, *Literary Criticism: A Short History* (New York, 1957), pp. 610 ff.

30 This paragraph and succeeding ones are a synthesis of the following: John M. Bradbury, *The Fugitives* (Chapel Hill, 1958); Louise Cowan, *The Fugitive Group* (Baton Rouge, 1959); John L. Stewart, *The Burden of Time* (Princeton, 1965); and Alexander Karanikas, *Tillers of a Myth* (Madison, 1966).

But shortly after the group began meeting, one decisive event made a more coherent program seem necessary. That was the famous "monkey trial" in Dayton, Tennessee, where John Scopes was prosecuted for teaching evolution in the public schools. Most people remember the trial for the fiasco it was, with William Jennings Bryan and Clarence Darrow arguing about the accuracy of the Bible, and H. L. Mencken writing nasty articles about the yokels in the area. This was all very well for Northerners, but it made Vanderbilt and its poets furious. They viewed the trial as a preposterous travesty of the South they knew and insisted further that the North was hardly much more enlightened in comparison. In reaction to this event, the best-known of the Fugitives began to plan some kind of defense of the South and its way of life. This new defense appeared in their poetry, their prose, and their critical work. As their chief weapon, they began to fashion a new vision of the South that would symbolize certain eternal values that had all but vanished from the North, and that, they feared, were in the process of disappearing from the South as well. This new picture concentrated on the Old South before the Civil War and found in it values essential to civilization. It had been an aristocracy, a society where everyone knew his place, as lords and serfs had known their places in the Middle Ages, innocent of status-seeking and the lust for material wealth. It was made up of a homogeneous people, with a reasonably uniform code of conduct, and this code had been enforced privately, by and large, without the need for government and the law to intervene. But above all, it had had a religion, a mythology, and a ritual, and a sense of mystic order that gave meaning to the lowliest life; a meaning, these men insisted, that life could not have under industrialism.

Much of this vision of the past was merely a projection of their own ideals. The South before the Civil War was in most places thoroughly uncivilized and as full of social climbers trying to get rich as any other part of the country. It was religious only spasmodically, and then chiefly in the three decades before the Civil War; Thomas Jefferson was typical of many Southerners in having only the most minimal religious beliefs. But the facts did not really matter. The myth was there if enough people came to believe it, and men like Tate and Ransom added a few corollaries to round out their conservatism. They hated all science, because it was precise and empirical and thus an enemy to myth; they disliked any sort of abstraction and rationalism. Instead, they praised the farmer and rural life, while attacking the cities, the new inventions, and the business existence of the age of Coolidge.

These views first came to national attention through works of history relevant to the Old South. Robert Penn Warren, for example, analyzed

John Brown over many pages, and condemned him along with most of the abolitionists for thinking of slavery "in terms of abstract morality, and never in the more human terms of its practical workings." Brown found "a situation which violated all justice," and he firmly believed "that every victim of the situation was ready to avenge himself by cutting a throat." Yet, Warren insisted, "the slave himself was at the same time more realistic and more humane; he never bothered his kinky head about the moral issue, and for him the matter simply remained one of convenience and inconvenience." Warren did not explain how he knew all those slaves were so happy and all the abolitionists so abstract. In his hands, the Civil War became the result of Northern pigheadedness about a misunderstanding. Likewise, when Allen Tate examined the career of Jefferson Davis, he found that the social system Davis defended was better than modern industrial civilization. "For society as a whole the modern system is probably inferior to that of slavery; the classes are not so closely knit, and the employer feels responsible to no law but his own desire. Industrialism comes in the end to absentee landlordism on a grand scale; this was comparatively rare in the Old South." The natural result of Tate's analysis was a condemnation of both industrialism and human nature: "Men are everywhere the same, and it is only the social system that imposes a check upon the acquisitive instinct, accidentally and as the condition of a certain prosperity, that in the end makes for stability and creates the close ties among all classes which distinguish a civilization from a mere social machine," Tate argued. "Only the agricultural order in the past has achieved this." Although Tate could be critical of Davis, and positively contemptuous in his description of the Confederate cabinet, he still had his usable myth of the old agrarian South to use as a stick to beat the North and its capitalism.[31]

These historical works were only a prelude to the well-known manifesto of the group, by now known as the Southern Agrarians. *I'll Take My Stand*, published in 1930, gathered together many of the themes explicit or implicit in the earlier books: the hatred of science and industrialism, the love of the rural and the individual, and the insistence that the South, especially the Old South, had something important to offer to civilization. As Ransom wrote: ". . . it is the character of a seasoned provincial life that it is realistic, or successfully adapted to its natural environment, and that as a consequence it is stable, or hereditable." But, on the other hand, "it is the character of our urbanized, anti-provincial, progressive, and mobile American

---

31 Robert Penn Warren, *John Brown: The Making of a Martyr* (New York, 1929), pp. 331–32; Allen Tate, *Jefferson Davis: His Rise and Fall* (New York, 1929), pp. 43, 55–56.

life that it is in a condition of eternal flux." So far, the picture was true enough; the Agrarians were hardly the first to find that whirl was king in the North, and that inevitable progress was a myth. But as the rest of the picture emerged, the result was increasingly debatable, and with the theories of Donald Davidson it left the factual historian simply gasping. Southern culture before the Civil War, he believed, was the ideal spawning ground for the arts. Industrialized society, on the other hand, "will extinguish the meaning of the arts, as humanity has known them in the past, by changing the conditions of life that have given art a meaning." Art and culture, Davidson continued, "have been produced in societies which were for the most part stable, religious, and agrarian; where the goodness of life was measured by a scale of values having little to do with the material values of industrialism; where men were never too far removed from nature to forget that the chief object of art, in the final sense, is nature." This sort of nonsense rolled rather easily off the tongue, but even these Southerners found it hard to make an intellectual garden out of the depressing, anti-intellectual swamp that was the Old South before the Civil War. If ever a culture had made men of literature or genuine learning outcasts, it had been the Old South; and only total blindness could prevent a man from seeing that ugly, industrialized New York was the intellectual center of the country, regardless of whether anyone wanted to live there.[32]

This sort of ruralism left itself open to parody, and the book did give rise to considerable laughter as well as serious criticism. It thoroughly deserved the former, for despite its merits as a critique of the idea that business was the sole criterion of value, it perpetrated much historical nonsense. The contributors did not really care, and in fact they rather invited derision by printing a piece by Andrew Nelson Lytle, which seemed almost beyond parody. Lytle advised Southerners to do "what we did after the war and the Reconstruction: return to our looms, our handcrafts, our reproducing stock. Throw out the radio and take down the fiddle from the wall. Forsake the movies for the play-parties and the square dances." He cautioned his readers to "turn away from the liberal capons who fill the pulpits as preachers. Seek a priesthood that may manifest the will and intelligence to renounce science and search out the Word in the authorities." The Southerner, he insisted, suffered from progress, from the North, and from the course of history:

He has been turned into the runt pig in the sow's litter. Squeezed and tricked out of the best places at the side, he is forced to take the little hind

---

32 Twelve Southerners, *I'll Take My Stand* (New York, 1962, c.1930), pp. 5, 29.

tit for nourishment; and here, struggling between the sow's back legs, he has to work with every bit of his strength to keep it from being a dry hind one, and all because the suck of the others is so unreservedly gluttonous.[33]

Many critics were content to leave Lytle and his friends there struggling, but the Agrarians did not give up so easily. The group, with some additions from English conservative thought, published another study five years later called *Who Owns America?* that eulogized Jefferson and called for a return to a true democracy of a multitude of small, yeoman landholders. But the book was clearly a swan song, a retrospective summation of a position rather than a breaking of new ground. Once more the key figures were moving on, this time into the field of literary criticism, where they made their greatest impact and left the future its greatest legacy from the movement. John Crowe Ransom had been a leader both of the Fugitives and of the Agrarians, and once again he was the leader in the formation of this school of "New Critics." The term came from Ransom's study of I. A. Richards, T. S. Eliot, Yvor Winters, and a few lesser-known practitioners of the new creed. Ransom was peculiarly appropriate to lead the group, for despite its aesthetic veneer, the new criticism was in many ways only further manifestation of Southern Agrarian religious and social views. Ransom's book *God Without Thunder* (1930) indicates the religious bias that tended to make the new criticism so controversial and so unattractive to liberal, Marxist, and Jewish critics. The book was a forceful, intellectual defense of fundamentalist Christianity, possibly the most intelligent example of its kind since the days of Jonathan Edwards. The tone of the book, as well as its content, is most clear in the italicized conclusion:

> *With whatever religious institution a modern man may be connected, let him try to turn it back towards orthodoxy.*
> *Let him insist on a virile and concrete God, and accept no Principle as a substitute.*
> *Let him restore to God the Thunder.*
> *Let him resist the usurpation of the Godhead by the soft modern version of the Christ, and try to keep the Christ for what he professed to be: the Demigod who came to do honor to the God.*[34]

The new criticism was in full flower even before Ransom published the book that gave the movement its name. In 1938, two of his most

33 Ibid., pp. 244–45.

34 See especially Herbert Agar and Allen Tate, eds., *Who Owns America?* (Boston, 1936); John Crowe Ransom, *The New Criticism* (Norfolk, 1941); and *God Without Thunder* (Hamden, 1965, c.1930), pp. 327–28.

brilliant disciples, Robert Penn Warren and Cleanth Brooks, produced in *Understanding Poetry* a textbook that revolutionized the teaching of college English and helped introduce an entirely new methodology into the writing of criticism. I. A. Richards had insisted that humanistic values quite probably depended on the intelligent study of literature and had put forward notions about complexity and form that gave would-be humanists a means of becoming human. The Agrarian movement had added a strong bias toward religion and anti-industrial values. The new textbook united these two attitudes and made them a force in schools everywhere. Do not merely paraphrase the logical content of a poem, the authors cautioned; do not concentrate merely on historical and biographical material; do not look for some sort of inspiration or message: "one must grasp the poem as a literary construct before it can offer any real illumination as a document." A satisfactory way of teaching poetry, they said, should embody the following principles:

1. Emphasis should be kept on the poem as a poem.
2. The treatment should be concrete and inductive.
3. A poem should always be treated as an organic system of relationships, and the poetic quality should never be understood as inhering in one or more factors taken in isolation.

As it developed, the New Criticism produced an emphasis on "concentration" and "intensity" in poetry, and insisted that "form" was very important. But religious ruralism was never long absent. The attitude of the critic to the text was that of a preacher to his Bible, and anyone who insisted on close analysis of the facts, the historical context, even the simple scientific truth, often found himself accused of what seemed like sacrilege. He would be overwhelmed by accusations, for example, about the heresy of the didactic, of paraphrase, or of the intentional fallacy, or some other heresy concerning the "unpoetic" aspects of the work of art. Clearly, the New Critics wished to exclude the dirty cities, the factories, the social problems of their environment, and concentrate only on the sublime and ineffable. Yet, as a rule, they regularly clothed their arguments in secular terms that the simplest English teacher could assent to. "The question of the value of poetry, then, is to be answered by saying that it springs from a basic human impulse and fulfills a basic human interest," Brooks and Warren wrote. Any complete answer would have to take into account the value of the impulses and interests, but for the moment that was largely irrelevant. "As we enter into a study of poetry it is only necessary to see that poetry is not an isolated and eccentric thing, but springs from the most fundamental interests which human beings have." No special training in literary analysis is necessary to detect the religious overtones behind that statement of the aesthetic creed of the New Critics.[35]

IX

By the early forties, despite all their own propaganda, most of the Agrarians and New Critics were heading north, into the wastelands of industrialism, tacitly admitting that the pay and working conditions at Yale or Kenyon or Minnesota were more conducive to the quiet pursuit of scholarly excellence than the impoverished and often intellectually arid South. Their migration was perfectly appropriate also for quite another reason: agrarianism, for all its identification with the South and the group around Ransom, was really a nationwide phenomenon, and the Southerners were only the most publicized and self-conscious group in a much larger movement of religious American conservatism. United after a fashion in the pages of magazines like Seward Collins's *American Review,* these writers produced an extremely peculiar and sometimes impressive school of thought, most notable in a sense because their work seemed so completely estranged from all the normal intellectual currents predictable in an American thinker. Collins and Lawrence Dennis, for example, developed what looks much like an American fascism; R. J. S. Hoffman and others like him adapted Roman Catholicism and English Distributism into a presumably American variety of theocratic state; T. S. Eliot attacked his strange gods; and a small horde of lesser-known writers went off on their own tacks, finding political, religious, and social ideas relevant to American life that had virtually never entered American writing before. This hothouse flowering of the Right was in many ways sterile, but it did produce foliage well worth examination and analysis.

One of the most able of the non-Southerners involved in this movement was the distinguished architect, Ralph Adams Cram. In the years after the war, with Frank Lloyd Wright in eclipse and the Bauhaus not yet come to America, Cram could have made an excellent case for himself as the most distinguished architect in America. He was a product of rural New England, son of a Unitarian minister, yet without the usual baggage of private schooling or a Harvard education. He had dabbled for a while in journalism, but soon decided that he was meant to be an architect, and in the 1880s had picked up informally, in a kind of apprenticeship, enough knowledge to qualify as one. But as a young man his chief enthusiasm had been the decadent romanti-

---

35 I. A. Richards, *Principles of Literary Criticism* (New York, 1925), p. 57; Cleanth Brooks and Robert Penn Warren, *Understanding Poetry* (New York, 1938), pp. iv–xv, 25, 167.

cism of Western Europe, and he combined many of the views then common on the continent into a hybrid that looked very odd in the Unitarian soil of Boston. He loved the music of Wagner, the art of Beardsley, the poetry of Wilde, and he and his friends reveled in the thought that they lived in a decadent age. Cram also read deeply in Ruskin and Morris and brought forth from this melange an American version of their ideas. He and his friends became High Church in religious views, royalist in politics, and socialist in sympathy; at times they even celebrated Jacobite holidays. The socialism of the handicraft movement appealed to them, but only in a society controlled by an elite and ruled by a king.[36]

In 1890, Cram found an able partner and settled down in Boston. In the beginning the firm built a few homes, but Cram wanted to specialize, and he soon found that the building of churches was one of the most neglected areas in American architecture. With the addition of various associates, chief among them Bertram Goodhue and Frank Ferguson, Cram's firm soon dominated the field. Cram deeply loved the Middle Ages, like most readers of Ruskin and Morris, so he decided to take up English Gothic as his chief style of design. He talked frequently about his ideas and published them as often as he could, and soon the firm was remarkably successful. It won a contract to remodel and expand West Point, and much of the modern campus still bears the marks of the secular Gothic forms that Cram and Goodhue devised. That award brought others. The Rice Institute in Houston asked Cram to develop a Spanish Baroque style for its new campus. The planners of the Cathedral of St. John the Divine in New York called in Cram, and he made it into one of the few modern church buildings comparable to medieval cathedrals. Perhaps most important, the authorities at Princeton University, eager to emulate the peaceful havens of scholarship in England, chose the Gothic for its chief form for future architectural development, and in 1909 made Cram supervising architect at Princeton. In that post he had a key role in creating a showcase for his own ideas about art and the contemplative life. In 1914 he became head of the architecture department at M.I.T., and chairman of the Boston City Planning Board, remaining in both jobs until the press of business in 1921 forced him to retire. He was also prominent in the formation of the Medieval Academy of America and the founding of the lay Catholic magazine *Commonweal*.[37]

---

36 Albert Stone, "Seward Collins and the American Review," *American Quarterly* 12, no. 1 (September 1960): 4–19; Ralph Adams Cram, *My Life in Architecture* (Boston, 1936).

37 Cram, *My Life,* passim.

Like Ruskin and Morris, however, Cram could never be content just doing. He had to be talking, writing, and converting, and his chief concerns were the quality of life that he saw lived around him and the political and religious ideas that he deemed responsible for it. He had grown up nurtured on Herbert Spencer and progress as well as Ruskin, and for a while he had apparently been a believer. But by the First World War, when the flood of his social writing began he had long since given up any idea of progress, any notions about the benevolence or ability of mankind, or about the value of the machine. His books are all repetitive and do not seem to change over the decades, and they can be summarized quickly. History to Cram moved in cycles of about 500 years. Out of virtually nothing, some odd mutation of force sparked itself into a great thrust of culture, an entire civilization would quickly flower, and then slowly die out, because the force of democracy would overwhelm the cultural aristocracy vital to any civilization. Ordinary men, inherently vicious, would slowly gain control of politics and culture, fill the air with democratic cant, and the civilization would die out, usually in a time of war, imperialism and dictatorship. For Cram, the First World War was the obvious sign of the coming of a new Dark Ages, and the activities in Russia, Germany, and South America during the years after the war did nothing to dissuade him. The cant of progress, of human equality, of progressive education, of the melting pot, of modernism in art—all the familiar targets of conservative attacks—appeared as forces destroying America and the West. Cram even went one step further than most conservatives and denied that the majority of the people were really human beings. Most people, he insisted, were nothing but a neolithic mob which at best contained only the biological possibility of, occasionally, producing someone worthy of being called a human being. Most people thus had more in common with anthropoid apes than with the really gifted men.[38]

What Cram wanted was not the rule of mass man that most modern people meant by "democracy," but rather a "true democracy," which he analyzed into three key parts: abolition of privilege, equal opportunity for all, and the utilization of ability. This ideal, he insisted, had reached "its highest point," and "was most nearly achieved" during the Middle Ages. Cram obviously used his own background and profession to form a mythical past as valid for him as the Old South was for the Agrarians. History reduced itself to conveniently simple analysis: "I must insist on these three factors in the development of society and its

---

38 R. A. Cram, *The Substance of Gothic*; *The Great Thousand Years*; *The Nemesis of Mediocrity*; *The Sins of the Fathers*; and "Why We Do Not Behave Like Human Beings," *Convictions and Controversies* (Boston, 1935), pp. 137–54.

present catastrophe," he wrote in 1922; "the great, predominant, central body of free men during the Middle Ages, their supersession during the sixteenth, seventeenth, and eighteenth centuries by a nonproducing bourgeoisie, and the creation during the same period of a submerged proletariat." Regardless of the myth, the diagnosis of the disease was strictly agrarian. The disease was still capitalism, with its notions of progress, perfectibility, imperialism, and democracy—together with Cram's private addition of every Protestant since Luther and Calvin—and the great cure was a return to the yeoman pattern of farm living, which was wholesome, close to the soil, with warm, devoted families living together. The whole dream really must have seemed charming to a man who had escaped the farm at his first opportunity and lived his life amid the bottled milk and delivered eggs on Beacon Hill. And no one, of course, could have persuaded Cram that some of the warm, devoted families of his ideal were living in those Irish slums not far from his home, however far they were from County Cork.[39]

X

Cram's views on politics perhaps indicate why artists should confine themselves to writing about art. But the strength of the conservative position was never in the political field. The truths of conservatism lay elsewhere, and when conservatives achieved greatness in art or in criticism they could often claim a following among people who would never style themselves "conservative" in any political sense. The supreme example of this kind of triumph was the major phase of William Faulkner, from about 1929 to 1942.

Cram often sounded as peculiar as he did because of his insistence on defining his beliefs and stressing their political consequences; Faulkner provided an excellent alternative to this definitional insistence. Indeed, in his very inability to write about politics and theology, he provided a case study of the conservative mind in its retreat from rationality, the machine, and progress. Without the formal education common among other conservatives, he nevertheless summed up the position of the conservative in the modern world, and he did it entirely by indirection, showing his ideas as they were embodied in people, and never systematizing them or attempting actively to persuade someone to follow him. He lacked the political sense of a Lippmann and the scholarly sense of a Flexner, but the rest was there: he used religion, myth, time, and geography to show people the fortitude

---

39 Cram, *The Nemesis of Mediocrity* (Boston, 1919, c.1917), pp. 23, 27; *Towards the Great Peace* (Boston, 1922), p. 7, passim; and *The End of Democracy.*

necessary to survive their times, and how their times came to be. His books are in no sense didactic, but they do stress indirectly the values of tolerance, of stoic survival, of Christian charity, and the pervasiveness of some kind of original sin and its embodiment in human greed and private property.

Faulkner grew up in Mississippi, in a family largely of the active capitalist class. The important thing about his background is not so much the economic or social status of his family, but the mythical, romantic atmosphere that permeated the very air he breathed. The Civil War and the legends of the South, especially the Old South and its decline in the face of modern industrial life, fascinated him and seemed to him far more interesting than mere reality. Unfortunately they did not point very clearly to a career for a young man, and after a rather aimless youth, and a brief, combatless training period for the Royal Air Force in Canada during the First World War, Faulkner found himself with little desire to do anything. He had a taste for bad romantic verse, and wrote some, but mainly he became a town hobo, taking occasional odd jobs and generally looking like more of a failure than was customary even in Mississippi. Eventually, largely due to friendship with the woman who later became Mrs. Sherwood Anderson, he worked his way to New Orleans and the bohemian world that centered around the local literary magazine, *The Double Dealer*. Later in life he was fond of recalling that Sherwood Anderson's easy life appealed to him so strongly that he, too, wanted to become a writer. Given Faulkner's love of myth, the accuracy of his memory should not, perhaps, be taken too seriously, but he did in fact begin writing at this time.[40]

Faulkner's later fame has obscured how excruciatingly bad his early work was. His reading in romantic poetry combined with the rhetoric so common in the Southern stump-speaking tradition to all but destroy an untrained writer's ability to communicate. Thus, in Faulkner's first novel, *Soldiers' Pay* (1926), we find images like: "After the immediate naked morning, the interior of the hall vortexed with red fire"; or, "Afternoon lay in a coma in the street, like a woman recently loved" —the examples could go on indefinitely. In addition, his whole sense of what writing could and should do was still to be developed, as this stirring example of the pathetic fallacy shows:

> She lay against him limply, weeping, and the rain filled the interval, whispering across the roof, among the leaves of the trees. After a long space in which they could hear dripping eaves and the happy sound of gutters

---

40 A responsible account of this early biography is given in Irving Howe, *William Faulkner* (New York, 1960 [revised], c.1952), part 1.

and a small ivory clock in the room, she moved and still holding her face against his coat, she clasped her father about the neck.

One has to go back to the domestic novel of the 1850s, like Susan Warner's *The Wide, Wide World*, to find a worthy ancestor for that passage.[41]

Mosquitoes, which followed a year later, was little better and at times even worse. The plotting was poor and the characterization unclear. The general theme of the book seemed to be the impotence and lack of direction people felt during the early twenties, unable as they were to get hold of their lives or do anything meaningful about them. The book was particularly cruel to women, painting them as mindlessly ineffectual adults or as selfish, boyish, and rather sexless flappers, capable only of physical functions and the corruption of men—they pet but don't spawn. The language was still precious, and often self-consciously arty. But like many bad novels, *Mosquitoes* can be quite helpful in guiding later readers to the source of the author's strength when he finally found it. What seems to be wrong with the bohemian "mosquitoes" that fly about in the novel is their lack of roots, of a past, and of a place in which they truly belong. The boat on which most of the action occurs is a symbol of a society set adrift, without family ties, without a past, and without conservable values. Just as the war separated a generation from its parents and thus destroyed life in *Soldiers' Pay*, so the postwar disillusionment and sense of meaninglessness isolated them in another sense. Faulkner's people absolutely had to have a home, a family, a past, and a sense of belonging or they could not survive. Nor was this merely the lack of experience of a young writer: by almost universal agreement, Faulkner's other "worst" novels are *Pylon* (1935) and *A Fable* (1954), and the same rootlessness and lack of connection with a specific place produce the same disastrous writing, characterization, and plotting.

But then, almost without warning, the major phase began in 1929 with the publication of both *Sartoris* and *The Sound and the Fury*. In the next few years virtually all of Faulkner's important work was written, apparently including, to judge from his own remarks, many of the best parts of the Snopes trilogy that were not actually published until long after the Second World War. No one questions any longer whether Faulkner is a major writer, and one way of illustrating his stature is to show how he could appeal to critics of many different persuasions. For the left-wing social critics, for example, Faulkner had more portraits of lower-class people, and more examples of the classes in conflict, than many belligerently proletarian writers. The Yok-

---

41 William Faulkner, *Soldiers' Pay* (New York, 1968, c.1926), pp. 46, 105, 92.

napatawpha series, the core of his work, can easily be read as the story of how a rising lower class takes power from a degenerate aristocracy. The Snopeses are hardly the hope of the socialist future, but this sense of class structure and conflict could not help but appeal to critics immersed in the dialectic. Likewise, a book like *As I Lay Dying* (1930) might well look like a prize example of the genuinely collectivist novel. The style is not always immediately appealing to the literary taste of the average stevedore, but the device of telling the story through numerous streams of consciousness within a lower-class family is certainly compatible with much social propaganda, and the problems the Bundrens meet are hardly those sexual and neurotic upper-class nonproblems that so offended Mike Gold. Faulkner knew the rural lower class, and he could paint them with considerable sympathy if he wanted to. He also condemned private property and gave leading roles to Negroes. It was thus only just that left-wing political figures, like Irving Howe and Malcolm Cowley, when they finally discovered Faulkner in the 1940s, should have played the important roles that they did in the development of his critical reputation.

Faulkner also appealed to the more psychological critics, who preferred stream-of-consciousness, experimental writing, art-for-art's sake, and the other categories of the critical life of the twenties. Faulkner had apparently been influenced by both Joyce and Conrad; the Benjy section of *The Sound and the Fury* is only the best known of the many places where Faulkner tried to write from the inside of his people, in manner of Conrad Aiken or Eugene O'Neill. He too was capable of stressing the traumatic youth of a character and showing how later life was often disastrously ruined by infant and adolescent experiences. The characters in *The Sound and the Fury,* except for Dilsey, are all neurotic or psychotic, and a disintegrated family life has scarred them all. Jason seems to be a parody of the anal-retentive personality, the boy Quentin is at least in part the victim of inadequate superego formation, Caddy seeks promiscuously for the love she was denied as a child, and the illegitimate girl Quentin combines many of the problems of the boy Quentin and Caddy—although she does manage to liberate Jason's hoarded and stolen money. It was thus appropriate that psychologically acute critics like Conrad Aiken and Frederick Hoffman were at least as important as the social critics in establishing Faulkner's stature.

But Faulkner's greatest appeal was undoubtedly to the New Critics and the myth critics, their first cousins, whose basically conservative and "religious" approach to the text, to time, and to eternal values finds such strong confirmation in Faulkner's work. One of his themes that most appealed to these conservatives, for example, was that of human rootlessness in the modern world. *Sanctuary* (1931), whatever else it is, is certainly an anatomy of man as cut off from his roots. Popeye, throughout the book, is without relation to the human community, and when at the end he turns out to have a mother whom he visits, this vestige of humanity leads to his arrest. The other members of his little bootlegging community have no "natural" connections to each other; in effect, they pollute notions of the family and the community in the way Popeye pollutes the landscape and the spring water. Temple Drake, when she falls among them, is an example of what happens to a girl when she cuts her ties to her family. The only relation she can establish to Popeye's "community" is via the bloody corncob, and all her other personal relationships are as unnatural as that singularly unappealing connection. Significantly, in a moment of terror, she neither prays nor does anything useful, but mutters in a kind of yearning, "My father's a judge; my father's a judge," as if the repetition of her one remaining connection to the family would help her survive. At the opposite extreme, Horace Benbow seems so entangled in the old and outworn customs of his communal roots that he has trouble acting at all, and when he does act he is usually impotent —his impotence is more genteel than Popeye's, but just as real. His sister Narcissa has become simply obnoxious, her rootedness has made her willing to risk everything to avoid scandal, even to the point of letting an innocent man die. And, of course, Temple's temporary refuge is singularly appropriate for her outcast status: Miss Reba's whorehouse indicates that rootlessness can even be institutionalized without ever giving any of the inmates a sense of belonging.[42]

In *Light in August* (1932) this theme of rootlessness controls the entire book. Gail Hightower has become an impotent minister, expelled from his congregation and deserted by his wife; Joanna Burden is the last abolitionist spinster, who somehow missed the last train back North, an outcast from the whites and a friend to the Negroes among whom she has no real place; Lena Grove has left her family while "in the family way," but she cannot find the man who has impregnated her and who could enable her to form a real family, so wanders witlessly in search of a home. The chief character is Joe Christmas, the most rootless of all. He thinks he may be part Negro in ancestry, but he is not sure. He passes for white, but his own doubts seem palpable, and eventually people think he is black and treat him accordingly. When Byron Bunch first sees him at the planing mill, he sees "something definitely rootless about him, as though no town nor city was his, no street, no walls, no square of earth his home," and this theme once announced becomes the key to Christmas's motivations, his flaws of character, and finally his murder. As Faulkner himself said many

---

42 William Faulkner, *Sanctuary* (New York, n.d., c.1931), see p. 50 for quotation.

years later, Christmas's tragedy was that "he didn't know what he was, and so he was nothing. He deliberately evicted himself from the human race because he didn't know" whether he was Negro or white. That was his tragedy and the "central idea of the story—that he didn't know what he was, and there was no way possible in life for him to find out." For Faulkner, that was "the most tragic condition a man could find himself in—not to know what he is and to know that he will never know." [43]

Like rootlessness, time is a recurrent theme that appeals to conservative critics of Faulkner's work. Much critical attention has been given to the time shifts in *The Sound and the Fury*: Benjy cannot distinguish the present from the past, or one time in the past from another, and it all flows through his head chaotically, evoked by the random sounds and smells of the present. The sequence of the chapters is purposely antichronological, as if the "present" were a contradiction in terms, something to be lived through as quickly as possible, so that it can become the past, and thus worthy of attention. The boy Quentin takes the hands off his Harvard clock, a premonition of the way he will soon arrest the movement of time by suicide. Dilsey, the stable center of the book, is the only one who can manage time: when the old clock strikes five, she automatically knows that it is eight o'clock. Faulkner himself explicitly recognized the significance of time in his work: ". . . to me, no man is himself, he is the sum of his past. There is no such thing really as was because the past is. It is a part of every man, every woman, and every moment." Everything that a person has in his ancestry or background "is all a part of himself and herself at any moment." Thus, "a character in a story at any moment of action is not just himself as he is then, he is all that made him." [44]

The corollary of Faulkner's sense of time, as he and his critics have since recognized, is his often involuted style, with its agonized rhetoric and endless sentences. Faulkner at times deprecated style as not really important, but since he showed many times that he could write simply, it is clear that he was trying to do something intentional and obviously different when he wrote intricately. In one place, after explaining his sense of the past, he talked of the long sentence as an "attempt to get his past and possibly his future into the instant in which he does something." This is as clear an explanation as any. If a man's past, present, and future were all in a sense present, then the temptation stylistically was to try to give the prose sense of what was happening at the same time that the author tried to evoke the past and presage the future.

---

43 William Faulkner, *Light in August* (New York, n.d., c.1932), p. 27; F. L. Gwynn and J. L. Blotner, eds., *Faulkner in the University* (New York, 1959), pp. 72, 118.

44 Gwynn and Blotner, *Faulkner*, p. 84.

The result could often be chaotic and at times quite obviously went out of the author's control.[45]

Combined with these notions about time, Faulkner apparently had a somewhat less exotic interest in the detective story, and this too influenced his style. The normal detective plot dropped clues to the reader throughout the story, but the entire rational explanation of the mystery had to wait until the end of the book. At times, as in *Sanctuary*, the detective devices are relatively transparent, but the book gives useful lessons for later and more difficult works. Many of the characters' motives come out only in bits and pieces. More significantly, Faulkner here uses most effectively his favorite device of having most of the important events happen off-stage. Instead of being present at Temple's rape, the reader is present until it is about to happen; then he finds her bleeding in a car, riding with Popeye. Only at the trial, long after, does he discover that the impotent Popeye has used a corncob as a substitute. In *Absalom, Absalom!* (1936), this detective methodology combines with Faulkner's use of time to produce a book in which the present seems almost entirely absent, and events never really "happen": Shreve and Quentin talk, and the "plot" comes out slowly by second- and third- and fourth-hand stories, many of which may or may not be mythical, or distorted by the variety of the tellers. One discovers the past in the present, as Benjy in *The Sound and the Fury* sometimes perceives phenomena by mirrors. Events occur in the present that are the sum of past experience, sublimated into neurosis. Nothing is clearly visible in the simple light of day because nothing simply "is." [46]

In addition to the need for roots, the role of the past, and the appropriate style, conservatives also naturally venerated Faulkner for his constant emphasis on religion and its importance in the South. Faulkner obviously and intentionally used Christian symbolism in several of his books, most notoriously in *The Sound and the Fury* and *Light in August*. But his most effective use of Christian and religious symbolism came in what may well be his greatest work, "The Bear" section of *Go Down, Moses* (1942). In this story, particularly, Faulkner's imagination has very effectively connected religious symbolism with his other key themes: property, the renewing value of nature, time, and the impact of the machine. Read on one level, "The Bear" is the story of the initiation of Ike McCaslin into just about every-

---

45 Ibid.; Malcolm Cowley, ed., *The Faulkner–Cowley File* (New York, 1966), pp. 14, 17.

46 See, for example, Faulkner's *Paris Review* interview, p. 82, and the article by Jean-Jacques Mayoux, pp. 166–67, both collected in F. J. Hoffman and O. W. Vickery, eds., *William Faulkner: Three Decades of Criticism* (New York, 1963, c.1960).

thing: the hunt for the bear himself, as a way of communing with nature; the initiation into manhood, when Sam Fathers uses the blood of a newly killed deer to baptize Ike (actually in the preceding story in the book, "The Old People"); the hunt as religious retreat. As Ike learns of these themes, he slowly absorbs the values of the conservative consciousness and of religion.

But the critics who stop here miss the point of both this story and Faulkner's religious vision as a whole. For behind the obvious theme of Ike's initiation lies a utopian social "theory," or "vision," that is basically a variation on the doctrines of Christian stewardship, and that very much resembles a modern version of the ideas behind the early Christian communal sects, with their poverty, common property, and deep sense of how the original sin in man can combine with private property and greed to produce a hell on earth. The basic sins in the book are committed when old Carothers McCaslin preempts the communal property of the Indians and the bodies of his slaves. He has a daughter by one of his slaves, and then later commits incest with this daughter to produce a child, a one-quarter-Negro slave, of which he is both father and grandfather. Thus Faulkner inextricably ties together the sins of property—of private property in land, which violates God's preferences for his people; and of private property in people, slavery, which violates God's plan for individual salvation and responsibility. Negro slavery becomes quite literally a symbol of the dark side of human nature, a kind of objective correlative of original sin. Ike McCaslin, after the slaves have been freed, discovers the sins of Carothers in old ledger books, and renounces his claims to the family property in order to imitate Christ by becoming a carpenter. Other stories in which he plays a role indicate that he is far from a true Christ figure in any developed sense, but he is trying to be like Christ, and that is the important thing.

Unfortunately, conservative critics have not been able to leave it at that. Christ symbols to them must mean Christian lessons, must mean the author is a Christian, and presumably must mean we should all become Christians. But Faulkner, if he was a Christian, was one only in the loosest and least doctrinal sense possible. When asked about his personal reading habits, for example, Faulkner consistently replied that he reread the Old Testament regularly, but ignored the New: "To me the New Testament is full of ideas and I don't know much about ideas. The Old Testament is full of people." True conservative that he was, Faulkner could not bear ideology even in the Bible, and turned always to people, to families in history, as they worked out their destinies. Likewise, his stories are full of his venomous dislike for much of the religion that he encountered in Mississippi. McEachern, Joe Christmas's foster-father in *Light in August,* is clearly a religious fanatic whose piety helps lead Joe to the murder of Joanna Burden; and she herself, as Joe insists, is killed because she insisted on praying over him, as if to reintroduce him to a religion he abhorred. Indeed, if Faulkner had a religion, he was what Cleanth Brooks has acutely called a "protestant anticlerical," a man full of some kind of Protestantism yet violently opposed to most institutionalized forms of the church. It is important always to remember that Faulkner did not have theological notions in mind when he wrote, he had people in mind. Thus, when asked about his views of Southern Baptists, he replied: "Well, they're Southern Baptist. I think that is an emotional condition that has nothing to do with God or politics or anything else." [47]

Faulkner certainly understood his Christian symbolism, and he used it not as an ideological means of conversion nor as a demonstration of faith, but because it was a genuine part of his usable past, like the Civil War or Reconstruction. The writer, he said, "must write out of his background," out of "what he knows, and the Christian legend is part of any Christian's background, especially the background of a country boy, a Southern country boy." Most of his life had been passed in a small Mississippi town, and so "I grew up with that. I assimilated that, took that in without even knowing it. It's just there. It has nothing to do with how much of it I might believe or disbelieve—it's just there." When he was asked about the Easter symbolism in *The Sound and the Fury,* he disclaimed anything resembling a "purpose": "I'm sure it was quite instinctive that I picked out Easter, that I wasn't writing any symbolism of the Passion Week at all." The choice of symbols was "a tool that was good for the particular corner I was going to turn in my chicken-house and so I used it." As for his own Christianity, Faulkner was fully as vague and unideological:

> Why, the Christian religion has never harmed me. I hope I never have harmed it. I have the sort of provincial Christian background which one takes for granted without thinking too much about it, probably. That I'm probably—within my own rights I feel that I'm a good Christian—whether it would please anybody else's standard or not I don't know.

It certainly would not please everybody, certainly not a believer in Christian dogma, or one of the dogmatic critics who think Joe Christmas is a Christ symbol, and Benjy an example of the state of Christianity in the modern world. The perfect Christian in Faulkner's work is Dilsey, the emotional, unideological Negro who simply endures—faithful, devoted, and with scarcely an idea in her head worthy of the name.

---

47 Gwynn and Blotner, eds., *Faulkner,* pp. 167, 189; Cleanth Brooks, *William Faulkner: The Yoknapatawpha Country* (New Haven, 1963), p. 62.

Christianity was a part of Faulkner's usable past, and for the modern, often secular, conservative, the usable past was almost all that was left.[48]

In his frequently opaque way, then, Faulkner helped to unify the two traditions of American conservatism between the world wars. On the one hand, he knew religion and myth from birth, and instinctively penetrated the mind of the believer. On the other hand, his understanding did not compel his own personal belief, and he apparently remained skeptical at least throughout the thirties. In addition, in his psychological insight and his social consciousness, he gave added elements to his essentially conservative vision, and thus enabled conservatism to leave a legacy to the years after the Second World War that was not necessarily the prisoner of capitalist greed that liberals and radicals so loved to dwell upon.

---

48 Gwynn and Blotner, eds., *Faulkner,* pp. 86, 68, 203.

V

THE
LOST
PROGRESSIVES

By the middle 1930s, one thing was clear about American intellectual and cultural life: the party was over. The disparate group that could gather at Mabel Dodge's so happily before the First World War had splintered irretrievably, and nothing short of another war could repair the damage. Those bohemians of the twenties who wished to survive found that they had to imitate Ernest Hemingway and adopt a stance of social and revolutionary relevance; if they did not, they risked the derision and rejection Scott Fitzgerald was subjected to when he published *Tender Is the Night;* or that a singularly unrepentant E. E. Cummings found when virtually every New York publisher turned down his next volume of verse. The reigning editors and critics of the thirties, like Mike Gold, Malcolm Cowley, or Granville Hicks, proved quite intolerant of the views of others and found no need to associate with people they disagreed with. Truth had been revealed, and he who was not with them had to be against them. The conservatives, regarded as nostalgic aesthetes or political incompetents, repaid the compliment by opting out of most public forums entirely, as they devoted themselves chiefly to literature and aesthetic theory. The American intellectual community had become fragmented; intellectuals were no longer able to cross-fertilize each other, and bitterness enveloped virtually all social relations among people who could not agree. One result was that hysteria became a kind of reigning tone for much writing in the period.

The positions held by intellectuals became increasingly opposed to one another, and the lines between them solidified in direct proportion to the one-sidedness of the position, and sometimes in direct proportion to its essential triviality. Everyone seemed to have a solution. Communism, overrated as a threat to American democracy, did have a great appeal to many; but its force lessened as the decade wore on, and the Moscow trials, the reports of travelers, the Spanish Civil War, and finally the Hitler–Stalin pact tried the intelligence of all but the blindest communist. Fascism was less fashionable, although occasionally figures like Lawrence Dennis or Seward Collins attempted to make a public case for their views on the subject. The coalition around the New Deal was in no way coherent, supporting as it did the collectivism of a Tugwell, the "Keynesian" theories of an Eccles, the atomism of a Brandeis, and the urban welfare-statism of a Robert Wagner. Just as ex-communist sympathizers like Max Eastman and William Henry Chamberlin were slowly moving to the right, so disillusioned New Dealers like Donald Richberg, Lewis Douglas, and Raymond Moley were finding more and more wrong with Roosevelt, and less and less wrong with basic American capitalism.

Some solutions were purely visionary, like those of Upton Sinclair to End Poverty in California, of Dr. Francis E. Townsend to end old-age insecurity, of Huey Long to make every man a king, or of Howard Scott to make America a technocracy. Still others found an overwhelming issue not essentially economic and spent their time trumpeting their new ideas. Lewis Mumford (*Men Must Act,* 1939; *Faith for the Living,* 1940) called for military intervention against nazism and fascism. Bernard De Voto (*The Literary Fallacy,* 1944) and Archibald MacLeish ("The Irresponsibles," 1940) condemned the irresponsible behavior of bohemian intellectuals, as if somehow free sex and opposition to the First World War were the sources of both Hitler and the depression. Van Wyck Brooks (*The Flowering of New England,* 1936, and its successors) began a campaign for benevolent approval of all things American. This strident nationalism really did not fully emerge until during and after the Second World War, and even then it contributed only marginally to the world's store of wisdom and knowledge.

In one sense, this fragmentation was misleading: intellectuals did not really disagree about everything. Even those who cordially loathed each other could endorse certain attitudes or plans as long as they were not aware that some enemy had also approved. One book, which helped give a name to the period, brought together one area of common agreement into a reasonably coherent and accepted whole. Stuart Chase's *A New Deal* (1932), argued that America had already evolved an economy of abundance, and that its main problem was its inability to distribute its production. Current American capitalism was operating not for the public good but for private profit, and he pointed specifically at the monopolies, the interest rates, the deceit, the artificial stimulation of demand through advertising, the stock-rigging, to show the unproductiveness of the great majority of American economic activity. The great trouble with previous writers, he asserted, was that they had never asked what was the purpose of an economic system. He could tell them that it was "to provide a means, without excessive waste and loss, whereby those who live under it may eat." Its chief function was "to provide food, shelter, clothing and comforts in as dependable and adequate quantities as natural resources and the state of the technical arts permit. . . ." The system known as laissez-faire, based as it was on a rural economy of scarcity, was irrelevant to modern industrial economy, and the remnants of its ideology were grains of sand in the wheels of the economy. Large parts of America were already collectivized: the tariff, unemployment insurance, the government payroll, the regulation of the currency, co-ops, trade unions. Chase insisted he was only demanding what was inevitable anyway, since "modern industrialism, because of its delicate specialization and interdependence, increasingly demands the collectivism of social control to keep its several parts from jamming." Governments must inevitably meet these demands, whether consciously or unconsciously, "by continually widening the collective sector through direct ownership, operation and regulation of economic functions." [1]

Chase was far less dogmatic than many other intellectuals of the period, and he seemed always willing to adapt his methods to the given conditions of his time. He suggested, for example, that an easy way to take over an industry would be to buy out the common stock of a company at a fair price and then run it much as it had been run before. The preferred stock would still pay its dependable dividends, managers would run the place on salary, and the profits could be put, say, to erecting new mass housing. Such a procedure would eliminate the need for fraudulent business arrangements, excessively high prices, and perhaps most important, stock speculation. Taken at their face

---

1 Stuart Chase, *A New Deal* (New York, 1932), pp. 22–23, 59.

value, many of Chase's proposals seemed mild indeed. He wanted, as general public policy, such measures as a managed currency to end inflationary cycles, higher income and inheritance taxes for the rich, higher wages, an end to tariffs, control of foreign investment, drastic curbs on speculation, more planning and clearer allocation of national priorities, a shorter work week, unemployment insurance, and public works. In short, what Chase wanted was a planned and collectivized economy, thoroughly worked out by experts for the greatest economic rewards possible to the largest number of people. He saw his path as a middle way between fascism on the right and communism on the left.[2]

Much of Chase's plan became law in some form during the New Deal, and all of it excited widespread debate. Conservatives, if they considered it, doubtless disliked the economic bias, the assumption that mere bounty was the end of life, and the rigid planning involved. Radicals doubtless distrusted the lack of dogma, the adaptability of the plan to capitalism, and the emphasis on experts. By the late thirties, however, most intellectuals were friendly to many parts of Chase's scheme. But one heterogeneous group was not friendly at all. Poets like Robert Frost and E. E. Cummings retained their individualism and seemed to prefer at least "emotional" laissez-faire. Writers like John Chamberlain, John Dos Passos, and William Henry Chamberlin, were well on the way to being the defenders of economic laissez-faire that they became after the Second World War. Ex-New Dealers like Raymond Moley and Donald Richberg were increasingly disillusioned with Roosevelt's planning schemes. Social thinkers like Albert Jay Nock, Oswald Garrison Villard, and Francis Neilson saw their old liberal and radical ideals threatened by the garrison state, and dug in their heels against any further expansion of state action.

In its political form, this group stood at least tacitly for the old economic liberalism of William Graham Sumner. In its philosophical form, it apparently also accepted the somewhat incompatible pragmatism of fifty years before, seriously questioning whether these plans would work, and if they did work, whether the results would be worth the effort. At times, the members of this group could endorse certain policies of the New Deal, collective social thought, or collective art. But for all their very real differences, both in age and in intellectual outlook, they seem to form a coherent whole that said "no" to many of the basic tendencies of their times. In return they were often condemned, misunderstood, or ignored. These men were the lost progressives. If they were old enough, they were not represented in Mabel Dodge's salon, untouched as they usually were by the newer social

---

2 Ibid., pp. 190–92, 213.

science, Freud or Marx. If they were younger men, coming to intellectual maturity in the twenties and thirties, they found themselves born
out of their time. Like Dos Passos, Chamberlin, and Villard, they
might well have been familiar with Marx, yet they became "premature"
in their disillusionment. They became trust-busters in an age of con-
solidation, relativists when the majority was absolutist, pragmatists
when everyone else was a true believer, or elitist when the cant of the
day was democratic egalitarianism. Such was the atomism of the day
that these men normally did not know each other, did not even agree
with each other, and would have marveled at even being in the same
chapter with each other.

II

Of the elder generation, Albert Jay Nock was perhaps the
ablest. In his last years, Nock looked to many like nothing more than
a benighted conservative, but in fact his roots and biases were genuinely
in the old Jeffersonian and mugwump traditions. A former Episco-
palian minister and a follower of Herbert Spencer and Henry George,
he had been a free-lance writer for the *American Magazine* in the days
when Lincoln Steffens, Ida Tarbell, and Brand Whitlock were contributors. Nock himself contributed quite a few articles, particularly
on single-tax subjects. But the war had soured him on the subjects of
democracy and reform, and in his postwar journal, *The Freeman,* he
frequently expressed his contempt for all politics and politicians, and
concentrated instead on cultural subjects. He left the magazine in
order to write a distinguished book on Jefferson, and followed it with
a scholarly edition of the works of Rabelais. All the while, he continued to comment sarcastically on the follies of Coolidge, Hoover,
and Roosevelt. He also displayed his growing concern for American
culture with a book on its educational theory that said most Americans
were capable of only technical training, and that a truly liberal education was possible only for a few. In this way, he slowly cut himself
off from the progressive egalitarianism of his prewar days and established ties to American conservatism rather different from those being
established by the repentant collectivists.[3]

Irving Babbitt had once written that the duty of an educated man
was to rid his mind of the cant of his time and discover what was
eternally true. For Babbitt the cant of his time was philanthropy; for
Nock, it was collectivism and materialism, and with them democracy
and anything else that smacked of pandering to the masses. Nock
expressed his agony over the state of culture in a collectivist age by

---

3 Robert M. Crunden, *The Mind and Art of Albert Jay Nock* (Chicago, 1964).

reasserting the elitist position that most men were incapable of culture, and that educated men must keep learning and art alive to enable them to rebuild after the deluge. While genuine conservatives like Abraham Flexner tended to be mild in their comments about the incapacities of average men, and to stress the reform of institutions to further the education of the elect and the training of the masses, Nock was far more critical, savage and despairing. For him, the survival of the fittest and the free play of the market economy had applications in the study of human nature that were really most "unconservative" in any historical sense. The mass man to Nock "is one who has neither the force of intellect to apprehend the principles issuing in what we know as the humane life, nor the force of character to adhere to those principles steadily and strictly as laws of conduct. . . ." The "Remnant," on the other hand, "are those who by force of intellect are able to apprehend these principles, and by force of character are able, at least measurably, to cleave to them; the masses are those who are unable to do either." From where he sat Nock could see only the professional prophet hawking his wares, playing on the whims of the masses. That was all very well, if useless, but it did hold a real danger: the message tended to be "so heavily adulterated with trivialities" that "its effect on the masses is merely to harden them in their sins." The Remnant, meanwhile, turn away in contempt "and will have nothing to do with him or his message." The man of culture, Nock insisted, need only keep his message pure and make it public; the Remnant would find him, hear it, and remember when a new day dawned.[4]

Like most followers of Henry George, Nock found himself in opposition both to the New Deal and to the capitalists who hated it. Herbert Hoover, the most eminent conservative in public life until Robert Taft entered the Senate, Nock regarded as a man almost totally devoid of any vestige of civilization, and he was not sorry to see him leave office. He expected some improvement from Roosevelt, but was never optimistic, and he soon classed Roosevelt also as a barbarian, different from the philistine Hoover only by virtue of his higher birth and gentler upbringing. Nock had opposed the capitalist Right because of its greed, its economic goals, its willingness to use government subsidies like the tariff even while chanting devoutly about laissez-faire, its total ignorance of the purpose of life. But the New Deal, as he saw it, offered little improvement. Nock himself seldom had any money, and he did not find poverty a disgrace. He remained unmoved by Roosevelt's economic nostrums, and instead condemned the whole operation as a vote-getting boondoggle. Roosevelt was pandering to

---

4 Albert Jay Nock, *Free Speech and Plain Language* (New York, 1937), pp. 248–65, esp. pp. 251, 256.

the masses, and meanwhile erecting a collectivist society that would make life all but impossible for the Remnant. "What ought to be understood, and is not understood, is that Rooseveltism, Hitlerism, Stalinism, are all only local variants of the common doctrine that man has no natural rights but only such as are created for him by the State. . . ." Yet when he heard of the formation of the American Liberty League, he could only snort: "I have heard of several people as being keen about it, not one of whom I believe to have an honest hair in his head." In short, the progressive single-taxer was still smiting the trusts, still believing in eternal principles, still believing in Jeffersonian self-reliance, still convinced that a beautiful life was possible if only corrupt businessmen and their kept politicians could be removed. But now the tone was shrill, the mood black, and the debacle just ahead. Neither the optimism nor the faith in human nature he had possessed in 1914 remained. He was in a kind of intellectual exile.[5]

III

Other old Progressives managed to survive with more of their old optimism and enthusiasm for social change. They frequently disliked the events of the modern world as much as Nock did, but they did not really despair. The most obvious example of this variety of lingering progressivism was the later career of Frank Lloyd Wright. Wright shared with Nock a devout Jeffersonianism: he was intellectually a rural yeoman, distrustful of the city and its values, enraptured by nature, an individualist seeking only freedom from the state. Like Nock too, he found considerable support for his views in the works of Henry George. George shared his concern for the social value of land, his willingness to formulate radical schemes requiring the government to protect both society and the individual without aggrandizing itself, and his complete inability to find any political or economic means capable of realizing these utopian plans. Instead of confronting the practical problems involved, Wright all too often continued the old radical habit of making his demands for reform merely rhetorical and hortatory. Wright had always had the bearing and tone of a prophet, but by the 1930s he seemed at times almost incapable of writing rational prose. His books became littered with capital letters, exclamation marks, and visions, as if somehow or other the added emphasis would bring insight without the intervention of mere logic.

Like many Progressives, Wright had long cherished a vision of the city beautiful—a city that had no obvious connection with the mod-

---

5 Crunden, *Nock*, pp. 149–57; Albert Jay Nock, *The Memoirs of a Superfluous Man* (New York, 1943), passim.

ern, hectic, densely populated cities which architects like Gropius, Le Corbusier, and Mies were attempting to make habitable. Long before, Wright had had a pronounced effect on the Bauhaus school of architecture, but he never liked the way their ideas and building methods had developed, and throughout the twenties he had studiously ignored them. Somewhat against his will, he did see some of their work in the early thirties, and his buildings later in the decade indicate that he definitely absorbed some of their insights—regardless of how vehemently he denied it. But spiritually, for all the similarities between them, Wright was never even a guest of the Bauhaus, for he hated its emphasis on group collaboration, its dislike of architectural individualism, its insistence on city architecture, its lack of any sense of the organic, and its willingness to coop people up in huge factories and tall apartments. Like an old populist, Wright ranted against the cash-nexus society, against interest on money, against the materialism of gadgetry, and against speculation in land—in short against the basically inhuman way in which American business had constructed the American environment for living. Americans, he said, had given up their "native pastimes with streams, woods, fields, and animals" in trade for "the taint of carbon monoxide rising to a rented aggregate of cells upended on hard pavements." They had become slaves to the herd instinct, and their sex lives, their business relations, their dependence on machines, their waste of resources, and their high rent all were evidence of their loss of innocence. While the Europeans were trying to make the inevitable as decent as possible, Wright quite plainly wanted to destroy the whole mess and start over. He found emotional safety in a "New Principle" of "natural horizontality," which he saw as the obvious cure for the vertical habits of city living. "Natural horizontality—the line of human Freedom on Earth—is going or gone, and the Citizen condemns himself to unnatural pig-piling—aspires to a sterile verticality. He is upended and suspended by his own excess. He is calling it Success." [6]

Yet for all his rejection of the urban environment, or perhaps because of it, Wright enjoyed a startling renaissance that began in the middle 1930s and lasted until his death. His much-publicized marital misadventures were over, he was legally tied to a woman whom he deeply loved, and his earlier problems combined with his sartorial extravagances to make a kind of folk hero out of him. Never averse to idolization, he suddenly gave the world legitimate reasons to revere

6 Frank Lloyd Wright, *When Democracy Builds* (Chicago, 1945), pp. 1–3; see also the *Autobiography*; N. K. Smith, *Frank Lloyd Wright* (Englewood Cliffs, 1966); Peter Blake, *Frank Lloyd Wright* (Baltimore, 1965), a partial reprint of *The Master Builders* (New York, 1960); and Edgar Kaufmann and Ben Raeburn, eds., *Frank Lloyd Wright: Writings and Buildings* (Cleveland, 1960), pp. 255–61.

him and his work, and each new triumph in turn seemed to symbolize his differences from other contemporary architects and trends, and to reemphasize his status as the chief lost progressive of the day. The renaissance of Wright's reputation began in 1936 with the considerable publicity produced by the completion of the famous Edgar J. Kaufmann House at Bear Run, Pennsylvania. The house was a beautiful example of Wright's organic principles: it seemed to grow out of the rocky ledge and cast a kind of blessing over the flowing water that ran beneath a part of it. Like most Wright buildings, it used many modern construction devices and in no sense demanded "old-fashioned" or "quaint" building methods. Yet the house managed to reject all the dogmas of the 1930s. It was rural, not urban, built for a rich man for a weekend retreat and not for the poor worker; it was organic, possible only in one location, instead of mass-produceable for any area; it enhanced the landscape and blended with it, instead of merely perching where it happened to land. Ideologically, it belonged more to the world of Walden Pond than to depression America.

His new status also brought Wright industrial commissions, and to some observers these new buildings showed that Wright was willing to use Bauhaus methods when they suited his purposes. Yes and no. Wright loved the naked concrete that Le Corbusier used so often, and the *pilotis* [a modern variety of pillar] so frequent in contemporary European designs, but the building materials concealed the two vastly different kinds of cultural influence. No building demonstrated this better than the Johnson Wax Company Administrative Offices, built at Racine, Wisconsin, chiefly between 1936 and 1939. In many ways, this building seems to belong in the International Style, with its long expanses of undecorated stone, the sheathing of glass for the tower, and its frankly industrial appearance. In fact it does not. As Norris Smith has pointed out, the building is more like a monastery than a factory: it turns its back to the street and the outside world, and has the air more of a retreat than of an open place of industry. The office tower is more a bell tower, calling the faithful to pray by working, than a harsh statement of modern capitalism. What Smith does not point out makes his case even better: Wright's use of the cantilever method, here as in the Kaufmann house, has an intensely personal meaning for him. Wright's familial vision, ever since his days as a young father, had always pictured the family as centered about the private home, and for him the architectural counterpart of family unity was the fireplace. The central core of each of his homes, the fireplace, was the firm spine that unified the basic living area of the family, brought its members together, and warmed them. It was the perfect expression in stone of the organic concept; it was built out of the material of the land, and it grew upwards like a tree, holding the branches together and nourishing them as if they were family members. When Wright came to build tall office buildings, he modified his basic design without giving up his emotional attachment to the hearth; instead of the warming and unifying tree trunk/fireplace, he substituted a simple principle of cantilever construction, using a central spine that supported each floor, ignoring the older method of using columns at the outside areas of stress to support the weight. As the tree trunk nourished and supported the branches and the fireplace drew together and united the family, so this central spine held the air-conditioning and heating equipment, the plumbing facilities and electrical lines, and quite literally was the nerve center of the factory. Here was Wright's answer to the urban glut: a decentralized factory for a small business, built in a city of reasonable size, and looking like an overgrown family home rather than an anonymous factory. It only completes the picture to learn that the Johnson company was a small-town, family-run affair, antiunion in its labor policies and paternalistic in its social views.[7]

Wright's next act of symbolic rebellion against his time was in his master plan for city planning, widely publicized at the time as "Broadacre City." Wright the city planner was in his most rhetorical and illogical guise, and many of his writings on the subject made little logical sense. He obviously wished to decentralize the hated city, to make America into one huge suburb, with over/underpasses to speed traffic, shopping centers, and hordes of small businessmen and farmers composing the great majority of the people. Having defined freedom and individuality as somehow synonymous with horizontality, he came up dextrously with the rule of thumb that each man needed an acre of land to live on if he were to attain his individuality and full organic growth. He always insisted that his plan could work for rich and poor alike, and did in fact spend a great deal of time developing mass-produceable "Usonian" houses that could cheaply house all his stalwart yeoman democrats. Like most Edenic utopias, however Broadacre City was economically ridiculous and politically laughable. No plan that failed to take into account the contemporary state of land settlement, private property rights, and established political and legal processes was worth the reading, let alone the attention, Wright's plans received. Intellectually, however, the plan was an excellent means of seeing once again how Wright expressed his progressive outlook.[8] Each

---

7 See especially Smith, *Wright,* pp. 136 ff., and Blake, *Wright,* pp. 87–90.

8 On Broadacre City see, *inter alia,* Smith, *Wright,* pp. 148 ff.; Blake, *Wright,* pp. 111–14; and Wright's *The Disappearing City* (New York, 1932), *The Living City* (New York, 1958), and *When Democracy Builds* (Chicago, 1945). The key articles were in *The Architectural Record* (April 1935), *Architectural Forum,* (January

man on his grassy acre, beholden to no one, growing up under the best of influences far from the immoral city: Jefferson at Monticello condemning the immorality of the French! Now that many of America's greatest cultural wastelands are its more affluent suburbs, complete with the three cars of each family polluting the air over the family acres, Americans can perhaps judge more clearly the value of Wright's contributions to city planning.

IV

A third old progressive served as a kind of moderator between the frank intransigence of Nock and Wright, and the far greater flexibility of the younger progressives. Carl Becker had been active in a small way in progressive intellectual life, although he did not achieve his position of real eminence in the historical profession until after the First World War. As a graduate student at Wisconsin and Columbia, he had come under the influence of the "New History" of men like Frederick Jackson Turner and James Harvey Robinson, who, with their colleagues, urged students to write history in such a way as to make it relevant for modern needs. No longer, they insisted, should historians emulate Leopold von Ranke and attempt to line up fact after fact in the manner of science, nor should they waste their time trying to discover biological or physical laws in history. Instead, if the present concerns were economics and reform, historians should rediscover their past by emphasizing the role of economics and reform in the history of their country; if peace were uppermost in their minds, they should examine past wars to see if a study of what caused them could help keep the country out of war in the future. Temperamentally, Becker was too detached and disillusioned to pattern his career after the more outspoken of the new historians like Charles A. Beard and Harry Elmer Barnes. He chose instead to follow after his own fashion in the footsteps of Turner, not publishing much, virtually never agitating for anything, but writing thoughtful essays that frequently posed more questions than they solved. Becker had lost faith in the Methodism of his early youth, and the pragmatists had opened up all sorts of problems about the nature of the world and the possibility of God's existence. But while the progressives even at their most skeptical had never directly denied God, Becker soon found that he had to. For him, God, if he really existed, must be extremely confused and disorganized, since that was the way the world looked to Becker. He thus took the social and economic and present-day concerns of

---

1938), and in the book, with Baker Brownell, *Architecture and Modern Life* (New York, 1937).

the new history, united them to his great skepticism about God and the existence of progress and order in the world, and began to probe for answers that his whole generation needed. Nock withdrew from society and condemned it; Wright preached at it; Becker suffered with it and tried carefully to help it, and himself, out of the painful dilemmas of the time.[9]

His problem was severe: how to act like a liberal, pragmatic progressive, in an illiberal, totalitarian world? The whole ethos of progressivism had been permeated by the assumption that almost all men were basically of goodwill, and that improved environmental circumstances would nourish a generation able to create a better world. But in the 1930s, with the rise of Stalin, Hitler, and Mussolini, the assumptions of the Progressives proved so irrelevant as to appear dangerous even to men like Becker who valued them as much as life itself. Philosophically, the dilemma was just as serious, for it seemed to require a man to believe in two contradictory views. On the one hand, people like Becker or John Dewey insisted that absolutes were bad, and that truth was relative to current needs and social problems. Yet both these men, for all their insistence on relativism, expressed in their writings a devout belief in certain absolutes, rationality for one. Dewey the philosopher and Becker the historian were always rationally explaining how things are to their readers, praising the virtues of liberal democracy, and feeling offended and even appalled by the tactics of the fascists and communists. Yet, considered dispassionately, if Stalin were getting "good" results, however defined, why should not a pragmatist support him? The answer, at least in part, was that the irrational use of force and power was really intrinsically evil, that it ultimately kept men from rationally examining problems and alternatives and thus from solving social problems as well as developing their own minds. But to state the answer this way is to return to the dilemma: if absolutes do not exist, how can a pragmatist argue that regardless of result, irrational and brutal behavior cannot be permitted? Becker and Dewey obviously thought, even when they did not say it, that freedom, enterprise, social problem-solving, and reason were all intrinsically good, and they acted as though their faith were justified even when the results appeared to turn out badly.

Becker expressed his ideas on these problems in connection with historical writing as early as 1910. In the essay "Detachment and the Writing of History," he took up in a deceptively simple way the question, What is a historical fact? The scientists said that a man need

---

9 My chief secondary sources throughout this section are Burleigh T. Wilkins, *Carl Becker* (Cambridge, 1961); and Cushing Strout, *The Pragmatic Revolt in American History* (Ithaca, 1966, c.1958).

only gather the facts, put them together, and the result would be "truth," or "scientific history." For Becker, the problem was not that simple. He chose the example of the stabbing of Caesar in Rome. That was a fact that everyone attested to, it had been accepted by experts everywhere, and was presumably unshakable. But really, he said, it was not a simple fact at all. It was a statement that was made up of a whole collection of facts: the senators standing around, the words people said, the scuffling, the twenty-three dagger strokes—all these, he said, were included within the simple statement that Caesar was stabbed in the senate. In addition, no one could write about the act except in the most misleading way unless he included the information that Antony, Octavius, and Lepidus were the people who replaced Caesar as the government—and what role if any did they play in that presumably simple act of murder? "While we speak of historical facts as if they were pebbles to be gathered in a cup, there is in truth no unit fact in history," he argued. "The historical reality is continuous, and infinitely complex; and the cold hard facts into which it is said to be analyzed are not concrete portions of reality, but only aspects of it." He concluded that "the reality of history has forever disappeared, and the 'facts' of history, whatever they once were, are only mental images or pictures which the historian makes in order to comprehend it." He then went on to discuss certain problems relating to evidence, the preconceptions of historians, and similar technical problems, but the main point was obvious: historical truth was as slippery a concept as absolute truth, and neither was really a usable tool, or a worthwhile goal for the historian. The historian should establish his present needs and then search the past for help in solving his problems.[10]

Becker once more took up this line of reasoning in the early 1930s, in one of the most famous essays written about the writing of history, "Everyman His Own Historian." The essay finished the job of painting old liberals and Progressives like himself into a corner from which there seemed to be no escape. Here is the figure of Mr. Everyman, who stands both for the historian and the old progressive, as he goes about his affairs. Mr. Everyman's world is like everyone else's, full of memories, current concerns, irritations, and all the things he has to do. Like most people, he tends to think about and remember only those things which have some connection or relevance to what has to be done when he gets up in the morning. This morning he has a problem, a coal bill which he has to pay. He immediately remembers his foresight during the summer, when he ordered the coal. He remembers the process of

---

10 Phil L. Snyder, ed., *Detachment and the Writing of History* (Ithaca, 1958), pp. 3–28.

delivering it, and he knows he has a lot of coal in his cellar and that some of it is keeping him warm. So, he goes down to the man who sent him the coal, when he finally finds out who it was, and pays his bill. Then he stops thinking about coal, money, last summer, and the current winter and goes on to another problem.

In this little story, Becker explained, he had attempted to reduce history to its basic parts, "first by defining it as the memory of things said and done, second by showing concretely how the memory of things said and done is essential to the performance of the simplest acts of daily life." But the affair has certain important implications. Mr. Everyman was paying his coal bill, but "in the realm of consciousness he has been doing that fundamental thing which enables man alone to have, properly speaking, a history": Mr. Everyman "has been re-enforcing and enriching his immediate perceptions to the end that he may live in a world of semblance more spacious and satisfying than is to be found within the narrow confines of the fleeting present moment." In other words, for Carl Becker the "present" does not really exist; it is what he called the "specious present." No one has a real present because time keeps flowing, and no event that is happening has any meaning without its past, without the cause of it, men's memories, and men's understanding of the causes and memories of other events they have experienced. Nothing is really real, and everything is deceptive.

The liberal dilemma reappears once more. For Mr. Everyman, history and life are the same thing. History is the tool a man uses to pay his coal bill; he remembers what he did, what followed, and what he must do. This, Becker says, is the function of history: people have problems, and they search the past for answers to these problems, for guides in how to live. Obviously, then, each historian, and each generation, will have different problems and will write different histories. History is, he writes, "an imaginative creation, a personal possession which each one of us" makes "out of his individual experience, adapts to his practical or emotional needs, and adorns as well as may be to suit his aesthetic tastes." The historian is thus "of that ancient and honorable company of wise men of the tribe," to whom "has been entrusted the keeping of the useful myths." The historian's function is "not to create, but to preserve and perpetuate the social tradition; to harmonize, as well as ignorance and prejudice permit, the actual and remembered series of events"; and "to enlarge and enrich the specious present common to us all," so that society "may judge of what it is doing in the light of what it has done and what it hopes to do." [11] Becker's dilemma should be obvious: if the work of a historian

---

was really only an expression of the climate of opinion around him, then there was absolutely no limit on what he could legitimately say. Historians in nazi Germany could rewrite European history to find the Jews everywhere at fault and, so long as the raw material was not altered, find comfort if they wished in Becker's discussion of Mr. Everyman. On the other hand, Becker's own preference for Jeffersonian freedoms could be no bastion against the onslaught of totalitarianism. If freedom were an absolute value, it contradicted all of Becker's relativism; if it were not an absolute value, its disappearance was of small importance to a generation that found security or military power more to its liking. In the end, Becker and his fellow Progressive relativists, or pragmatists, had to conclude that some values were absolute; that freedom to choose and think and worship could not be included in the mere flux of time; and that however much man might be willing to rewrite history to suit his times, he would not be able to write at all under a totalitarian regime. By the Second World War, the Progressive pragmatists, admittedly or not, had adopted these absolutes at least.[12]

V

The agonizing dilemmas that Becker and his fellow pragmatists faced in the thirties had parallels in the most vigorous movement within the progressive tradition itself during the thirties. Although conservatives like Chief Justice William Howard Taft had been the majority voice on the Supreme Court during the twenties, they had not been particularly popular in the better graduate schools, and by the thirties the influence they represented had given way most conspicuously to the supporters of ideas that resembled those of Taft's opponent in the Court, Oliver Wendell Holmes. At Harvard, Holmes's fellow progressive reformer Roscoe Pound was the most conspicuous legal educator in the field; at Yale and Columbia, the related group of legal thinkers, known under the loose term "legal realists," were strongly in command. The natural result of these influences was a stream of lawyers into aging law firms and, particularly, into the state and federal governments, who did not find ideas like those held by Taft of much interest or relevance to the problems they faced. Deeply influenced by the naturalistic philosophy of John Dewey and the pragmatic methods of William James, these legal realists soon managed to cast doubt on the whole tradition of abstract legal thought. The formal, deductive nature of the old law, with its insistence that some-

---

12 In addition to Wilkins and Strout, cited in note 9, see also Becker's *Modern Democracy* (New Haven, 1941); *New Liberties for Old* (New Haven, 1941); and *Freedom and Responsibility in the American Way of Life* (New York, 1945).

how its categories were binding for all cases that fit them, its faith in written precedents, its belief in the abstract judge unsullied by personal prejudice, fell into disrepute as the legal realists became the most vigorous thinkers in the field. They discovered "sociological jurisprudence," and insisted that the social effects of a given legal habit were relevant; they demanded large quantities of raw, factual data, so they could reach decisions inductively; they thought lawyers and judges needed training in allied social sciences like psychology, economics, and sociology; and they filled the air with new terms and standards of value: "rule skepticism," "fact skepticism," relativism, behaviorism—all anathema to their elders.[13]

By the middle thirties, Yale was the unquestioned hotbed of the movement, particularly in the work of Walton H. Hamilton and Harold Lasswell. As far as the public was concerned, the chief propagandists for the movement and its leading symbol was a new and singularly unconventional Yale professor, Thurman Arnold. Arnold was the son of a Wyoming rancher and lawyer who had gone east to school, taking a B.A. from Princeton and an LL.B. from Harvard. For a while, he was active in local politics in Laramie, as well as in business organizations, and his manner resembled far more that of a Lion or chamber of commerce man than it did a legal scholar. But Roscoe Pound never forgot his fascinating student and recommended Arnold for a post at the University of West Virginia, and after a brief time there, Arnold was soon active both in the New Deal in Washington and on the faculty at Yale. As a New Dealer, he was the antithesis of the communitarian, planning, managerial bureaucrat of the type personified by Rexford Tugwell, with his visions of a static society at economic maturity, highly centralized in Washington and benevolently caring for the outcasts of capitalistic society. Like Thomas G. Corcoran and Benjamin V. Cohen, Arnold represented the progressive side of the New Deal, the booster, pragmatist, capitalist, and little-man side whose most conspicuous elder statesman in the law was Justice Brandeis.

At Yale, this side of Arnold's personality expressed itself in his fascinating if garrulous and often irrelevant lectures, which he gave at the side of his dog, who usually accompanied him to class. In Washington, where he moved in 1938 to become assistant attorney general, it expressed itself in his general cheerfulness about capitalism in an administration generally pessimistic, in his Wilsonian belief in the small businessman, and in his willingness to offend labor as well as capital when he thought the good of the country depended on it. One

---

13 Wilfrid E. Rumble, Jr., *American Legal Realism* (Ithaca, 1968), passim; see the footnotes for a bibliographical guide to the movement, esp. pp. 1–3.

newsman confronted Arnold, and said that he looked "like a small-town storekeeper" and talked "like a native Rabelais." His friend, Justice Robert H. Jackson, remarked that "Thurman is a cross between Voltaire and a cowboy, with the cowboy predominating." Arnold clinched his reputation among New Dealers, perhaps, when he sat conspicuously in his Washington office and declared that Herbert Hoover was probably right when he said that the ordinary American would soon have two chickens in his dinner pot and two cars in his garage. Franklin D. Roosevelt was notorious for appointing men of wildly varying ideologies and mixing up their ideas in a peculiar brew of his own, but even in this environment, Thurman Arnold looked a bit odd.[14]

Arnold looked odd at least in part because he was a genuine Progressive and pragmatist in an administration that made bows toward this tradition, but whose chief economic and political leaders were on the whole communitarian and planning oriented. At first, in his books, Arnold seemed to resemble these planners, for by and large they agreed with him when he talked about the psychology of big business and the courts. In his first and best book, *The Symbols of Government* (1935), Arnold made a sardonic and Veblenesque anatomy of the mental sacred cows revered by the majority of his fellow Americans. Americans would not think of looking to ancient medical texts when they wanted to cure a disease, he noted, yet they insisted on the rule of precedents when they wanted a cure for a legal grievance. Obviously influenced by his colleague Lasswell, as well as by John Dewey, even though he mentioned neither, Arnold saw American legal thinking as a quest for certainty motivated more by psychological insecurity than by an objective desire for justice. The result was a kind of paralysis, since these principles, "once formulated into a logical system, and accepted, seem to paralyze action in the actual arena of human affairs." Law schools, monastic institutions that they are, seemed determined to pursue learning only when they were sure that both the process and the result would be irrelevant for social application. Arnold thought the results absurd. He insisted that general principles were unnecessary for the creation of justice and unobtainable for the forseeable future anyway. In Arnold's view, the legal scholar should examine inductively each case on its own merits, determine the most beneficent results obtainable by any decision, and then decide accordingly. This approach, in other words, was "a formulated theory against all formulated theories." Men insisted on their theories and principles

---

14 "Thurman Arnold," *Current Biography,* 1940, pp. 26–28; Joseph Alsop and Robert Kintner, "Trust Buster: The Folklore of Thurman Arnold," *Saturday Evening Post* 212, no. 7 (August 12, 1939): 5–7, 30–34; William B. Huie, "Thurman Arnold: Prophet of Prosperity," *American Mercury* 54 no. 222 (June 1942): 679–87.

because they received a religious comfort from the sense of order they created; Arnold suggested that they forge ahead with confidence and let the cosmos take care of itself.[15]

Arnold then wrote the book that gained him a rather spurious fame as a reform thinker. *The Folklore of Capitalism* (1937) gave its author the opportunity to enjoy mocking the way the business world resembled the legal and political worlds in its reverent attitude toward dead economists, in its puritanical notions of salvation through labor, and in its intellectually ridiculous devotion to both laissez-faire and the tariff. But while the book was popular, it was also something of an intellectual disaster, for it showed that Arnold was really in the same dilemma as Carl Becker. The pragmatist emphasizing results and facts, and rejecting theories and principles, could have some amusement showing how business defeated itself by its silly pieties, how Americans regularly voted against their own interests, and how judges regularly ruled against justice in a particular case to reenforce some abstract concept of justice they believed in. This process, however, did not produce anything of value unless the pragmatist in question presupposed certain values. Becker ultimately found that generalities like "democracy," "reason," and "liberty" still glittered absolutely, and Arnold found himself forced to postulate similar absolutes even if he disliked admitting it. Business was thoroughly corrupted by its orgy of reorganizations, stock-watering, and monopoly patenting, but many New Dealers, as Arnold soon came to realize, also had their own folklore that inhibited constructive reform. The disaster of the NRA had not taught many of them anything about the problems of planning, and the propaganda for labor and against business had created prejudices that only decades could mitigate. Fortunately, Arnold came to Washington and found himself in one of the few places where his unspoken absolutes could work themselves out to the benefit of the whole country; in the Sherman and Clayton Antitrust Acts of the earlier reformers, he found progressive laws of an earlier time his most useful tools.

Arnold's openness to change, his basic fairness and intelligence, naturally brought him condemnation when he began prodding the sacred cows of the land to increased milk production. One of his most publicized exploits was to take on the Chicago milk monopolies, using the force of the courts to bring down substantially the retail price of milk. When he did so he offended farmer, laborer and manufacturer alike. Arnold was soon everywhere, with his greatly enlarged corps of lawyers, using the Sherman Act to break down monopoly pricing and patenting arrangements in fields as diverse as aluminum, oil, and

---

15 Thurman W. Arnold, *The Symbols of Government* (New Haven, 1935), quotations from pp. 5, 30.

housing. As his plans matured, Arnold plainly showed that he was an old progressive, friendly to business and capitalism and to the little man and his individual initiative, opposed to any bottleneck that would prevent this man both as capitalist and as consumer from participating in the economy of abundance. Here, in terms of consumer reward and individual self-fulfillment, were Arnold's absolutes that fueled his attack on the absolutes, or "folklore," of others. There is, he said, "only one sensible test which we can apply to the privilege of organization, and that is this: Does it increase the efficiency of production or distribution and pass the savings on to customers?" The unlovely alternative to this bourgeois capitalism was the cartelization of the economy, and indeed, the ghost of the Weimar Republic and the rise of nazism haunt many of Arnold's writings. By 1941, he even allowed himself to use the word "ideals" without a note of sardonic condescension: "In the antitrust laws is found the only expression of our competitive ideals which we now have. Just as the Supreme Court represents the ideal of the rule of law, so do the institutions which center around the antitrust laws represent the ideal of a society of independent competing business men and farmers," he argued. This is what Americans mean by "Democracy," and "abandonment of the competitive ideal in favor of a centralized economic structure seems to us to be the abandonment of Democracy." He deeply believed that "if we do not center the development of tomorrow around the ideal expressed in the Sherman Act, ineffective though that ideal may have been in the past as a practical agency, the last obstacle to complete industrial autocracy will have disappeared." [16] The vast majority of those who voted for Theodore Roosevelt and Woodrow Wilson would have felt right at home.

VI

Arnold was, however, a distinctly modern type of "lost progressive." His skepticism and cynicism marked him off from a genuine progressivism, however much he found it useful to use progressive ideas in the New Deal context. But not all of the younger generation of lost progressives were so modern in their use of the older categories. One of these men, Arnold's colleague at Yale, Ralph Henry Gabriel, made the greatest contribution to the summing up of his school of thought within the American intellectual heritage and applied it to current events in a manner similar to that of Carl Becker.

16 Thurman Arnold, *The Bottlenecks of Business* (New York, 1940), p. 125; "Antitrust Law Enforcement, Past and Future," American Council on Public Affairs Pamphlet (Washington, 1941), pp. 8–9. See also Gene M. Gressley, "Thurman Arnold, Antitrust, and the New Deal," *Business History Review* 37, Summer 1964.

Gabriel's synthesis of intellectual history, *The Course of American Democratic Thought* (1940) was first of all an unblushing defense of the notion that ideas and ideals had definite consequences, and that they had been essential to the American experience. Gabriel obviously had one eye on writers in the communist and fascist traditions when he wrote, and he explicitly rejected their determinisms, economic or otherwise. "The principal purpose of cosmic philosophies" of whatever kind, he wrote, "is to give orientation to human life and to evaluate its significance." Because of this, "the reigning cosmic philosophy is as fundamental to a particular climate of opinion as are its economic foundations to a selected social scene." Man's social beliefs "adjust themselves to the ruling ideas concerning the cosmos in essentially the same manner in which the social institutions of that place and time adapt themselves to their economic substructure. As cosmic philosophies change, social beliefs change with them."

As Gabriel examined America for its own indigenous cosmic philosophy, he noted first the influence of the wilderness and the effect of dispersal on the American mind. Instead of the elaborate intellectual constructs of Hobbes, Locke, or Rousseau, Americans developed two ideas that were so ingrained they almost seemed not to be ideas at all: "The first was that human affairs should be thought of in terms of the individual; the second was that progress is normal and that the future promises more than has been realized in the present." Given these assumptions, the American cosmic philosophy developed in an atmosphere of relative military security and in time made the transfer from an agrarian to an industrial society with most of its tenets intact. It gradually picked up corollary doctrines of the kind always associated with America: the universal faith in reason of the Revolutionary generation, the atomism of farmers fiercely independent of outside constraint, the intense morality, and the importance of evangelism all made their mark.[17]

Given this basis, Gabriel then went on a headhunting expedition that, among other things, clearly demonstrated the great change in mood that separated the world of 1914 from the world of 1939. The generation of Mabel Dodge had been hopeful about life, glorying in rebellion against the past and in the challenge of a modern future, and it is doubtful whether they worried less about religion or about politics. Gabriel's generation could not be so blithe. The events in Spain, Russia, Germany, Italy and Ethiopia were too well known, and the horrors of the First World War were memory rather than an unknown future. Gabriel searched the American past for "heads" that could

---

17 Ralph H. Gabriel, *The Course of American Democratic Thought* (New York, 1940), esp. pp. 26, 4.

guide the nation through troubled times, and in so doing he produced a book that stressed what Mabel Dodge could hardly have conceived.

Gabriel's heads seemed to agree roughly on three general positions about the American past. "The foundation of this democratic faith was a frank supernaturalism derived from Christianity," Gabriel insisted. "The twentieth-century student is often astonished at the extent to which supernaturalism permeated American thought," but the democratic faith affirmed as a basic postulate "that God, the creator of man, has also created a moral law for his government and has endowed him with a conscience with which to apprehend it." Everywhere at the foundation of human society "is a moral order which is the abiding place of the eternal principles of truth and righteousness." The government of the natural world had its parallels in the government of the spiritual world, and the American Constitution was the best statement yet made of how God intended men to govern themselves. The appeal was so strong that even at the time of the Civil War, both sides argued about the moral law and the real meaning of the Constitution, rather than about the actual problems that faced them.

Gabriel's second doctrine was that of "the free individual." Most obviously portrayed in men like Thoreau and literary characters like Leatherstocking, this doctrine stressed personal liberty and of freedom from governmental restraint. It was derived from the idea of the moral order of human affairs, and from faith in progress. "This philosophy affirmed that the advance of civilization is measured by the progress of men in apprehending and translating into individual and social action the eternal principles which comprise the moral law." Somehow, by living in America, men would develop their civilizing capacities for reason and virtue, and the result would be a constant perfecting of God's democracy. The corollary view was that if this virtuous man should find himself in opposition to a State that demanded that he do something against God's will, rebellion was excusable, and even essential, both for personal and democratic salvation.

Gabriel's third idea within the democratic faith was "the mission of America." This was an American version "of those myths of unique origin and of unique destiny so common in tribal tradition." With this idea, Americans could feel that they were a chosen people, picked by God for the best form of government. They were expected to flourish and then by their example to light the way for lesser or unluckier people. Eventually the whole world could become as free as America, and every individual would be capable of perfecting himself and growing every day more like Christ.[18]

---

18 Ibid., pp. 14, 19, 22.

The book accomplished Gabriel's purpose and demonstrated his ideas extremely well. Assembling such diverse figures as Isaac Hecker, Calhoun, Carnegie, John Wesley Powell, Robert Ingersoll, and a host of other probable and sometimes improbable American thinkers, Gabriel did indeed show what Americans had apparently presupposed, whether they had been aware of it or not. Instead of the usual bleak procession of dead presidents and stirring battles, Gabriel produced a genuine text in intellectual history that really had no precedent in the history of American history. Vernon Parrington had written a pioneering if simplistic study that lined up writers into liberal and conservative schools; Woodbridge Riley had done a sounder job organizing American philosophers. But no one before Gabriel had actually confronted the whole of the American mind and come out alive, let alone with clarity of prose and sense of vignette. Quite aside from his theses, he had shown how Calvinism and its successors were at the very core of American life and thought, and how social science in all its varieties fitted into American history. Once revised since, the book remains in many ways the best single introduction to the subject.

Like Carl Becker, Gabriel had faced the problems of his day and come up with a usable past. He clearly did not like many of the varieties of statism that surrounded him, nor did he like the naturalism and pragmatism that had developed among the younger generation— the books of Thurman Arnold being an abomination singled out for special attention. The pragmatism of William James fitted his book neatly; the cynicism of Arnold seemed like the coming of the deluge. Gabriel was clearly a religious man writing about a country he saw as very much like himself, gathering what solace he could for the coming battle. And, unlike the members of Mabel Dodge's generation, he was very pessimistic.

VII

Time proved Gabriel's pessimism correct for the short run, but perhaps not for the long run. His sense of American religion and capacity for endurance proved accurate. The country survived the war with its faith largely intact, and it turned out that Gabriel's book, quite aside from its scholarly contributions, was but an influential contribution to a movement already underway and soon to become most important. Critics had been busily rediscovering American literature; historians like Charles Beard had excited a similar interest in the American past. With Gabriel's book, Americans could find themselves reintegrated with society once again, and thus more capable of meeting threats from abroad.

But that is another story.

BIBLIOGRAPHY

This bibliographic essay is chiefly an attempt to name a few of the more valuable secondary sources for this period in American intellectual and cultural history. Here as in the text of the book, the emphasis is on those intellectual currents that influenced more than one discipline in the culture. This approach neglects, on the one hand, books of largely technical interest for one discipline; and on the other, books useful for social history or popular culture.

For background reading, several textbooks are valuable for both content and bibliography. Two general surveys of superior quality are T. Harry Williams, Richard N. Current, and Frank Freidel, *A History of the United States* (New York, 1969), published in several versions, including a one-volume survey of America in the twentieth-century that is Prof. Freidel's portion of the larger text; and Samuel Eliot Morison, Henry Steele Commager, and William E. Leuchtenburg, *The Growth of the American Republic*, revised edition (New York, 1969), the first of the modern textbooks, and something of a classic in its own right. The best of the briefer surveys are both by William Leuchtenburg, *The Perils of Prosperity, 1914–1932* (Chicago, 1958), and *Franklin D. Roosevelt and the New Deal, 1932–1940* (New York, 1963). Arthur M. Schlesinger, Jr., and Morton White have also included a number of valuable surveys relevant to this period in their *Paths of American Thought* (Boston, 1963).

Recent American history is also extremely rich in autobiographical material. Considered as art, Albert Jay Nock's *Memoirs of a Superfluous Man* (New York, 1943), is the only American work that manages to challenge *The Education of Henry Adams*. Three others are of extraordinary importance as documents of the era: *The Autobiography of Lincoln Steffens* (New York, 1931), is best for the years before the First World War and still an important work in this period; Max Eastman, *Love and Revolution* (New York, 1965), covers both topics with passion and detail, and ranks with Joseph Freeman, *An American Testament* (New York, 1936), as the two key analyses of this period by participants. Of interest chiefly for the twenties are Mabel Dodge Luhan, *Movers and Shakers* (New York, 1936), probably the most entertaining single document for the era, the third volume of her interminable "Intimate Memories"; Claude McKay, *A Long Way from Home* (New York, 1937); Floyd Dell, *Homecoming* (New York, 1933); Frederic C. Howe, *The Confessions of a Reformer* (New York, 1925); Van Wyck Brooks, *An Autobiography* (New York, 1965); Conrad Aiken's difficult but rewarding *Ushant* (New York, 1952); Malcolm Cowley's very useful and analytical *Exile's Return* (New York, 1951); and Matthew Josephson's *Life among the Surrealists* (New York, 1962). Samuel Putnam, *Paris Was Our Mistress* (Carbondale, 1970) and Kay Boyle and Robert McAlmon, *Being Geniuses Together* (New York, 1968) are essential for Americans in Paris. For the thirties, see Granville Hicks, *Part of the Truth* (New York, 1965), and *Where We Came Out* (New York, 1954), both of which are dry and disappointing; Richard Wright, *Black Boy* (New York, 1945), which does not reach the thirties but helps show the source of some of its emotions, supplemented by Wright's essay in Richard Crossman, ed., *The God That Failed* (New York, 1950); Alfred Kazin, *Starting Out in the Thirties* (Boston, 1965); and Matthew Josephson's second volume, *Infidel in the Temple* (New York, 1967). Poets and musicians are infrequent autobiographers, but see especially *The Autobiography of William Carlos Williams* (New York, 1951); Virgil Thomson, *Virgil Thomson* (New York, 1967); and George Antheil, *Bad Boy of Music* (New York, 1945). Frank Lloyd Wright is, as usual, a similar exception for architects, in *An Autobiography* (New York, 1943). Conservatives have been traditionally more fluent. Joseph Wood Krutch, in *More Lives Than One*

(New York, 1962), and Mark Van Doren, in *The Autobiography of Mark Van Doren* (New York, 1958), are friends who were among the most civilized academic conservatives. *Abraham Flexner: An Autobiography* (New York, 1960), is by a similarly impressive critic of academia. James B. Conant, *My Several Lives* (New York, 1970) is useful for science, government, and higher education. Ralph Adams Cram, *My Life in Architecture* (Boston, 1936), demonstrates how even the most peculiar ideas can take root in American soil. No autobiographer is perhaps wholly accurate, but the prejudices and errors in *The Memoirs of Herbert Hoover*, 3 vols. (New York, 1952), are rapidly becoming a minor academic scandal.

Published letters for a period so recent are naturally scarce. Several collections stand out: Ella Winter and Granville Hicks, eds., *The Letters of Lincoln Steffens* (New York, 1939), contains illuminating material on why Steffens was attracted to communism; Guy J. Forgue, ed., *Letters of H. L. Mencken* (New York, 1961), contains much material valuable for literary history; Robert Spiller, ed., *The Van Wyck Brooks–Lewis Mumford Letters* (New York, 1970), is useful for cultural nationalism; and Holly Stevens, ed., *Letters of Wallace Stevens* (New York, 1966), and F. W. Dupee and George Stade, eds., *Selected Letters of E. E. Cummings* (New York, 1969), give some insight into those very difficult personalities. Andrew Turnbull, ed., *The Letters of F. Scott Fitzgerald* (New York, 1963), and two collections of Albert Jay Nock letters, Francis Nock, ed., *Selected Letters of Albert Jay Nock* (Caldwell, Idaho, 1962), and Frank W. Garrison, ed., *Letters from Albert Jay Nock* (Caldwell, Idaho, 1949), do not show either Nock or Fitzgerald at his best.

For the origins of many of the intellectual concerns of the twenties, Henry May, *The End of American Innocence* (New York, 1959), David Kennedy, *Birth Control in America* (New Haven, 1970), and Morton White, *Social Thought in America* (Boston, 1957), are useful. Howard Mumford Jones, *Guide to American Literature and its Backgrounds since 1890* (Cambridge, regularly revised), is a basically literary bibliography. Frederick J. Hoffman, *The Twenties* (New York, 1965), is the key survey of the meaning of the literature, while his *Freudianism and the Literary Mind* (Baton Rouge, 1957), is the pioneering work in that area; it should be supplemented by Louis Fraiberg, *Psychoanalysis and American Literary Criticism* (Detroit, 1960), Claudia C. Morrison, *Freud and the Critic* (Chapel Hill, 1968), and the relevant chapters in Stanley Edgar Hyman, *The Armed Vision* (New York, 1948). F. H. Matthews, "The Americanization of Sigmund Freud: Adaptations of Psychoanalysis before 1917," *Journal of American Studies* 1, no. 1, April 1967, is the most lucid introduction; for a more technical supplement with an extremely full bibliography, see David Shakow and

David Rapaport, *The Influence of Freud on American Psychology* (New York, 1964). Other books I found useful include: Walter Bromberg, *The Mind of Man: A History of Psychotherapy and Psychoanalysis* (New York, 1959); Nigel Walker, *A Short History of Psychotherapy in Theory and Practice* (London, 1957); Franz G. Alexander and Sheldon T. Selesnick, *The History of Psychiatry* (New York, 1966); Robert Thomson, *The Pelican History of Psychology* (Pelican original, Baltimore, 1968); and A. A. Roback, *A History of American Psychology* (New York, 1964). Philip Rieff, *Freud: The Mind of the Moralist* (New York, 1959), is easily the best book on Freud himself.

Many of the more important literary figures of this period have never been studied at length. A few exceptions are worth noting: Carlos Baker has written Hemingway's biography for his generation in *Ernest Hemingway* (New York, 1969), and Philip Young has done an admirable critical study, *Ernest Hemingway* (New York, 1966). Arthur Mizener in *The Far Side of Paradise* (Boston, 1965) and Henry Dan Piper in *F. Scott Fitzgerald: A Critical Portrait* (New York, 1965), have done the same for Fitzgerald. Of the studies of Wallace Stevens, Joseph N. Riddell, *The Clairvoyant Eye* (Baton Rouge, 1965), seems preferable. For E. E. Cummings, Charles Norman has given us a chatty memoir in *The Magic Maker* (New York, 1964), while the best critical introduction is Norman Friedman, *E. E. Cummings: The Growth of a Writer* (Carbondale, 1964). Irving Howe, *Sherwood Anderson* (New York, 1951), Mark Schorer, *Sinclair Lewis* (New York, 1961), Jay Martin, *Conrad Aiken* (Princeton, 1962), and Cleanth Brooks, *William Faulkner: The Yoknapatawpha Country* (New Haven, 1963), are all standard. On Thomas Wolfe, see Richard S. Kennedy, *The Window of Memory* (Chapel Hill, 1962). Of the many books on Robert Frost, Lawrance Thompson, *Robert Frost: The Early Years* (New York, 1966), is the first volume of the standard biography (a second volume is announced as this book goes to press), while Reuben Brower, *The Poetry of Robert Frost* (New York, 1963), is perhaps the best book-length criticism. For the literary history of the period as a whole, Alfred Kazin, *On Native Grounds* (New York, 1942), is still superior, although the author has since changed some of his earlier opinions; and Robert Spiller, et al., *Literary History of the United States* (New York, 1963), for all the exasperatingly erratic nature of many of its essays and judgments, is still unavoidable, especially for bibliography.

For the critical background, see Walter Sutton, *Modern American Criticism* (Englewood Cliffs, 1963); William Van O'Connor, *An Age of Criticism* (Chicago, 1952); Charles I. Glicksberg, *American Literary Criticism, 1900–1950* (New York, 1951); Floyd Stovall, ed., *The Development of American Literary Criticism* (Chapel Hill, 1955); John P. Pritchard, *Criticism in America* (Norman, Okla., 1956); and Morton

D. Zabel, *Literary Opinion in America* (New York, 1962). Sherman Paul, *Edmund Wilson* (Urbana, 1965), is very disappointing. Robert A. Bone, *The Negro Novel in America* (New Haven, 1965), is standard. W. K. Wimsatt and C. Brooks, *Literary Criticism: A Short History* (New York, 1957), is in many ways brilliant, but extremely skewed in its standards of judgment and interpretation. On the Agrarians, four books are useful: John M. Bradbury, *The Fugitives* (Chapel Hill, 1958); Louise Cowan, *The Fugitive Group* (Baton Rouge, 1959); John L. Stewart, *The Burden of Time* (Princeton, 1965); and Alexander Karanikas, *Tillers of a Myth* (Madison, 1966). Richard Foster, *The New Romantics* (Bloomington, 1962), is valuable on the New Critics during their full flowering in the years after the period studied in this book.

For good introductions to the background of life among the intellectuals in the thirties, see especially Charles Forcey, *The Crossroads of Liberalism* (New York, 1961), A. A. Ekirch, *Ideologies and Utopias* (Chicago, 1969), and Daniel Aaron, *Writers on the Left* (New York, 1961). Granville Hicks, *John Reed* (New York, 1936), is both a fine biography and a good example of what it took to be a hero in the period. Arthur M. Schlesinger, Jr., is still writing his *Age of Roosevelt*, which will prove invaluable both for intellectual and political history. The three volumes to date, *The Crisis of the Old Order* (Boston, 1957), *The Coming of the New Deal* (Boston, 1958), and *The Politics of Upheaval* (Boston, 1960), are, however, written with great partisanship and a really marvellous inability to find anything wrong with New Deal liberalism or its culture heroes. Those wishing a more balanced picture must wait for the next volumes of Frank Freidel's *Franklin D. Roosevelt*, which will correct many of the more imaginative romanticisms in this period of scholarship. Donald D. Egbert and Stow Persons, eds., *Socialism and American Life*, 2 vols. (Princeton, 1952), provide the best introduction and bibliographies on that subject, while Theodore Draper is the most reliable student of communism, in *The Roots of American Communism* (New York, 1957), and *American Communism and Soviet Russia* (New York, 1960). Whittaker Chambers, in *Witness, Whittaker Chambers* (New York, 1952), gives an unequaled picture of communism's attractions from the inside, whatever a person may think of his subsequent career. The most recent surveys of intellectual currents in the period are Frank A. Warren, *Liberals and Communism: The "Red Decade" Revisited* (Bloomington, 1966), a model monograph; and James Gilbert, *Writers and Partisans* (New York, 1968), a study that concentrates chiefly on the *Partisan Review*.

Robert G. McCloskey, *The American Supreme Court* (Chicago, 1960), is a serviceable introduction with bibliographical essay, while Fred Rodell, *Nine Men* (New York, 1955), is a spirited and thoroughly biased romp through Supreme Court history that I found extremely entertaining as well as full of insights. Leon Freedman and Fred L. Israel, eds., *The Justices of the United States Supreme Court, 1789– 1969* (New York, 1970) is a mine of information. Wilfrid E. Rumble, *American Legal Realism* (Ithaca, 1968), is the best guide to that subject. Merlo Pusey, *Charles Evans Hughes,* 2 vols. (New York, 1951), is the standard life. The rest of the legal history of the period belongs to Alpheus T. Mason, in his series of able but awkwardly written studies: *William Howard Taft: Chief Justice* (New York, 1965); *The Supreme Court from Taft to Warren* (Baton Rouge, 1958); *Brandeis—A Free Man's Life* (New York, 1946); and *Harlan Fiske Stone, Pillar of the Law* (New York, 1956).

On the general subjects of isolationism, revisionism, and foreign policy, the following are basic: William L. Langer and S. Everett Gleason, *The Challenge to Isolation* (New York, 1952); Robert A. Divine, *The Illusion of Neutrality* (Chicago, 1962); and Foster R. Dulles, *America's Rise to World Power, 1898–1954* (New York, 1954), which includes a lengthy bibliography. Selig Adler, *The Isolationist Impulse* (New York, 1957), is long, detailed, and essential, but extremely biased in its interpretations, and should be used with care; Manfred Jonas, *Isolationism in America, 1935–1941* (Ithaca, 1966), is brief and superficial. Two of the better diplomatic memoirs of the period are George F. Kennan, *Memoirs, 1925–1950* (Boston, 1967), and Robert Murphy, *Diplomat among Warriors* (New York, 1964). Wayne S. Cole, in *America First: The Battle against Intervention, 1940–1941* (Madison, 1953), and *Senator Gerald P. Nye and American Foreign Relations* (Minneapolis, 1962), has produced two valuable studies of popular isolationism. Robert M. Crunden, *The Mind and Art of Albert Jay Nock* (Chicago, 1964), and Michael Wreszin, *Oswald Garrison Villard: Pacifist at War* (Bloomington, 1965), examine more intellectual figures. Warren I. Cohen, *The American Revisionists* (Chicago, 1967), is good enough so that one wishes he had attempted a study of the entire movement, instead of concentrating only on major figures. Arthur A. Ekirch, *The Decline of American Liberalism* (New York, 1967), is full of essential background material.

Unfortunately, Joseph Dorfman did not carry his monumental *The Economic Mind in American Civilization,* 5 vols. (New York, 1946–59), past 1933. Two basic introductions to Keynes are Seymour Harris, *John Maynard Keynes* (New York, 1955), and Robert Lekachman, *The Age of Keynes* (New York, 1966). Bernard Sternsher, *Rexford G. Tugwell and the New Deal* (New Brunswick, 1964), is so disorganized that it drags on to double its proper length. John K. Galbraith, *The Great Crash, 1929* (Boston, 1961), is brief and lucid.

Turning to music, Gilbert Chase, *America's Music: From the Pil-*

grims to the Present (New York, 1966), now much revised, is the best place to begin for both history and bibliography. English critic Wilfrid Mellers's *Music in a New Found Land* (New York, 1965), is considerably more interpretive, and to me one of the really important and imaginative books in recent musicology. Aaron Copland, *Our New Music* (New York, 1941), is both history and memoir. W. W. Austin, *Music in the Twentieth Century* (New York, 1966), gives the world perspective to American music, also with extensive bibliographies. Elliott Schwartz and Barney Childs, eds., *Contemporary Composers on Contemporary Music* (New York, 1967), and Gilbert Chase, ed., *The American Composer Speaks* (Baton Rouge, 1966), are invaluable collections of primary materials.

The place to begin for architectural history is Sigfried Giedion, *Space, Time and Architecture*, 5th ed. (Cambridge, 1967), supplemented for a more American emphasis by John Burchard and Albert Bush-Brown, *The Architecture of America* (Boston, 1961). For Walter Gropius, see especially the article by William Jordy in Donald Fleming and Bernard Bailyn, eds., *The Intellectual Migration: Europe and America, 1930–1960* (Cambridge, 1969). On Frank Lloyd Wright, Peter Blake is straightforward in *The Master Builders* (New York, 1960), and Norris K. Smith is stimulating and interpretive in *Frank Lloyd Wright* (Englewood Cliffs, 1966), even when misguided.

Oliver Larkin, *Art and Life in America* (New York, 1959), is the best introduction to American painting as a whole, while Barbara Rose, *American Art since 1900* (New York, 1967), and Sam Hunter, *Modern American Painting and Sculpture* (New York, 1959), are the best books devoted to the twentieth century. Still more focused are Milton Brown, *American Painting: From the Armory Show to the Depression* (Princeton, 1955), and J. I. H. Baur, *Revolution and Tradition in Modern American Art* (Cambridge, 1951). Irma Jaffe, *Joseph Stella* (Cambridge, 1969), and Parker Tyler, *The Divine Comedy of Pavel Tchelitchew* (New York, 1967), are examples of what can be done with biography in art history.

For the drama, Arthur and Barbara Gelb's *O'Neill* (New York, 1962), contains all the biographical detail this generation is capable of absorbing; John H. Raleigh, *The Plays of Eugene O'Neill* (Carbondale, 1965), contains the best sustained criticism. Joseph Wood Krutch, *The American Drama since 1918* (New York, 1957), is the best survey of the whole period; Gerald Rabkin, *Drama and Commitment: Politics in the American Theater of the Thirties* (Bloomington, 1964), and Morgan Y. Himelstein, *Drama Was a Weapon* (New Brunswick, 1963), are both competent on the thirties. John Mason Brown, *The Worlds of Robert E. Sherwood* (New York, 1965) is the first half of a biography that will unfortunately never be completed.

The basic source for research into American religion is that edited by James W. Smith and Albert L. Jamison, *Religion in American Life,* 4 vols. (Princeton, 1961). Three brief surveys are Winthrop Hudson, *American Protestantism* (Chicago, 1961), John T. Ellis, *American Catholicism* (Chicago, 1956), and Nathan Glazer, *American Judaism* (Chicago, 1957). William McLoughlin, *Modern Revivalism* (New York, 1959), is exemplary on a controversial topic. Two relevant surveys are Paul A. Carter, *The Decline and Revival of the Social Gospel . . .* (Ithaca, 1954), and Donald B. Meyer, *The Protestant Search for Political Realism, 1919–1941* (Berkeley and Los Angeles, 1960). Meyer's *The Positive Thinkers* (New York, 1965), covers material I have neglected in this book. None of the books on Reinhold Niebuhr so far is worth reading; the best historical introduction, although somewhat infatuated and more than slightly motivated by current concerns, is A. M. Schlesinger, Jr., "Reinhold Niebuhr's Role in American Political Thought and Life," in Charles Kegley and Robert Bretall, eds., *Reinhold Niebuhr: His Religious, Social and Political Thought* (New York, 1956). Norman F. Furniss, *The Fundamentalist Crisis, 1918–1931* (New Haven, 1954), is standard for its subject. The best study of Walter Lippmann is Charles Wellborn, *Twentieth Century Pilgrimage: Walter Lippmann and the Public Philosophy* (Baton Rouge, 1969).

Brand Blanshard has surveyed recent American philosophy in Spiller, *Literary History of the United States,* ch. 76. For a world perspective, see Albert William Levi, *Philosophy and the Modern World* (Bloomington, 1966), and John Passmore, *A Hundred Years of Philosophy* (London, 1957). For a more American focus, W. H. Werkmeister, *A History of Philosophical Ideas in America* (New York, 1949), is an introductory textbook with far more modern material than is customary in such books; John E. Smith, *The Spirit of American Philosophy* (New York, 1963), is brief and lucid on the major figures; Paul Conkin, *Puritans and Pragmatists* (New York, 1969), is similar in method but more detailed; Herbert Schneider, *A History of American Philosophy* (New York, 1963), is long, erratic, and often painful to read. Andrew Reck has concentrated on very contemporary work in *Recent American Philosophy* (New York, 1964), and *New American Philosophers* (Baton Rouge, 1968). Sidney Hook, *John Dewey* (New York, 1939), is the best longer study of Dewey. Merle Curti, ed., *American Scholarship in the Twentieth Century* (Cambridge, 1953), examines philosophy as well as social science, history and literature.

The best scholarly introduction to the history of anthropology is Marvin Harris, *The Rise of Anthropological Theory* (New York, 1968); H. R. Hays, *From Ape to Angel* (New York, 1958), is more readable and less technical, as is Abram Kardiner and Edward Preble,

They Studied Man (New York, 1961). Melville J. Herskovits, *Franz Boas* (New York, 1953), is a brief life that scarcely exhausts its subject, while Margaret Mead, *An Anthropologist at Work: Writings of Ruth Benedict* (Boston, 1959), is a model of scholarly editing. Theodora Kroeber, *Alfred Kroeber* (Berkeley, 1970) is a useful memoir. Both Hays and Harris have extensive bibliographies.

In sociology and social psychology, Roscoe and Gisela Hinkle have written a brief introduction to the history of the subject in *The Development of Modern Sociology* (New York, 1954). Harry Elmer Barnes has edited *An Introduction to the History of Sociology* (Chicago, 1948), and E. S. Bogardus has written *The Development of Social Thought* (New York, 1940, regularly revised); both tend to peter out for the period after the First World War. John Madge, *The Origins of Scientific Sociology* (Glencoe, 1962), is far more useful for the later period, and has the best introduction to Robert Park and the Chicago school; Robert E. L. Faris, *Chicago Sociology, 1920–1932* (San Francisco, 1967), is a good start on an institutional history of the best sociology department in the country at the time. Martin Birnbach, *Neo-Freudian Social Philosophy* (Stanford, 1961), is fairly technical on neo-Freudianism, while J. A. C. Brown, *Freud and the Post-Freudians* (Penguin original, Baltimore, 1961), is the best general introduction. Alvin Johnson, *Pioneer's Progress* (New York, 1952), is the autobiography of one of the more eminent men in social science. Bernard Crick, *The American Science of Politics* (Berkeley and Los Angeles, 1964), is an Englishman's history of American political science.

In the history of education, Lawrence Cremin is setting new standards of scholarship, most notably in his admirable *The Transformation of the School* (New York, 1961). The best introduction to the university is Frederick Rudolph, *The American College and University* (New York, 1962). For background to the twentieth century, Merle Curti, *The Social Ideas of American Educators* (Paterson, 1963), is very helpful; Isaac L. Kandel, *American Education in the Twentieth Century* (Cambridge, 1957), covers the social side of educational thought, and Rush Welter, *Popular Education and Democratic Thought* (New York, 1962), covers the political and cultural foundations. Samuel E. Tenenbaum, *William Heard Kilpatrick* (New York, 1951), is more an act of adoration than of scholarship, but C. A. Bowers, *The Progressive Educator and the Depression: The Radical Years* (New York, 1969), is a sign that more legitimate scholarly work is now being done in the field. Richard Hofstadter, *The Progressive Historians* (New York, 1968), is hopefully the last word on Parrington, Turner and Beard.

Outside of its strictly academic variety, as in the New Criticism, American conservatism has never received its due from the scholarly world. Clinton Rossiter is somewhat bemused about the whole subject, but his *Conservatism in America* (New York, 1962) is on the whole a fair assessment by a political scientist. Russell Kirk's *The Conservative Mind* (Chicago, 1960), only gets as far as the New Humanism, and is more of a passionate defense of religious conservatism than a scholarly survey of the whole subject. The most recent addition to the literature, Allen Guttman's *The Conservative Tradition in America* (New York, 1968), is completely mistitled; it is little more than a series of disconnected essays with no real methodological unity. Richard Hofstadter has a good discussion of Hoover in *The American Political Tradition* (New York, 1948), but we have no similar studies of Flexner, Krutch, the conservative poets, or the origins of the post-Second World War New Right.

Students of American studies should also be aware of the large amounts of scholarship available in periodicals and dissertations. Much of the better periodical work that has appeared in the *American Quarterly* is now available in two texts, edited by Hennig Cohen, *The American Culture* and *The American Experience* (both Boston, 1968). That magazine and *American Literature* publish dissertation titles regularly; James Woodress has collected all those he can find through 1966 in his book, *Dissertations in American Literature, 1891–1966* (Durham, 1968). The American Historical Association also publishes cumulative lists of dissertations in progress or known to have been completed; the latest of these, dated fall 1967, edited by Robert L. Zangrando et al., is titled "List of Doctoral Dissertations in History in Progress or Completed at Colleges and Universities in the United States since 1964," and is available from the Association, 400 A St., S.E., Washington, D.C.

INDEX

DATE DUE

4/20			
GAYLORD			PRINTED IN U.S.A.